GOING UNDERGROUND
BURY ST EDMUNDS

MARTYN TAYLOR

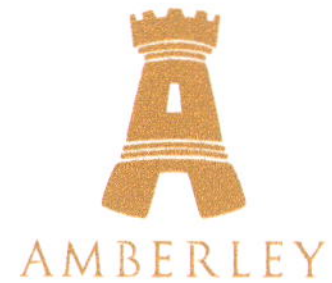

First published 2022

Amberley Publishing, The Hill, Stroud
Gloucestershire GL5 4EP

www.amberley-books.com

Copyright © Martyn Taylor, 2022

The right of Martyn Taylor to be identified as the Author of this work has been asserted in accordance with the Copyrights, Designs and Patents Act 1988.

British Library Cataloguing in Publication Data.
A catalogue record for this book is available from the British Library.

ISBN 978 1 3981 0508 9 (print)
ISBN 978 1 3981 0509 6 (ebook)

Typesetting by SJmagic DESIGN SERVICES, India.
Printed in the UK.

Appointed GPSR EU Representative: Easy Access System Europe Oü, 16879218
Address: Mustamäe tee 50, 10621, Tallinn, Estonia
Contact Details: gpsr.requests@easproject.com, +358 40 500 3575

CONTENTS

INTRODUCTION

In 2020, Bury St Edmunds had visions of celebrating a millennium since the founding of its abbey of St Edmund by King Cnut; however, the worldwide Covid-19 pandemic put everything on hold – strange times. As you would expect, stories concerning the now dissolved abbey feature significantly within this book. Speculative tunnels leading from the abbey to various destinations can be ruled out because of topography, as can tales of subterranean medieval ghostly figures occupying the town – or can they?

As for tunnels, these are mainly associated with the chalk mines to the east, west and central parts of the town, especially Jacqueline Close. Here, devastating consequences saw the demolition of houses built above these mines. Fortunately, the town has not suffered too much from sinkholes, though there have been isolated collapses associated with mines.

While collating information on the subjects mentioned within this book, blocked-up doorways in ancient cellars feature prominently with an air of mystery, and the notion of what lay behind them contributing to further anecdotes. All of these accounts add to the rich history of our town, going back to when it was known as Beodericsworth in Saxon times. Some of these Anglo-Saxon ancestors of ours were discovered in a cemetery when building works were well underway on the western edge of town. Burials have formed an important part of this book – the wealthy, famous and those without a memorial anymore. You never know what lies below.

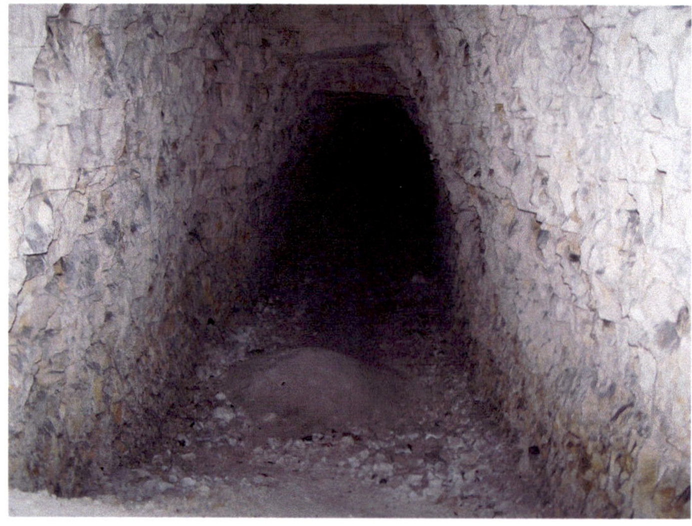

Chalk mine, off Mount Road.

1

TUNNELS

Under Greene King

Since its formation in 1887 with the amalgamation of Edward Greene's Westgate Brewery and Fred King's St Edmunds Brewery, Greene King has grown to its present size through the acquisition of other breweries. Wealthy Hong Kong company CK Asset Holdings completed a takeover in 2019. A major asset though of Greene King is the brewhouse fronting Westgate Street. In 1936, following a scathing report on the then unsafe brewhouse, a cracked mash tun and loading facilities, it was decided that replacement work would start in December of that year. The capital to enable the work to proceed was raised from issuing 25,000 ordinary unallocated shares, with a bankers' overdraft of £50,000. The project

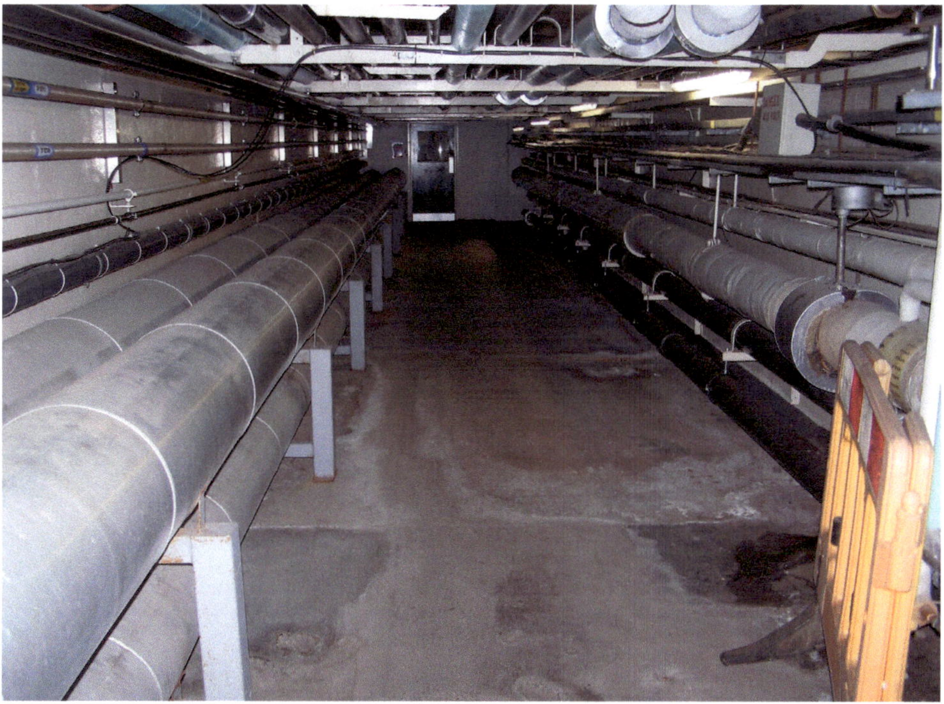

Under Greene King.

was planned and conceived by a committee mainly consisting of managing director Major Lake, head brewer Colonel Oliver, engineer Mark Jennings and architect Bill Mitchell.

However, things did not go smoothly: the work estimate doubled to £80,000, with severe problems caused by the gravel and chalk substrata. This meant piling was required to enable work to proceed, causing lengthy delays along with the shortage of building materials because of the prospect of another world war. The new facilities included a long, wide tunnel (shown) from the brewhouse under Crown Street to the original Westgate Brewery fronting Westgate Street to allow free passage of staff. Finally, the facilities opened in January 1939.

At one time Greene King had a subterranean rifle range from the Westgate Brewery that went under part of Bridewell Lane near to the Guildhall Feoffment School, foundry and school maltings (now Heaton Mews), on the corner of Westgate Street and Bridewell Lane.

Former Masonic Lodge, No. 37 Churchgate Street

Once a well-used coaching inn with roots going back to the seventeenth century, the Six Bells ceased trading in 1885 to become the Masonic hall in 1890. This moved to Ashlar House in Eastern Way, being consecrated in September 2014 with the former lodge converted into luxury apartments. During the refurbishment work I was fortunate to be given permission to look into the cellars, which are quite ancient, probably predating the building itself, which was 'Georgianised' from at least the middle of the eighteenth century. The 1997 Grade II listing describes: 'INTERIOR: Extensive cellars run below both parts of the property with walling which includes stone blocks and rubble flint with old render; various brick tunnel vaults.'

Two interesting facts are mentioned here: stone blocks, which suggest they came from the abbey, and various brick tunnel vaults. After the dissolution the abbey site was used as a quarry for the town, so this is likely where these blocks originated. The other fact is certainly thought-provoking because on the cellar's north wall, by means of four small openings in brickwork, a vaulted ceiling can be seen.

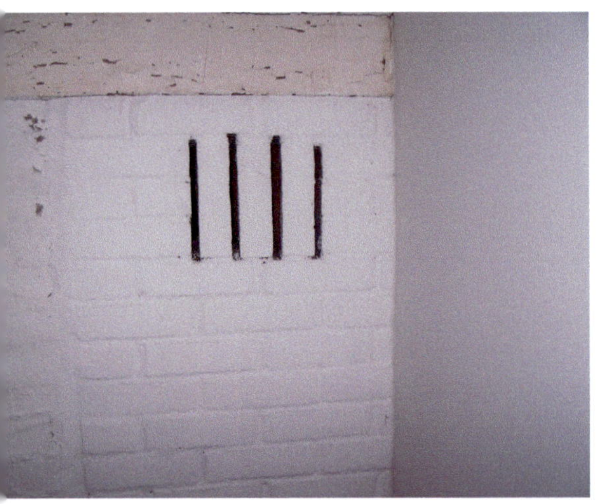
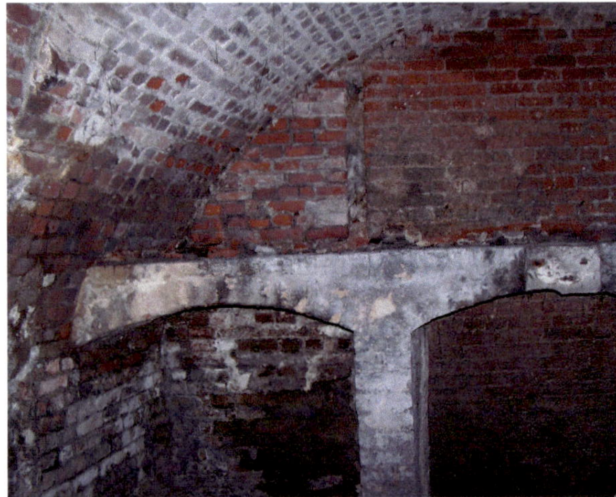

Above left and above right: Former Masonic Lodge, No. 37 Churchgate Street.

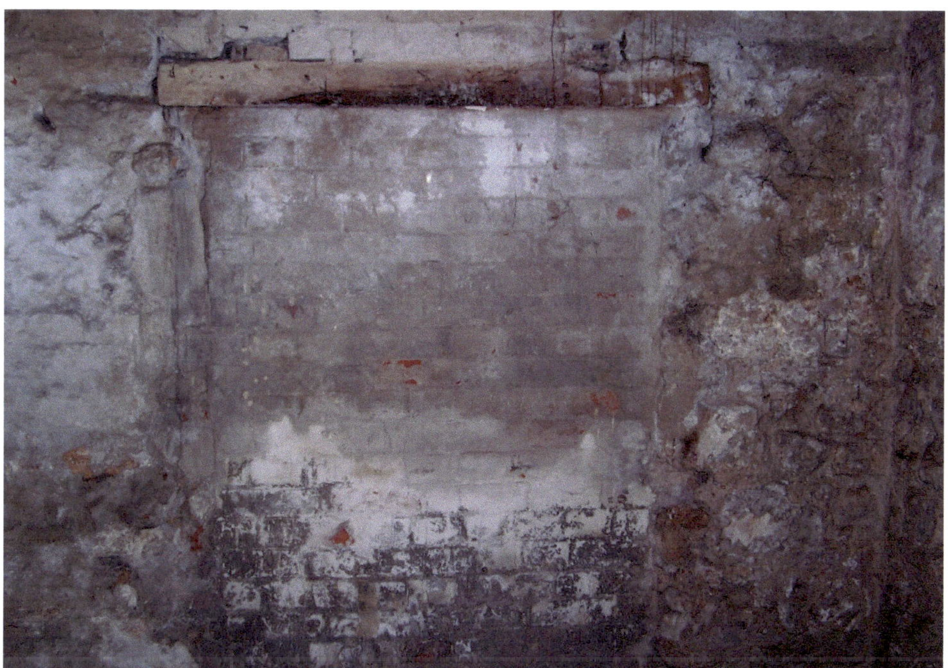

A further blocked-up dooway?

Inside, are items of furniture such as Lloyd Loom chairs and heaters left when this doorway was bricked up post-1997 after the listing had been carried out. A substantial wooden lintel sits above the former doorway. Not wishing to propagate many stories about long-lost tunnels under the town, I have been reliably informed by a former mason's son that as a child he would enter a tunnel via this entrance, going under Athenaeum Lane where it stopped at a metal gate with numerous wine bottles propped against it, on the Angel Hotel side. Wine bins in a cellar for storing wine at constant ambient temperatures are often erroneously associated with tunnel entrances because of their curved construction.

On another part of the north wall of the cellar there is possibly a further blocked-up doorway. Is the proof of this the wooden lintel, as both sides of the doorway are of rubble construction but in between are bricked up? A classic interpretation of what appears to be an entrance to somewhere once.

Death of Humphrey Plantagenet, 1390–1447

In far-off days, care of the soul was more prevalent than the body, medical care being minimal. The ruins of St Saviours, a medieval hospital founded by Abbot Samson during 1184–86, can be seen today in Fornham Road. As was his wont in 1447, Henry VI called Parliament to the town. Henry resided at the abbey, while Humphrey Plantagenet lodged at St Saviours.

Humphrey Plantagenet, the 'good' Duke of Gloucester, brother of Henry V, uncle and guardian of the king, and Lord Protector of the Realm, was regent, in essence de facto ruler, of England during Henry VI's minority. This role would put Humphrey at odds with his own uncle, Cardinal Henry Beaufort. Humphrey was also a great patron of the arts, supporting St Edmundsbury Abbey's poet monk John Lydgate, who had presented to the young king a fabulous, illuminated manuscript of the life of St Edmund at Christmas in 1433.

Being the fourth son of Henry IV, Humphrey had partly followed a militaristic career but did not make friends easily and with his second wife, Eleanor Cobham, this intransigence would set him on a direct path of conflict with the now crowned Henry VI. Charges of witchcraft would be laid against Eleanor Cobham, and treason against Humphrey.

On 23 February, the good duke was found dead. The official cause of death was apoplexy, a stroke, but there were rumours he was poisoned. He was buried in St Albans Abbey. In 1907, the year of the splendid Bury pageant, George Gery Milner Gibson Cullum of Hardwick paid for a rectangular plaque to Humphrey on the front of St Saviours, part of a twelve-plaque trail around Bury celebrating people who have contributed to the town's rich heritage.

So, did Humphrey die from natural causes, or was it murder? Fact and fiction overlap, because in 1860 Margaretta Greene (of the Greene brewing family) supposedly discovered, hidden in the abbey's west front, an account of Humphrey's demise. Using the basic details of the intrigues of this tale she penned a novella called *The Secret Disclosed*, which was published in 1861. Maude Carew, a nun, is persuaded by Queen Margaret of Anjou to poison Humphrey, who threatens the queen with blackmail to avoid his charges. Maude, a court member, had entered Babwell Priory (today's Priory Hotel) to rid herself of fond memories for another prominent court member, Sir Roger Drury. He, by coincidence, had

St Saviours archaeological dig.

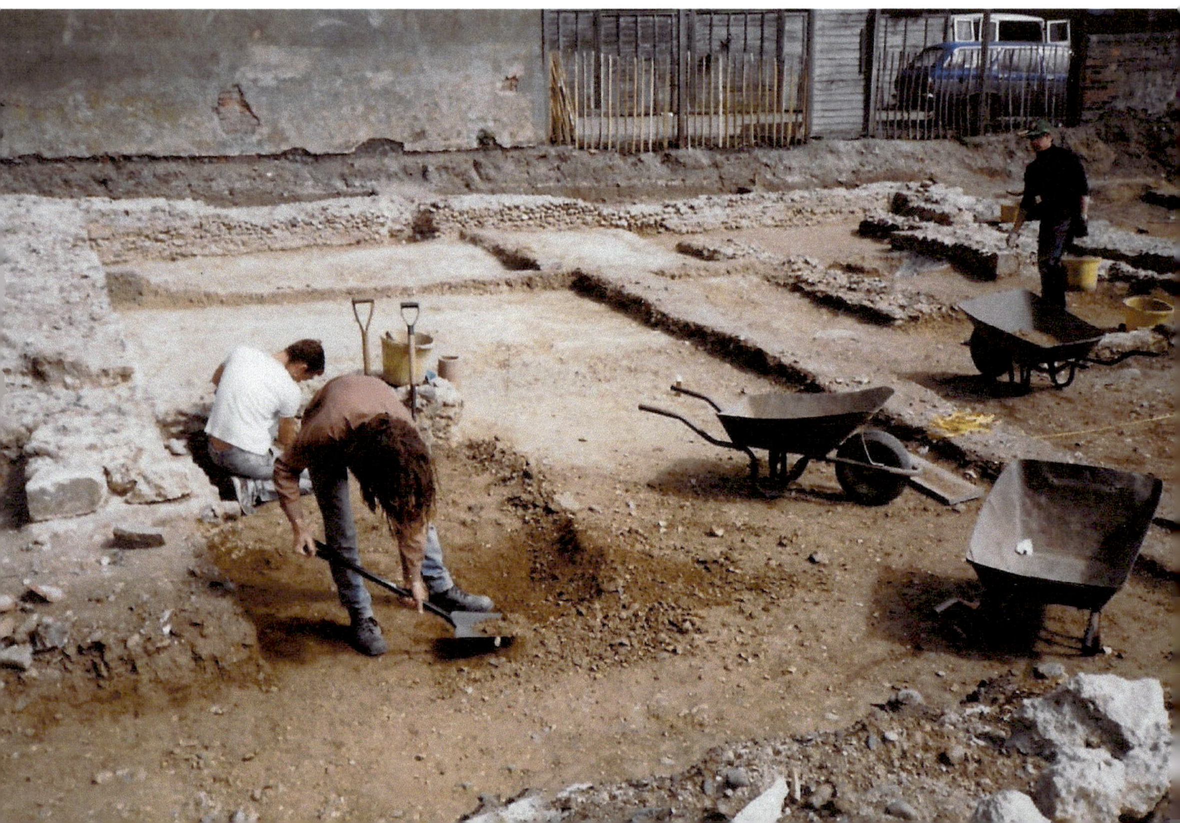

enrolled in Bury Abbey as Brother Bernard, a strange man versed in witchcraft. Via a secret tunnel that led from Babwell to St Saviours, Maude crept into Humphrey's chamber and administered poison to the sleeping duke. As he expires Maude carelessly spills some of the draught onto herself. Dying, she seeks out Brother Bernard, who on learning of her deed curses her to walk among the Great Churchyard forevermore as the Grey Lady Ghost.

Consider this though, Margaretta drew on local knowledge as Carew and Drury's effigies are represented in St Mary's Church, but surely anybody with knowledge of the Fornham Road area would realise how improbable it is for a tunnel to go from the priory to St Saviours. Is it believable, or just a good yarn?

Angel Hill

Le Mustowe, known as Angel Hill today, is where the famous Bury Fair was held until it was abolished in 1871 – Mustow, the place to muster, to meet. Could Angel Hill really have a warren of tunnels leading to and from the abbey, as we are led to believe?

There is story of an intrepid violinist at the end of the eighteenth century who supposedly left Angel Hill from Anderson's coffee shop on the south side via one such subterranean route, accompanied by other revellers. Heading in the direction of the abbey, fear overtook his companion's bravado, and they decided to follow his tune above. Left alone, no more was heard of him – his fiddle was silent.

The abbey at Bury was one of the most powerful and impressive in England. All that remains today are the flint core ruins and two massive entrances: the twelfth-century

The Personal History of David Copperfield film extract.

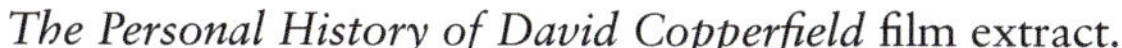

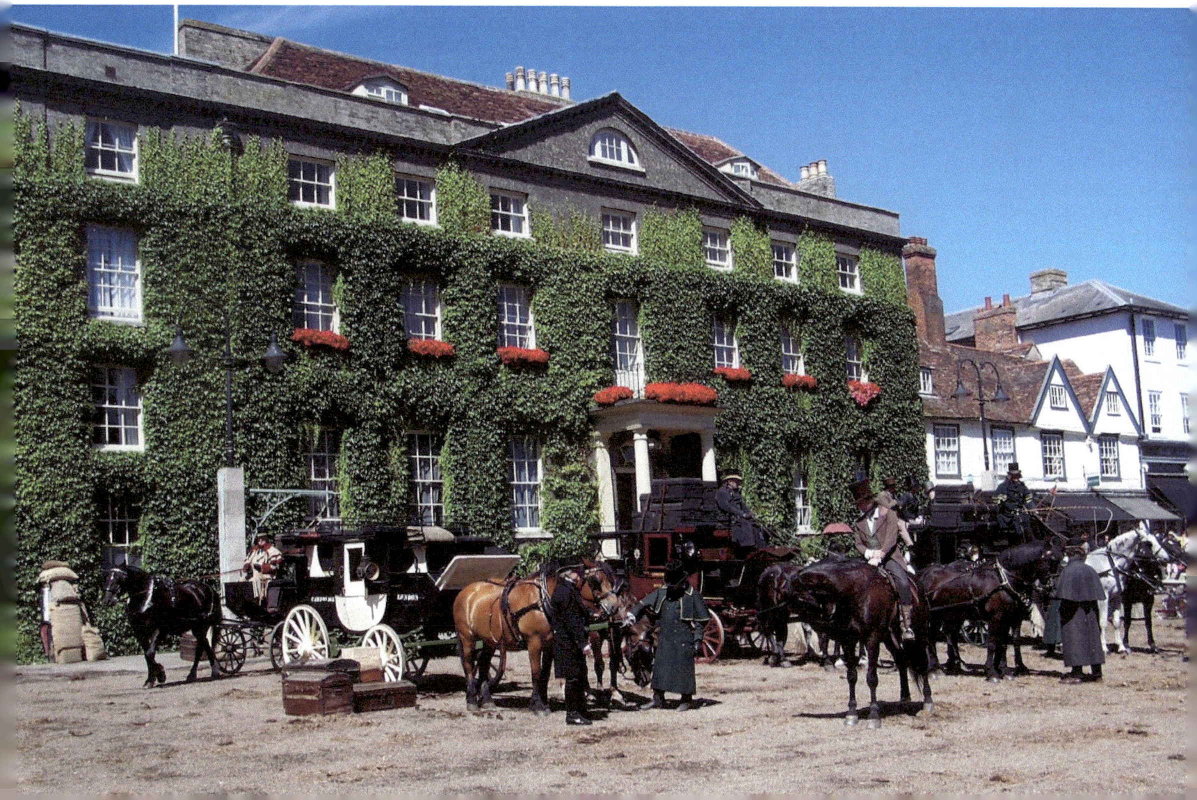

Norman Tower, the religious entrance, and the secular Abbeygate, the second of such due to the rioting townspeople destroying the first in 1327, which was situated opposite today's Abbeygate Street. The Norman Tower was the first made.

Angel Hill is said to be honeycombed with underground culverts and concealments originating from the abbey, formulating tales of ghostly monks being seen at various times in the cellars of interconnecting shops up nearby Abbeygate Street. Modern-day accounts tell of spectral monks in brown habits being seen, but as the abbey here at Bury St Edmunds housed Benedictine monks, who wore black habits, could people have been confused or mistaken?

The Angel Hotel

The Angel Hotel was a much-used coaching inn in the days before the coming of the railway, overlooking Le Mustowe. The Angel Hotel was built on the site of three adjoining inns, namely the Castle, Angel and White Bear, in 1774–76 to designs by Harleston architect John Redgrave. Records show an Angel Inn existed as far back as 1452, though its arched vaulted undercroft built in three bays with stone ribs and octagonal supporting pillars date from the thirteenth century. In 1859 and 1861, Charles Dickens stayed at the Angel Hotel, which a blue plaque now confirms. The 2019 film *The Personal History of David Copperfield* was also filmed nearby. The hotel was owned by the Guildhall feoffees until 1917. Anecdotally, secret tunnels are said to emanate from the undercroft, but no actual proof exists. It is now a popular restaurant/cocktail bar.

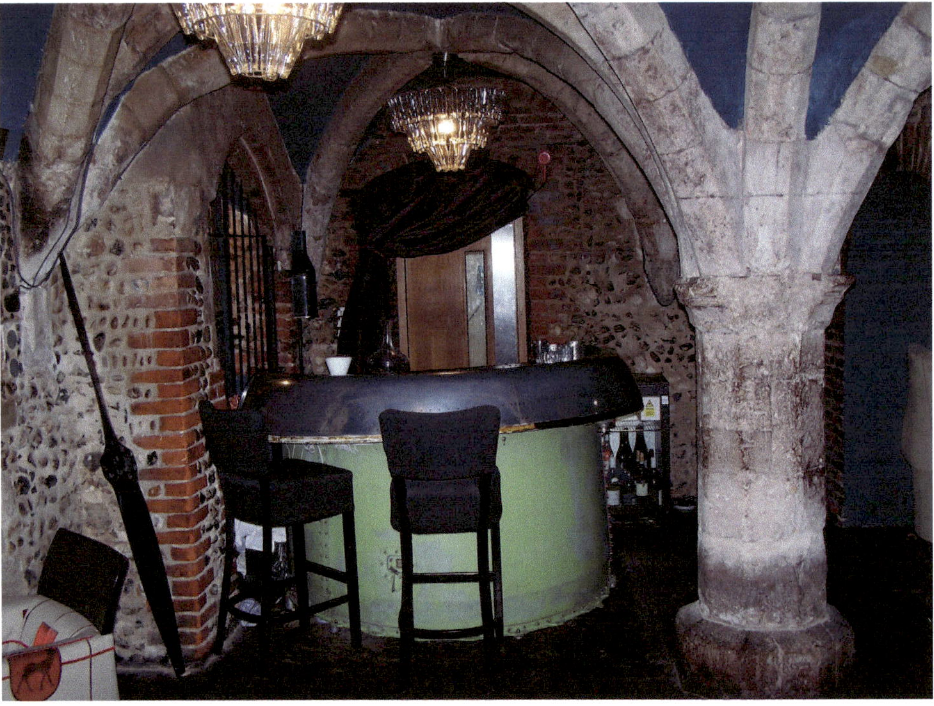

The Angel's undercroft.

Skinner Street Tunnel

Skinner Street is as near you can get to an authentic medieval street in the town. Its name derives from when animals were skinned of their hides prior to being butchered at the nearby Shambles, and is mentioned as far back in the 1295 rentals list. Narrow, cobbled, dark and foreboding at night, the street is not well used, probably because some businesses that back onto it from the Buttermarket and Traverse store their large wheelie bins here, around which unsavoury characters sometimes gather.

A tunnel once went under Skinner Street, between what is the rear of Unit A, Buttermarket (JD Sports in 2020, but subsequently relocated to the arc) and Toni & Guy, hairdressers of No. 5 The Traverse. Previously, Unit A was a branch of Debenhams, which sold clothing and drapery, and before then E. W. Pretty & Co. Ltd, selling the same sort of merchandise. Originally No. 13 Buttermarket, I wonder if someone could have been superstitious with the changing of the shop address to Unit A, Buttermarket? When Pretty's department store closed around 1978, Debenhams moved in, although for only twenty years. The year 2009 saw Debenhams back in Bury at the arc shopping complex. Debenhams had a homeware branch in the Traverse where Toni & Guy now are. A service tunnel, some 2 metres in height, allowed staff from their respective cellars to move freely under Skinner Street between the two branches of EW Pretty & Co. Edward Pretty had been trading from around 1885 in Bury with both branches, so may have been responsible for the tunnel, but is it still there?

Skinner Street.

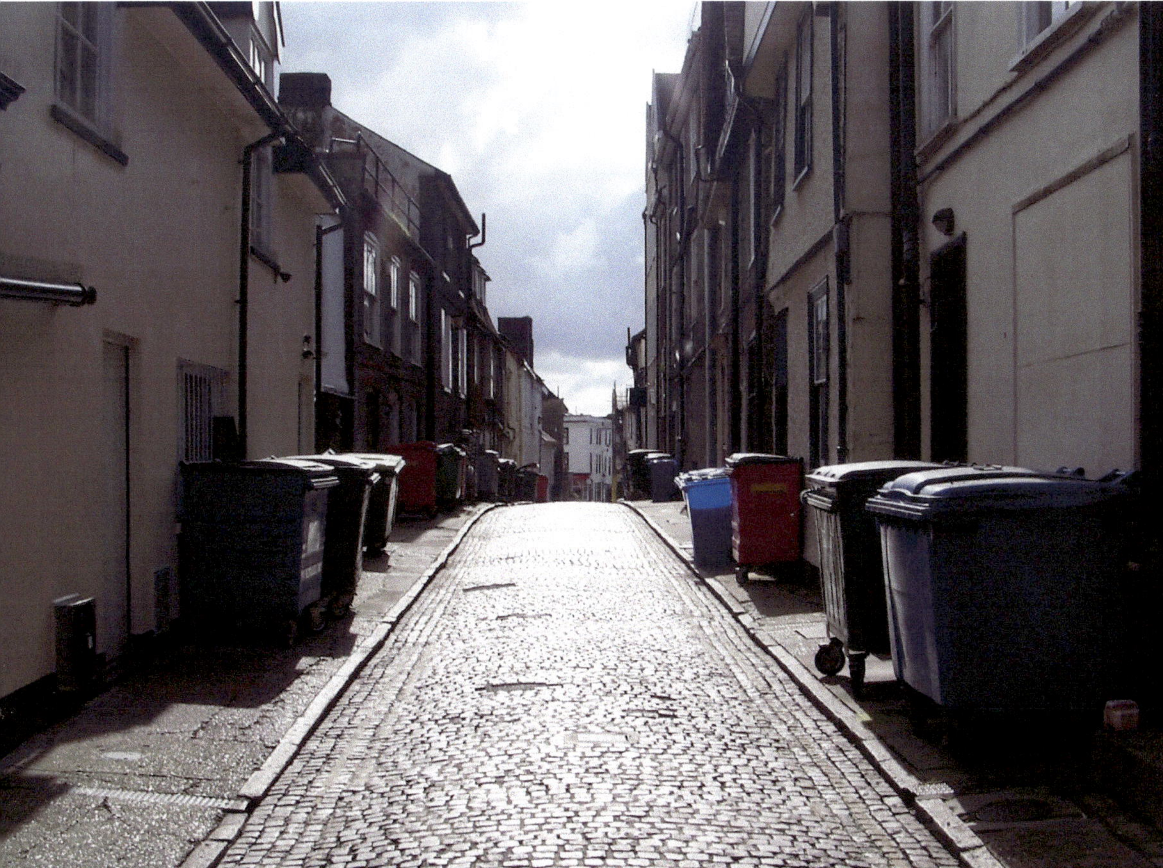

The Tunnel of W. E. Image, 1807–1903

The fine Georgian manor house on Honey Hill was built in 1736–38 by John Hervey, 1st Earl of Bristol, for his second wife, Elizabeth Felton, as a town house. To improve the vista from his wife's property the remnants of the abbey's St Margaret's Gate opposite were demolished. Fast-forward 100 years later and this setting was interrupted by another resident of the area, William Edmund Image. He lived with his first wife, Catherine, at No. 5 Schoolhall Street (Honey Hill), but appropriately known in deference today as St Margaret's Gate. A respected, principled man, his boundary wall near St Mary's Church in the churchyard has a plaque confirming his ownership: 'This Wall Belongs To W.E.Image 1836.'

William was a physician at the Suffolk Hospital in Bury, where he studied forensic medicine. He performed the autopsy on John Foster, the poisoned husband of Catherine Foster, the last woman hanged in Bury in 1847. Oddly, he was also a renowned early philatelist, later becoming a Justice of the Peace and High Sheriff of Suffolk.

On 1 July 1863 he applied to the borough corporation for a right of way tunnel underneath a new public roadway into the Great Churchyard, which bisected his garden, across to today's former Shire Hall small car park. An indenture (Suffolk Archives, HB504/1331/1) was drawn up between the corporation and himself, costing 2*s* 6*d* – the expenses split between them. One month's notice had to be given by the borough for the removal of the right of way. It would seem that Edmund wanted some privacy while traversing the two elements of his garden. Whether this cut and cover tunnel, whereby a deep trench was dug with an overhead support that was then backfilled, still exists is not known.

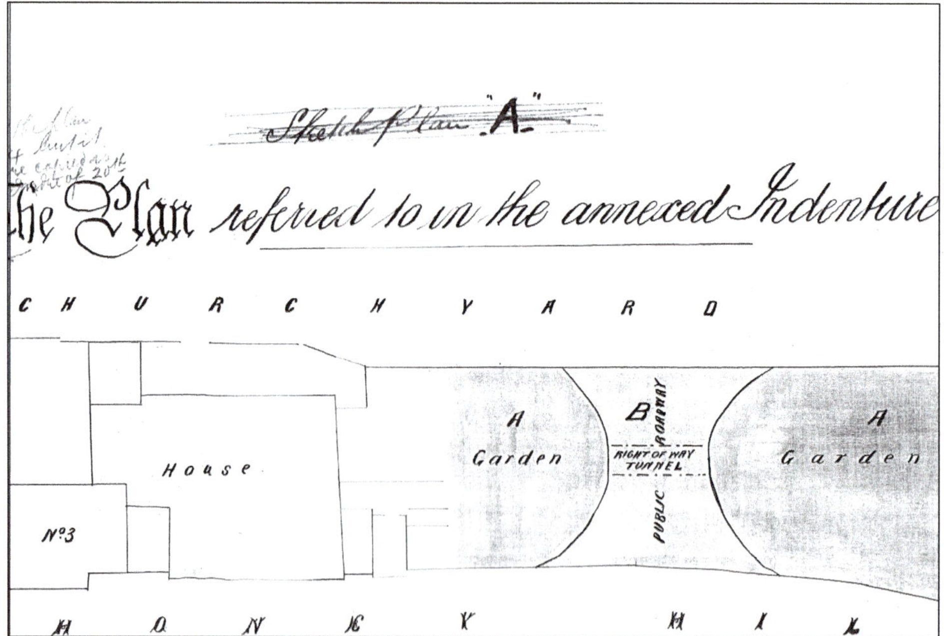

Plan of W. E. Image's tunnel.

St Botolph's Lane

This was initially known as Madam White's Lane after this lady rented South Hill House on the corner with Southgate Street. South Hill House was later a Victorian academy for young ladies, with Amelia Hitchins as its principal. An apocryphal story goes that this was the Westgate School that featured in Charles Dickens' famous novel *The Pickwick Papers*, but no actual proof exists.

Upon entering the lane, on the left, is a large, red-brick building known today as The Warehouse. This was once used as a boarding and day school for boys and was run by a widow, Mrs Susan Aldridge. Pupils under ten were charged 30 guineas per annum and those over sixteen, 50 guineas. Boarders had to provide their own clothing, including at least three pairs of 'drawers' (underpants).

The building still has the school bell on the roof, which contributed to its Grade II listing as it is an uncommon feature. There used to be a tunnel under the lane near the bend so pupils could have access to their exercise yard opposite, all the while kept under the school's jurisdiction. This tunnel would cause major problems when the Sexton Meadows estate was being built off Southgate Street. Services from the Haberdon were to come through the lane to the new estate but hit the now filled-in tunnel, resulting in their re-routing. After the building ceased to be a school it later became a furniture storage depot for Lands (furniture removers of Churchgate Street), then a Pickford's furniture repository until being turned into offices by Driver, Prior & Theobald (architects) in the 1980s. Subsequent building works there have identified that the original floor level was 3 feet lower – possibly to discourage the children from looking out of the windows.

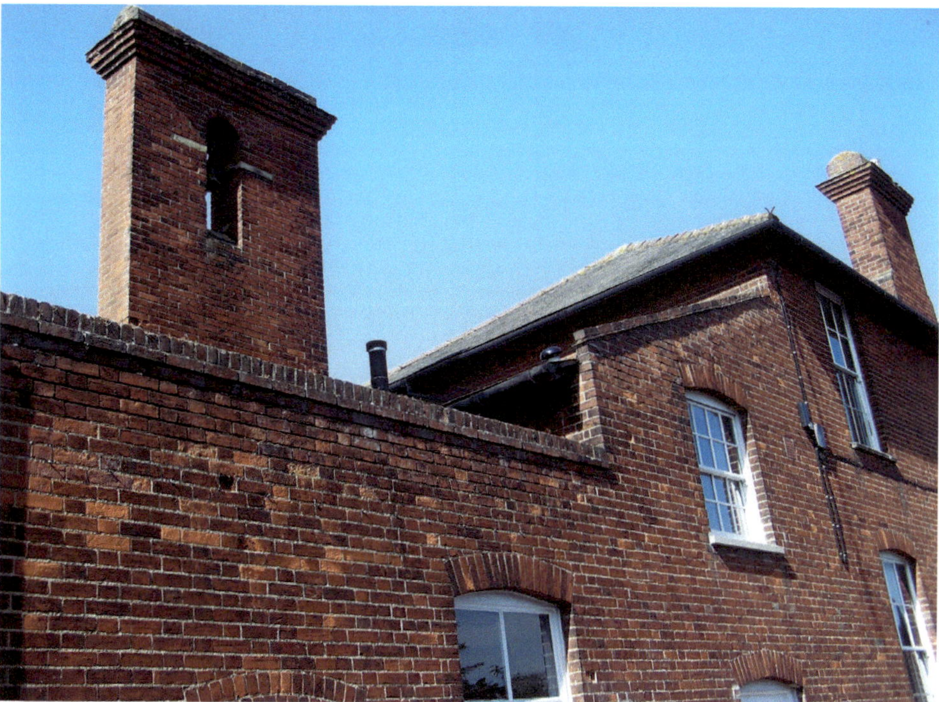

South Hill House.

2

BURIALS

The Charnel House, Great Churchyard

One of only a surviving handful in this country, this was a consecrated bone depository for skeletal remains uncovered when a new grave was being dug. Once two storeys, the chapel was founded by Abbot John de Northwold in 1300. Concerned for the irreverence shown towards the unwanted occupants, he observed 'they were indecently cast forth and left'. Two chaplains conducted services here on a regular basis. With the Dissolution of the Monasteries in 1539, Le Charnelle became an alehouse, but in 1637 it was described as 'a common nuisance'. It subsequently became a blacksmiths forge. Banker John Spink considered purchasing it as a family mausoleum; unfortunately, his bank in Buttermarket collapsed, the final transaction unfinished – a painting of around 1790 showing him holding the uncompleted conveyance document can be seen in the Guildhall.

The Charnel House, Great Churchyard.

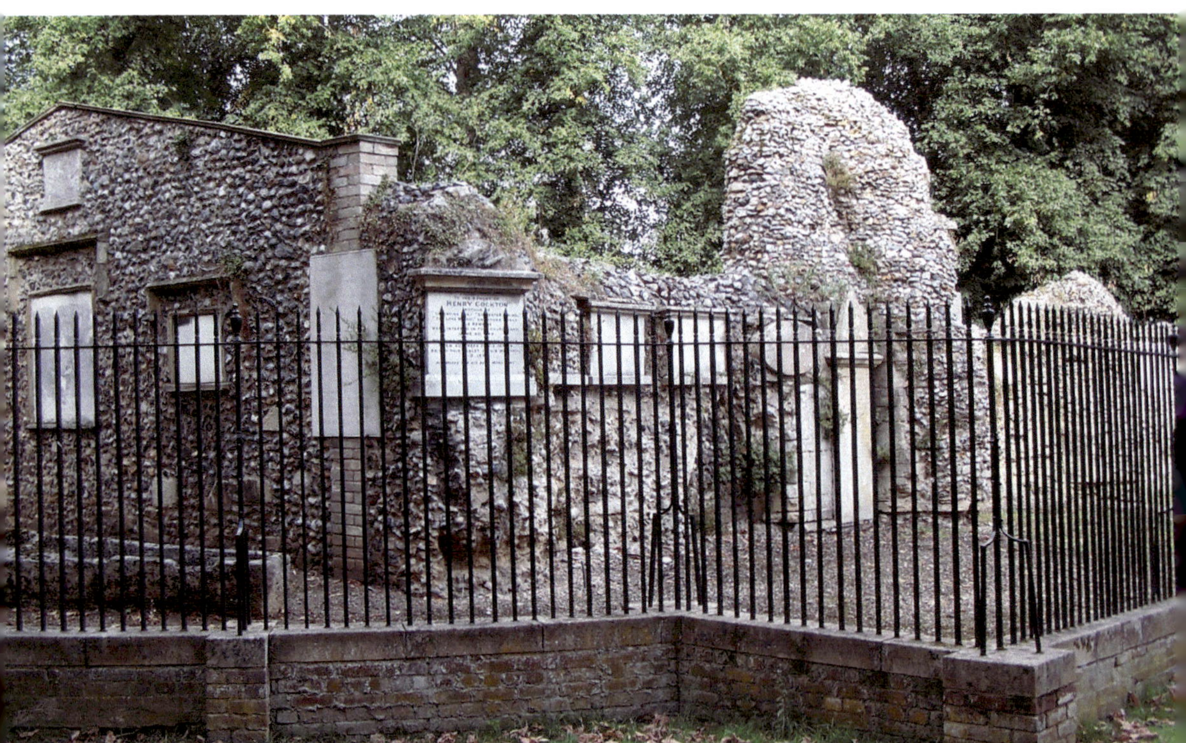

Commemorative plaques on the Charnel's exterior include John Boldero, gargantuan landlord of the Angel Hotel; Mary Haselton, who was struck down by lightening while saying her prayers at the tender age of nine years old; Henry Cockton, erstwhile Victorian author; and Bartholomew Gosnold, founder of Jamestown in 1607. Gosnold's daughter, Martha (Martha's Vineyard), is buried somewhere in the Great Churchyard, but where? However, the most poignant plaque is that of Sarah Lloyd, who was hanged in 1800 for burglary at the youthful age of nineteen. Her sombre epitaph here cautions those of errant ways: 'may my example be a warning to thousands'. The chapel, now surrounded by railings, had a very strange event occur here in 1844 when some poor soul walking across the crypt fell through the floor onto a bed of bones.

The Burials of Thomas Beaufort, 1377–1426

A son of John of Gaunt, Duke of Exeter was one of many titles bestowed on Thomas Beaufort, who commanded the rear guard of Henry V's English army at the Battle of Agincourt in 1415. Held in great esteem by all who knew him, he also became the executor of the king's will. Just before Thomas died, he left instructions to be buried next to his wife near the wall of the Lady Chapel (shown) in the abbey. It so happened that in February 1772, workmen working in the ruins came across his lead coffin. An eminent local physician, Thomas Gery Cullum, later a baronet, who had a surgery in Northgate Street, examined the deceased. He noted the extremely well-preserved state of the body, mainly due to the high-quality embalming, layers of cere cloth and the tight-fitting lead coffin. For

Lady Chapel of the Abbey of St Edmund.

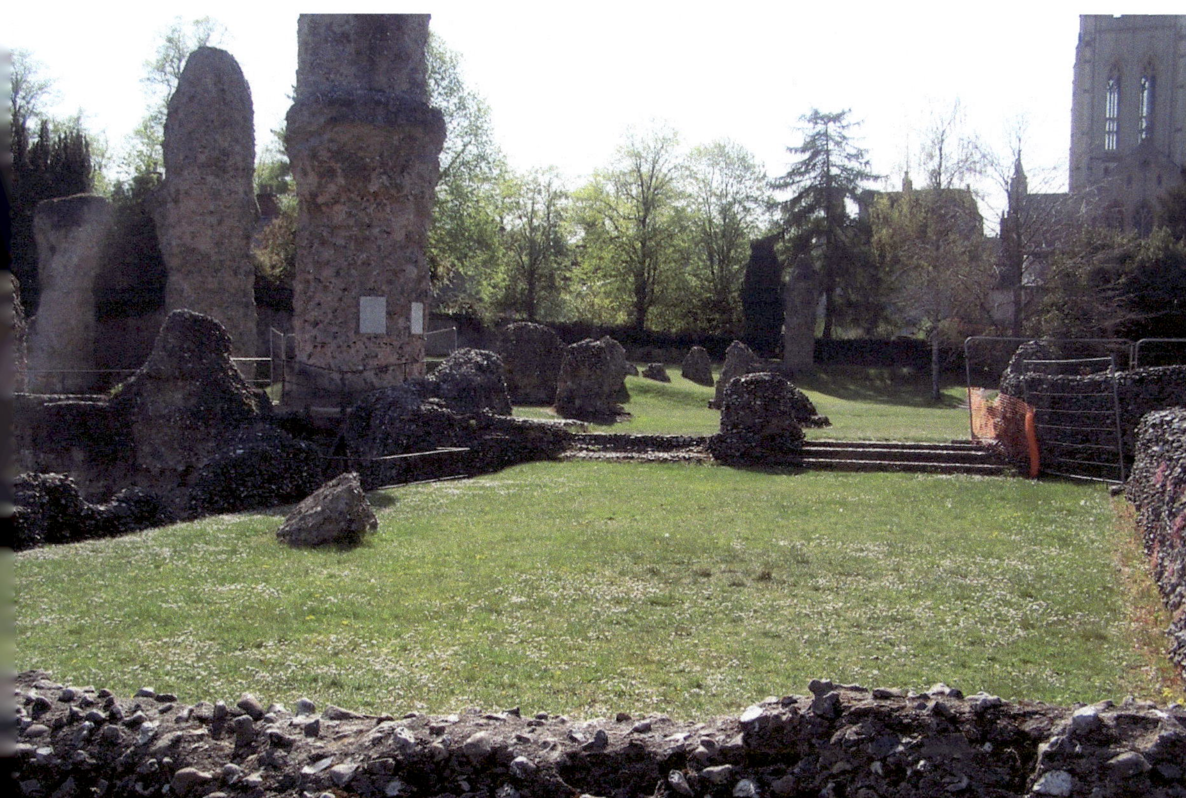

some inexplicable reason Cullum mutilated the corpse by severing its two hands, putting them into preserving fluid and sending them off to the Royal College of Surgeons. Many years later these hands disappeared despite a rigorous search for them. It also transpired that the 'good' doctor carried out further investigations on the body, also cutting off hair, now in Moyse's Hall Museum. As for the lead coffin, a local plumber paid around 15s for its scrap value, but what of the cadaver? It was reburied some 8 feet down in an oak casket. Apparently, a postscript to this occurred in 1834: the reburied coffin was exhumed again. The body within, now skeletal, had a bone removed and was shown at a meeting in 1849 of the Suffolk Institute of Archaeology and History. Hopefully, as far as is known, Thomas Beaufort has been finally laid to rest.

Abbots' Graves

Bury Abbey's dissolution and the destruction of its infrastructure would see books, manuscripts, texts and documents distributed far and wide. Hence why notable academic and ghost story writer, M. R. James, whose father Herbert was rector of St Peter's, Great Livermere, was able to discover in Douai, France, towards the end of the nineteenth century, the whereabouts of six abbots of St Edmundsbury Abbey. They were in the chapter house, the 'engine room' of the abbey; within these walls the monks were given the instructions for their day. With his local connections Montague knew the remains of the abbey intimately, even writing an acclaimed book on the subject.

On New Year's Day in 1903 the abbots' graves were uncovered. Five of the abbots were in coffins: Ording, Samson, Richard de Insula, Henry of Rushbrook and Edmund De Walpole, and Abbot Hugh I was without a coffin. Samson's coffin had a lead cross and the silver tip of a crozier inside (now in Moyse's Hall Museum). Common Christian practice then, as now, had people buried face up, looking east in expectation of the Second Coming

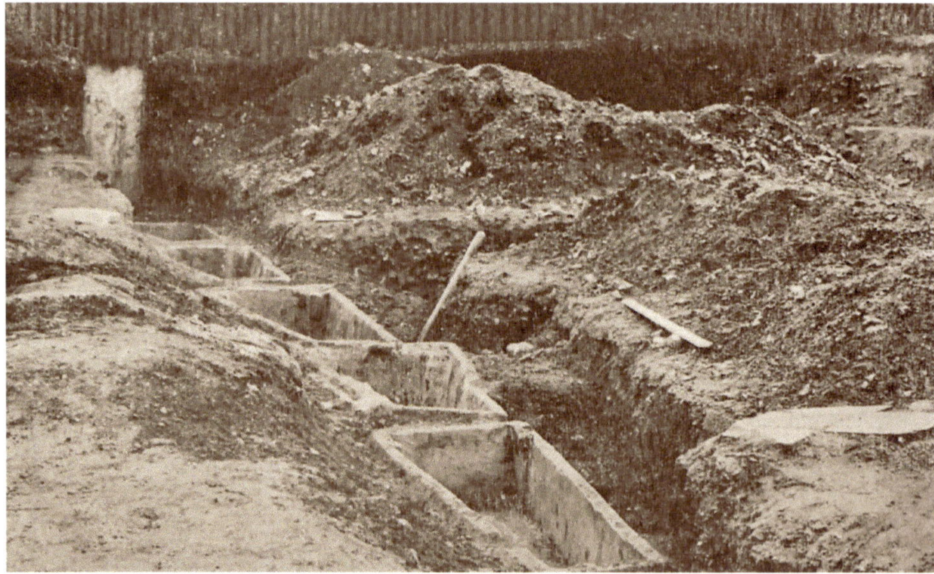

Abbots' graves.

of Christ, who would appear in Jerusalem. The abbots here faced west, in preparation for that glorious day to meet their flock. Apart from Abbot Hugh, the abbots were all reburied with new coffin lids of blue York stone supplied by local stonemason Hanchets for the princely sum of £8 12s. A curious add on is that any lettering change would incur an extra charge of 1 penny per letter. The bill was generously paid for by Henry Donne of Abbey Precincts in the Great Churchyard as his then garden included the chapter house.

Mary Tudor, Queen of France

Mary Rose Tudor, the stunning younger sister of Henry VIII, was married twice. The first, an arranged marriage to the elderly Louis XII of France, lasted just three months. A trusted courtier was sent over to France to fetch Mary, who was then in quarantine in Cluny in case she was pregnant with an heir to the French throne. Much to the chagrin of Henry, she remarried Charles Brandon, an upwardly mobile courtier who became Duke of Suffolk; she had four children with him. One daughter, Frances, married well. She married Henry Grey, 3rd Marquess of Dorset. It was this union that produced Lady Jane Grey, queen in name only for nine days in 1553, twenty years after the death of her grandmother.

In 1533, the attractive Mary died, at the age of thirty-seven, at Westhorpe, the family home, from the 'Tudor curse', or sweating sickness – possibly tuberculosis. The funeral was a very grand affair, befitting a person of royal rank. After her body had laid in state for a while at Westhorpe, a cortège led by French heralds and 100 poor men in black hoods and gowns made of rough cloth and carrying wax tapers, preceded to Bury St Edmunds. The hearse, drawn by six black horses, magnificently draped in black velvet, was followed by chaplains, mounted knights and family mourners, which included Frances and Henry Grey and Henry Brandon, Frances's brother. Winding their way to the still magnificent Abbey of St Edmundsbury, they went through the villages of Bacton, Wyverstone, Badwell Ash, Ashfield, Norton and Thurston. En route, peasants left the fields to swell the cortège – incentives of free ale, food and a few pence thrown in were not to be sneered at after all.

Into Bury St Edmunds the procession came, through what we know today as the Norman Tower, into the enormous Abbey Church of St Edmund. It was the last great procession to take this route. The French heralds proclaimed, 'Pray for the soul of the right high excellent Princess and right Christian Queen Mary, late Queen of France.' Neither her husband, Charles Brandon, nor the king attended the funeral, which in those days was not uncommon.

After a Requiem Mass on 22 July 1533, with Abbot Reeve probably officiating, she was buried in a handsome alabaster monumental tomb, which was destroyed at the dissolution. Six years later, Mary was moved to St Mary's Church. In 1758, professor of modern history at Cambridge, Dr John Symonds, later of St Edmunds Hill (todays Moreton Hall), paid for the repair of her tomb (now in the north-east of the chancel) and put an inscribed marble tablet to her on the wall there. Her rest was disturbed again in 1784 when her very plain grave was opened by St Mary's churchwardens accompanied by local dignitary Sir John Cullum of the noble family of Hawstead and later Hardwick. What only can be called an act of desecration occurred on her embalmed body, which was still in a reasonable state of preservation. Small locks of her golden/auburn hair, from near 2-foot-long tresses were trimmed off, eventually one being presented to the Duchess of Portland. Another wisp in a gold locket can be seen today in Moyse's Hall Museum. Not many parish churches in England, though, can claim such a royal presence – a remarkable visitor attraction.

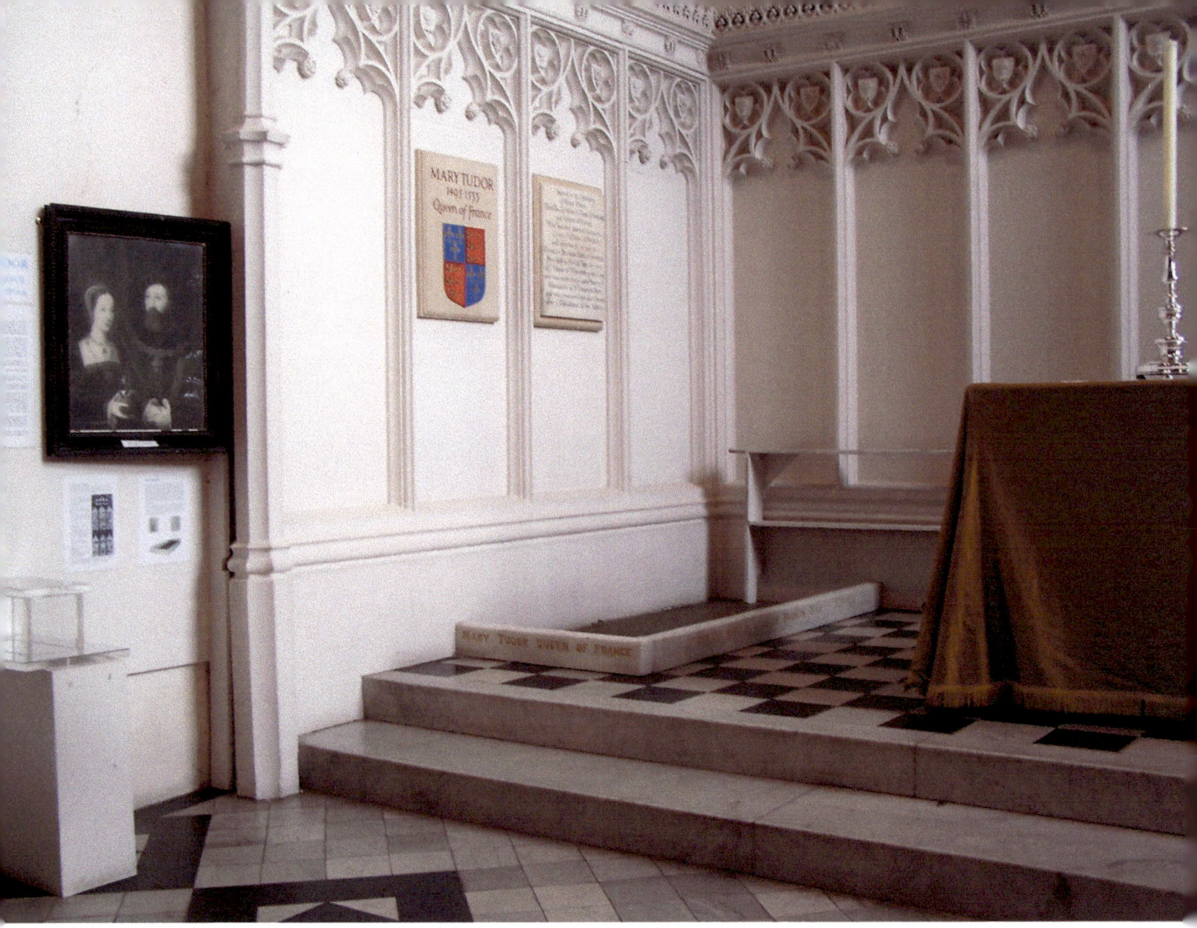

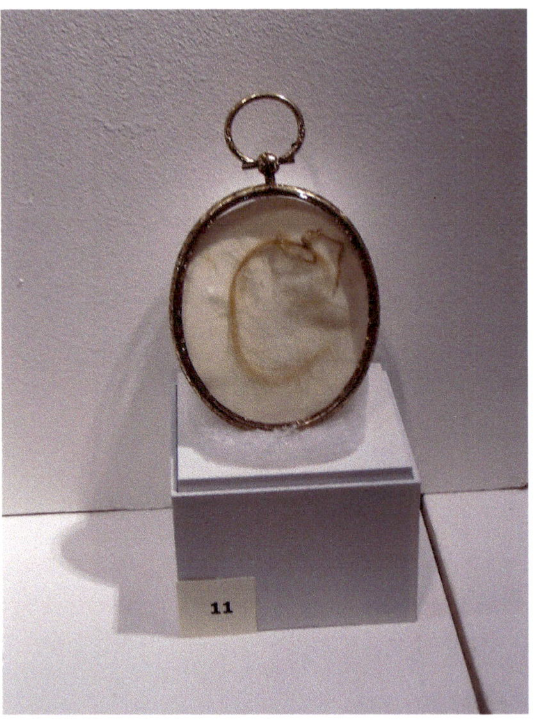

Above: The plain grave of Mary Rose Tudor.

Left: A lock of Mary Tudor's hair. (Moyse's Hall Museum)

Francis King Eagle

Designed by Cooper & Peck, architects of the cemetery lodge and chapels, this obelisk, now Grade II listed, was erected by public subscription in 1857 to the first mayor of Bury St Edmunds. The Borough Cemetery had opened in 1855 at the end of Field Lane, becoming appropriately Cemetery Road, then King's Road in 1912 to celebrate George V's coronation a year earlier. Francis King Eagle, born in November 1784 in Lakenheath, went to Bury Grammar School and then to Trinity College, Cambridge, in 1809. After qualifying as a lawyer, he later came back to Bury, residing at No. 19 Crown Street in 1831. With the widening a year later of the national franchise, which gave more men the vote, he stood as the Reform Party, candidate to represent Bury St Edmunds in Parliament, trying to upset the status quo, that of Lord Charles Fitzroy and Earl Jermyn, well-heeled local aristocrats. With nearly 600 voters instead of the thirty-seven members of the corporation that used to elect the two MPs to Parliament (you could say Bury was a 'pocket borough' then) there was a chance F. K. E. could succeed. Despite a recount on the grounds of alleged malpractice in as much some voters were bribed, F. K. E. lost. His supporters rioted, windows were smashed in Whiting Street, the house owner, a Philip Case, defended himself, firing a fowling piece resulting in a woman being injured. Before the town had a mayor, an Alderman led the corporation and the election of F. K. E. as the first modern-day mayor on 1 January 1836 following the Municipal Corporation Act turned out to be a foregone conclusion. This popular man went on to become a County Court judge and died on 8 June 1856.

Obelisk dedicated to Francis King Eagle, first mayor of Bury St Edmunds.

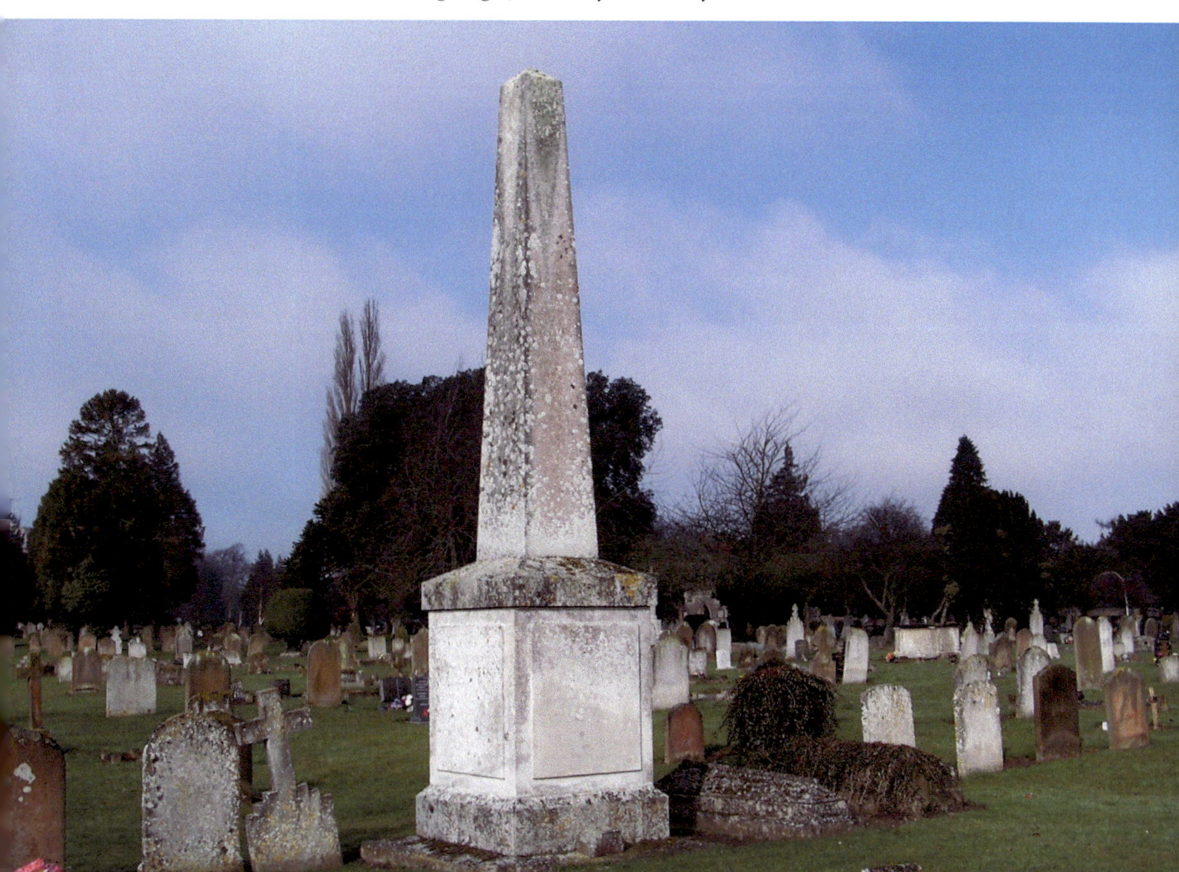

Frederic Gershom Parkington, 1886–52

Frederic Gershom Parkington was born above his father's military tailor's shop at No. 29 Abbeygate Street. A blue plaque is now there. No doubt the young Frederic, seeing the grammar school boys going past his first-floor window and carrying their violin and cello cases on the way to lessons inspired him to take up the cello, winning a scholarship to the Royal College of Music. He became prolific at arranging music early on in his career making music to fit the new age of phonograph records in the 1920s. Around then, he also became fascinated by time and started collecting timepieces. He formed a world-famous quintet and became popular on the wireless.

In the 1930s silver-screen actors and stars from the music world were used by cigarette manufacturers to promote their brand. Frederic was feted in this way. It would seem you had reached the pinnacle of your profession if your activities were published in a set of cigarette cards. With the coming of the Second World War he toured the country, performing for the armed services; however, this war tragically altered his life. His son, John, was killed in the North African campaign. Frederic died in 1952 in Jersey, but he kept his son's memory alive as his will of 1953 bequeathed his fabulous collection of clocks, watches, etc., to the town of Bury St Edmunds. A museum showing these was opened in 1954 at Angel Corner, but after two burglaries it moved to the Manor House Museum. On its closure the collection was temporarily put in storage at West Stow, but now can be seen in Moyse's Hall Museum. He is buried in Bury St Edmunds Cemetery in Compartment 69, space 251.

Grave of Frederic Gershom Parkington.

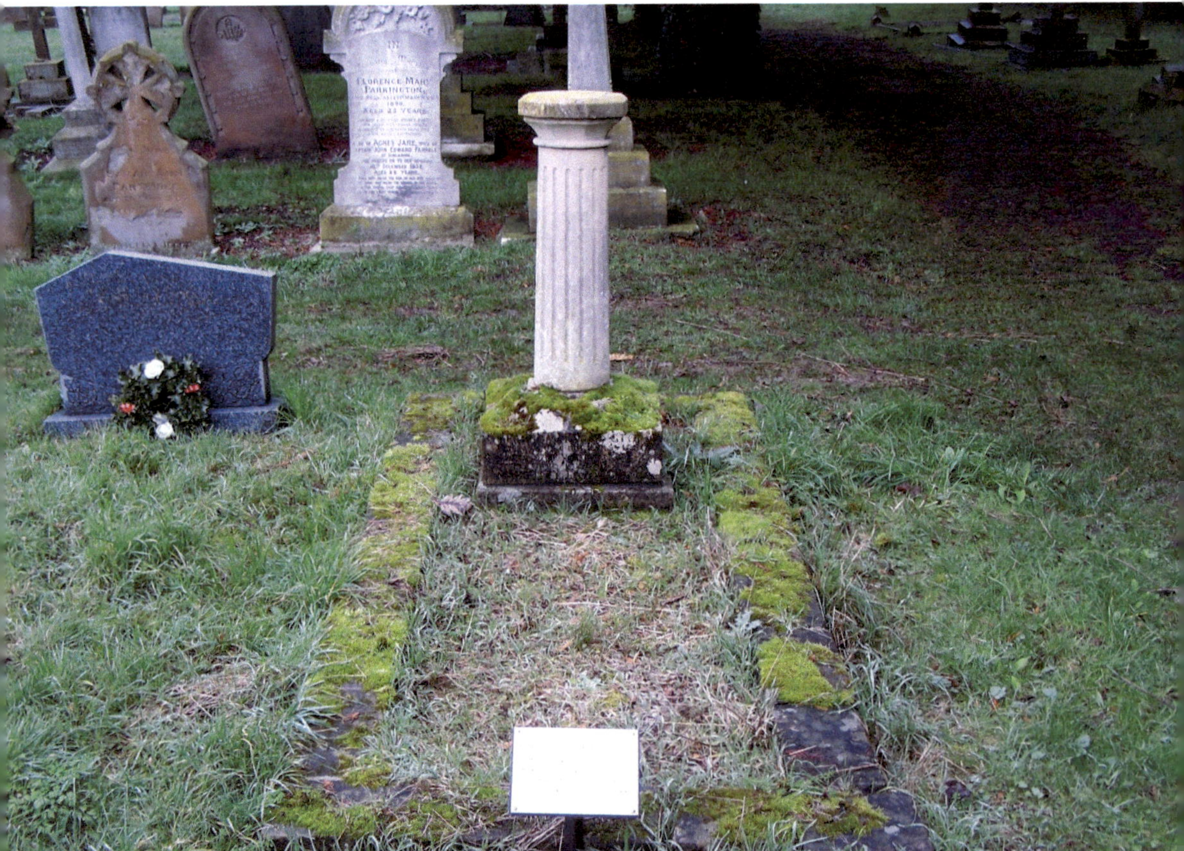

Where Is St Edmund?

Much has been written as to the whereabouts of the martyrdom of King Edmund of East Anglia, who became St Edmund the Martyr, first patron saint of England. His superb statue, by Dame Elizabeth Frink from 1976, is at the abbey's west front. We know for certain he was martyred at a place called Haegelisdun; modern-day thinking is that Bradfield St Clare is the location. This makes sense then for his body to end up at the nearest religious site – the monastery at Beodericsworth founded by King Sigeberht circa AD 635. Here he laid in a wooden church until Cnut ousted the secular monks there and built a stone rotunda church in 1020, installing Benedictine monks from Ely and Benet at Holme. Over time, thanks to the patronage of various monarchs and veneration by thousands of pilgrims, the abbey church housing Edmund's shrine eventually became the largest Romanesque church in northern Europe. As expected from such a devout man, miracles were forthcoming, even to the point of escaping a terrible fire in 1198, which saw much of his magnificent shrine damaged. Abbot Samson very humbly opened the coffin in the presence of several monks to check if any harm was done to Edmund's body, which amazingly was uncorrupted. With trepidation and reverence, Samson removed the cere cloth protecting Edmund's face, even commenting upon the largeness of his nose. This was the last time that Edmund's body was verified. When Henry VIII's commissioners came in 1539 to do their worst, Edmund had gone, and the shrine was empty. Clearly the monks knew they were coming, so did they remove Edmund to a place of safety? If so, where? To quote Shakespeare: 'There's the rub.'

Statue of St Edmund by Dame Elizabeth Frink.

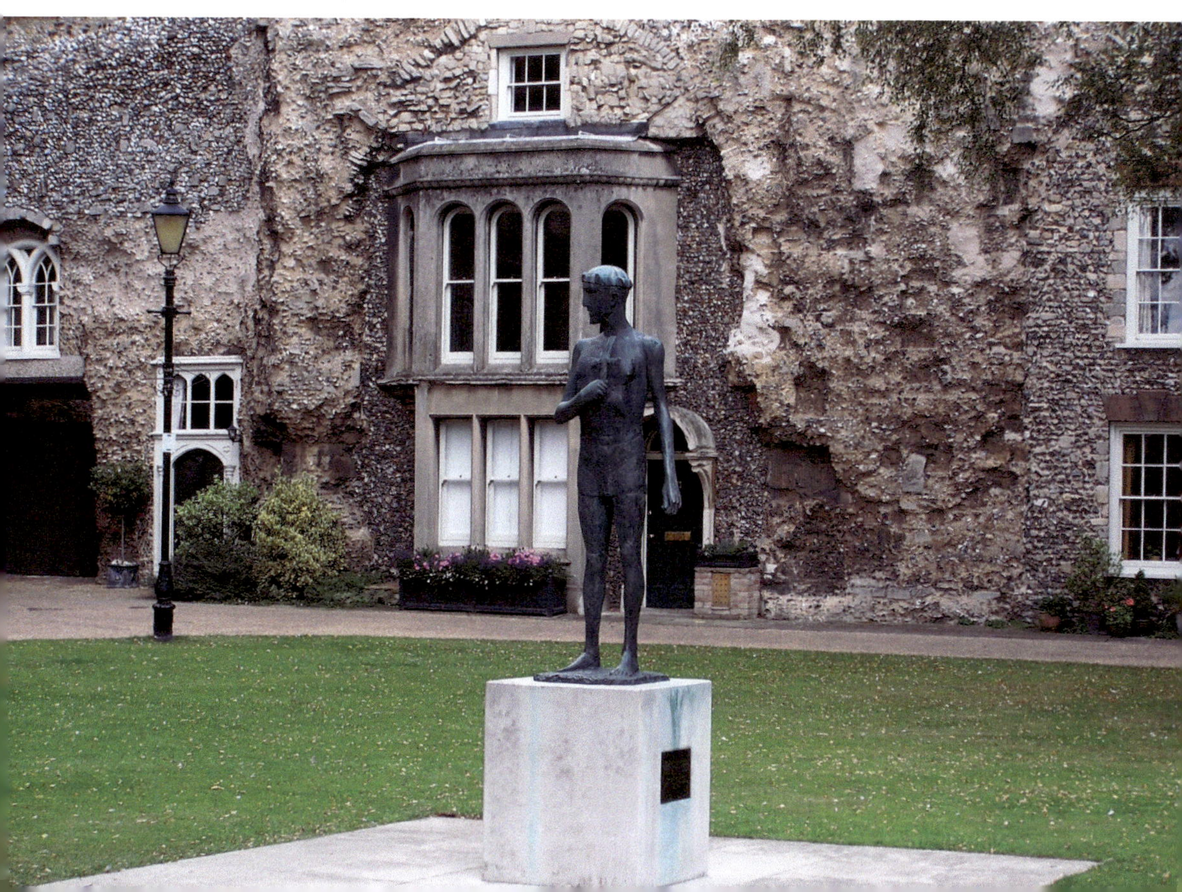

Saxon Burials

In July 1972, a development on former allotments on the west of the town, near Westgarth Gardens, was well underway. A combination of houses and chalet bungalows were being built by Decmar Properties under the guidance of foreman Jack Gladwell. As the site progressed on the south bank of the River Linnet, a startling discovery revealed itself – an Anglo-Saxon cemetery. Work stopped and the archaeologists moved in. It transpired that this was no ordinary burial site, such as the seventh-century graves that had been discovered in Northumberland Avenue and Barons Road. Altogether, sixty-nine graves were discovered dating from around the fifth to the seventh century. There were sixty-five burials, inhumations as opposed to four cremations, both Christian and Pagan, reflecting differing beliefs as time progressed. Unusually, there was a high proportion of weapons in the graves, with spears found in fourteen of them. However, one grave stood out from the rest – No. 62. It contained the remains of an adult male and some remnants of assorted weapons, but the most outstanding of the grave goods was a beautiful pale green glass bucket in near perfect condition. The small bucket, with two handles, was described as being of exquisite workmanship and similar to earlier Roman glass vessels. The bucket went on loan to Moyse's Hall Museum with some other finds from the site, but eventually sold at auction in 1977. The British Rail Pension Fund, who had purchased it, kindly then let it go back to Moyse's on loan. Ultimately, it went back to the sale room in 2004 where it sold for an astonishing £116,650, including premium at Bonhams. Appropriately, part of the housing site is called Saxon Rise. Many years later the following question was raised: were any graves were missed?

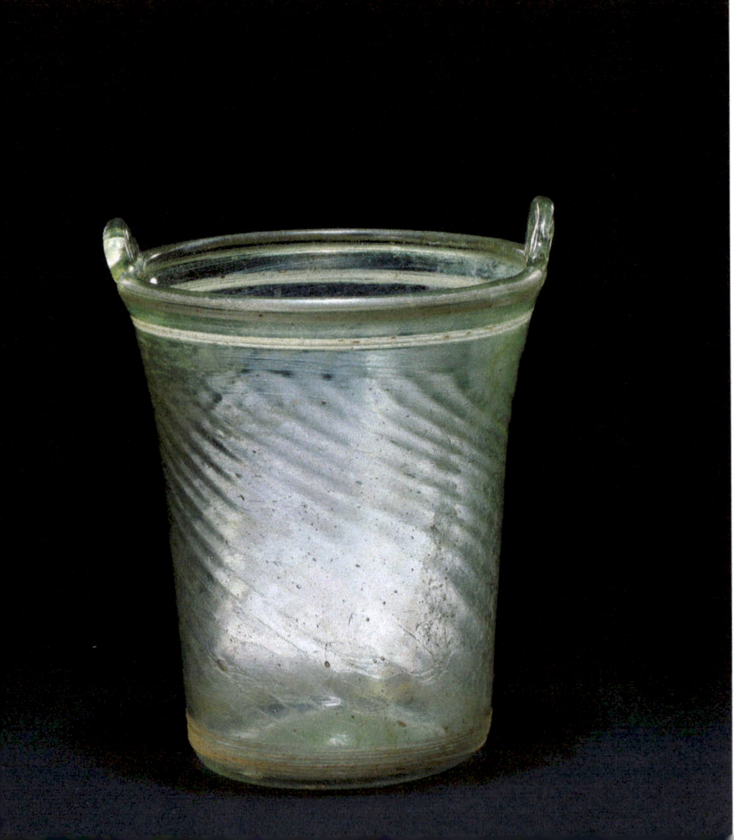

Pale green glass bucket found in a Saxon grave.

Buried Limestone

A few years ago a number of pieces of ashlar limestone, some carved, were uncovered in the garden of No. 35a Southgate Street, adjacent to the Abbey Hotel, formerly the Olde White Hart public house. Some have since been used to form a drystone wall there, and a small quantity have been donated to be part of the wolf statue on Southgate Green. This oolitic sedimentary rock dressed limestone from Barnack on the Northamptonshire border was part of St Botolph's Chapel. Richard Yates, a distinguished nineteenth-century antiquarian said this stood in the yard of the White Hart. Another historian, Edmund Gillingwater, in his *History of Bury St Edmunds* (1804) professed: 'In this yard stood St Botolph's Chapel. This building was standing about three years since but is now wholly taken down and demolished.' So, it would seem not all the stone was reused as building material as in other parts of the town. However, Southgate Street was a suburb of the town and a processional route much used by pilgrims on the way to St Edmund's shrine; while nearby St Botolph's Lane in medieval times was called Yoxfore Lane. St Botolph, aka Botwulf, a patron saint of travellers, was an English saint who died in AD 680. Little is known of this abbot, but he is described in the *Anglo-Saxon Chronicle* as having several churches dedicated to him. Cnut even had Botolph's remains transferred to Bury for a time and later there would be a chapel dedicated to St Botolph in the abbey church. In the town the Guild of St Botolph used to meet at the College of Sweet Jesus in College Street.

Ashlar limestone found in the garden of No. 35a Southgate Street.

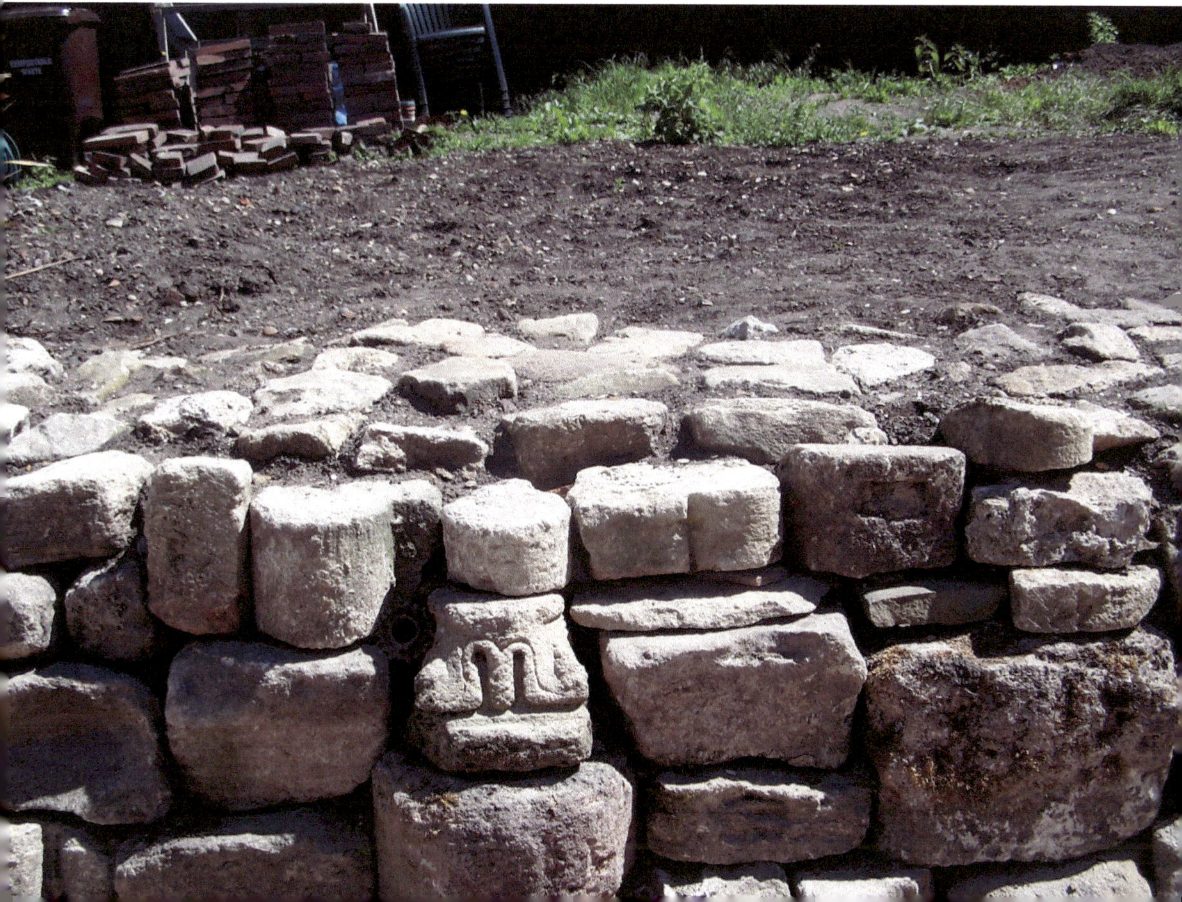

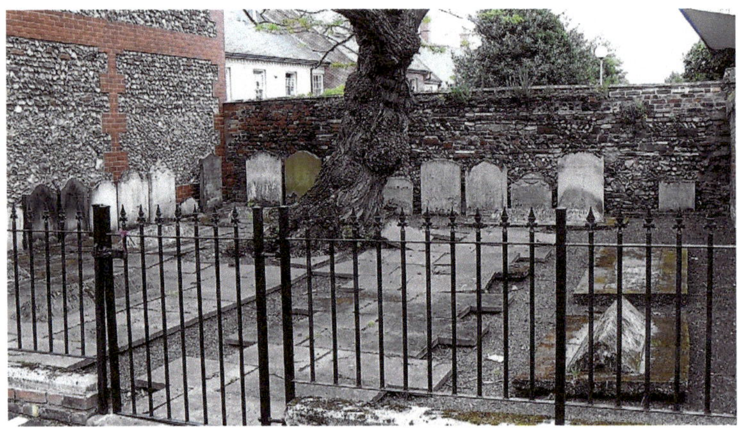

Baptist Chapel Graveyard, Lower Baxter Street.

Baptist Chapel Graveyard, Lower Baxter Street

The inaugural Baptist Chapel, founded in 1800 in the then named Nether Baxter Street, saw its expanding congregation move to a new chapel in Garland Street in 1834, known as the Eberneezer Chapel. Hidden away at the rear of a council car park is the Baptist Chapel graveyard. The gravestones consolidated here after January 1956 when the graveyard was sold for £250 to the council.

Rehoboth Baptist Chapel, Out Westgate

A breakaway Rehoboth Baptist Chapel was opened in 1840 in Out Westgate for a stricter interpretation of the Bible. Its name means 'open spaces'. Sold off by the Evangelical Trust in 1989, during subsequent building work at the rear unexpected graves were discovered.

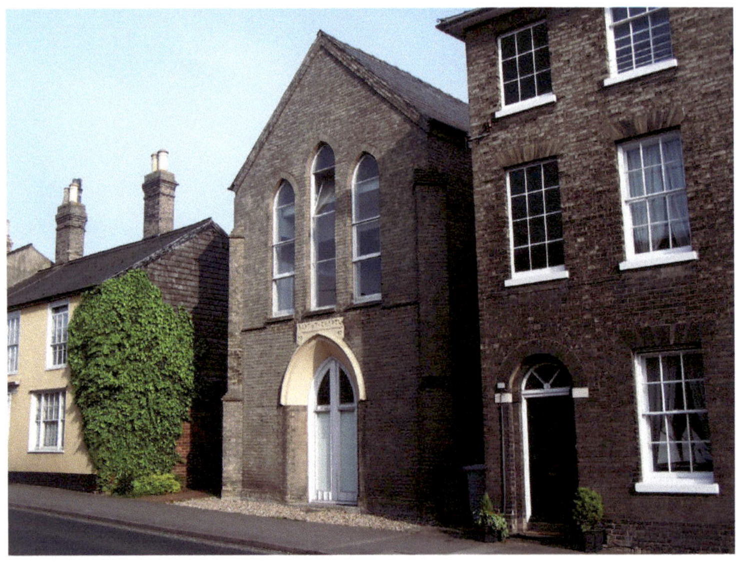

Rehoboth Baptist Chapel.

Quaker Burials

Quakers have been meeting on this site since 1682. The street was then known as Long Brackland. In 1751 a meeting house was built. It was refronted in Victorian times and then in 2007–08 an extension was added.

Sarah Bott, the beneficiary of the wills of Sarah and Samuel Fennel, was given burial land to the rear in St Andrew's Street North. Bott's purpose-built flats, the Fennel Homes, opened in 1874. In the rear of houses to the north of Well Street, Quakers also met. Their burial ground (now gone), shown here on a map of 1885, opened in 1748.

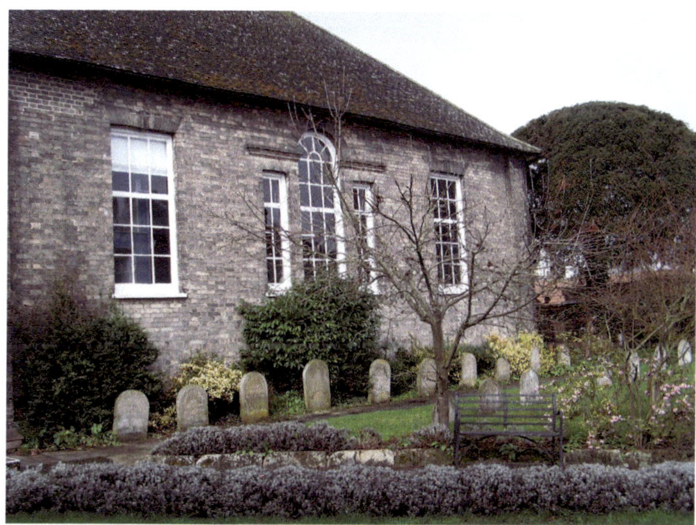

Right: The Friends Meeting House.

Below: Map of the former Quaker burial ground.

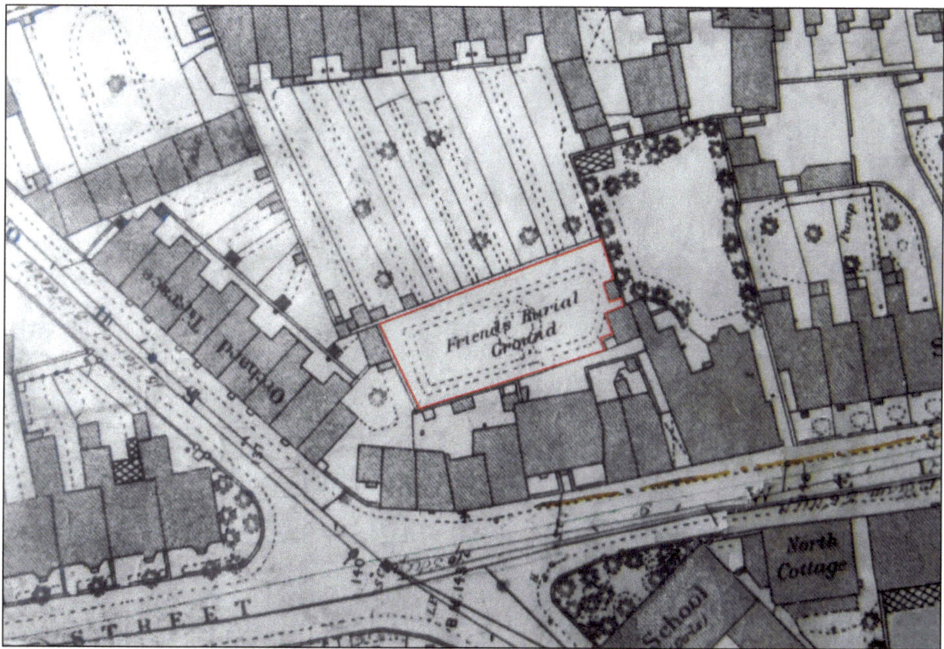

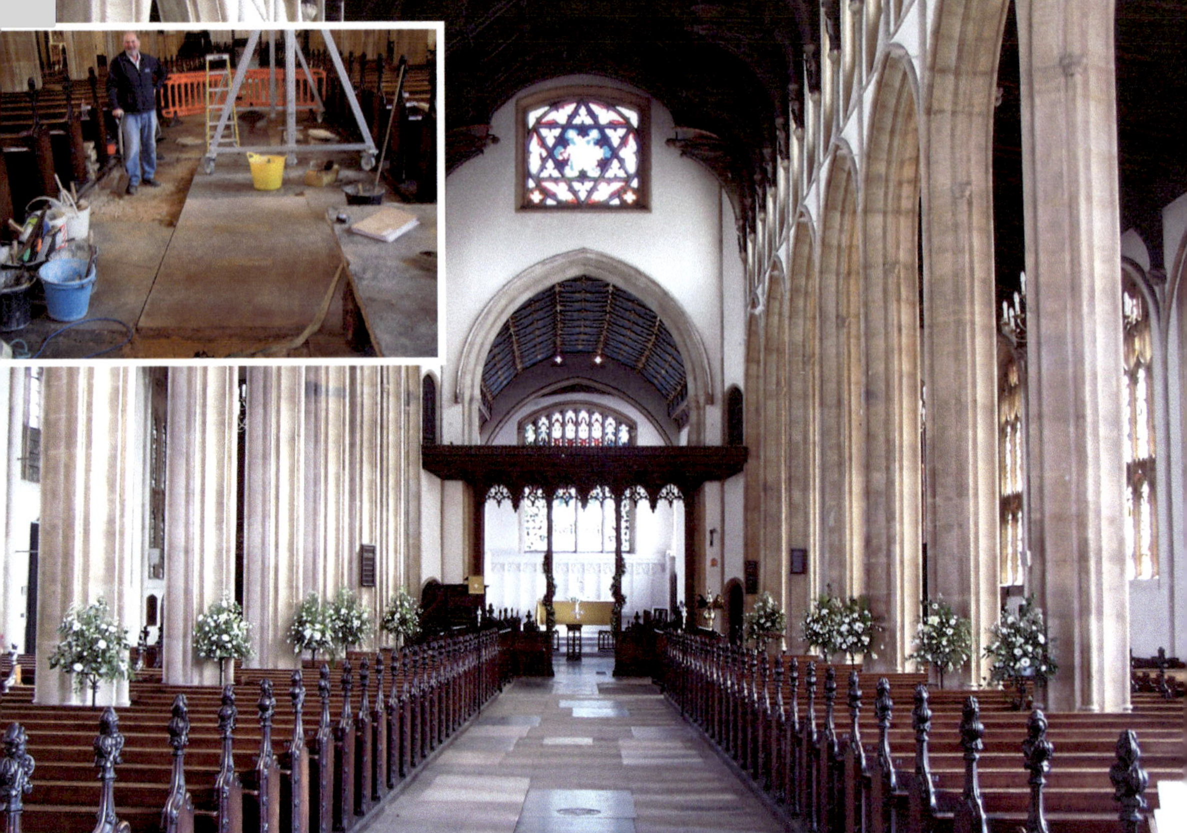

Nave burials in St Mary's Church.

St Mary's Church

According to a historical account of St Mary's Parish Church by notable historian Samuel Tymms in 1854, there are twelve memorials in the nave, which is one of the longest of any parish church in England. With its magnificent angel roof above, to be buried in the town's civic church carried some kudos. However, a physical count up of graves in the nave's central aisle numbers twenty-seven – an error on Tymm's part or are they grave memorial slabs from elsewhere? In February 2020, some paving slabs were realigned by Abbeygate Masonry due to subsidence on their sandy bed.

Abbot John Reeve, aka de Melford (Abbacy: 1514–40)

John Reeve, from the Order of St Benedict, has a melancholic honour: he was the last abbot of the fifth-richest Benedictine abbey in the country. In 1533 the lavish funeral of Mary Brandon, Queen of France, was the last significant event at the abbey church prior to its dissolution in 1539. The Act of Supremacy in 1534 saw Henry VIII established as the head of his newly created Church of England and avariciously looking to the wealth of the monasteries. In 1538 his commissioners arrived at the abbey, surprised at its administration, a testament to John Reeve. Attempting to prise away jewels and precious metals from Edmund's magnificent shrine they commented that 'it was exceedingly cumbrous to deface'. On 4 November 1539, Abbot Reeve and forty-one monks signed the abbey's deed

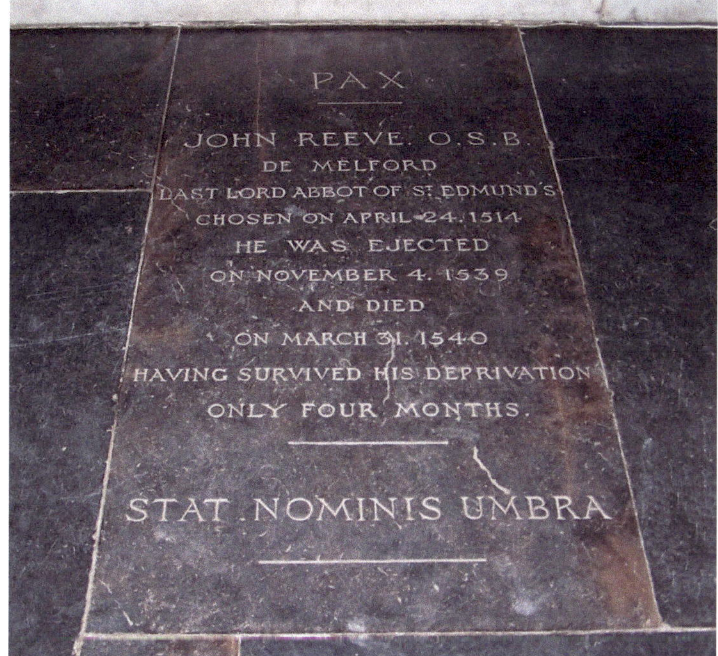

Abbot John Reeve. The Latin inscription 'STAT. NOMINIS UMBRA' literally means 'the shadow of a name' – one whose early greatness has been attenuated.

of surrender. He received a house in Crown Street and an enormous pension of 500 marks, though he never collected it. He was rumoured to have died of a broken heart and was buried in St Mary's, His brass, removed in 1643, showed his coat of arms.

Another epitaph says:

Here rest the sepulchred bones of that man who Bury formerly acknowledged Lord and Abbot, born at Melford in Suffolk, named John, his father and family Reeves. He was magnanimous, prudent, learned, benignant, and upright, loving the religion to which he was dedicated. Who, when he had seen the 31st year of the reign of Henry VIII on the 31st of March, sunk untimely to the grave, spare his soul, O gracious God! 1540.

Priory Hotel Burial, Mildenhall Road

Franciscan monks came to Bury St Edmunds in 1238, settling in what we know today as Friar's Lane. Abbot Henry de Rushbrook objected to these potential rivals and had them removed. In 1262, with the help of Gilbert de Clare, the friars settled in at the Babwell Fen, just outside the Banleuca – the area of jurisdiction of St Edmundsbury Abbey. The Priory Hotel is built on part of the friary site that is now a scheduled monument. Franciscans were mendicant monks, travelling around preaching and doing good deeds. They were not popular with the wealthy, powerful Benedictine abbey, whose abbot saw his role as the guardian of Edmund's shrine. The town was taxed and controlled by the abbey and because of this some of the townspeople supported the friars, even leaving bequests to them.

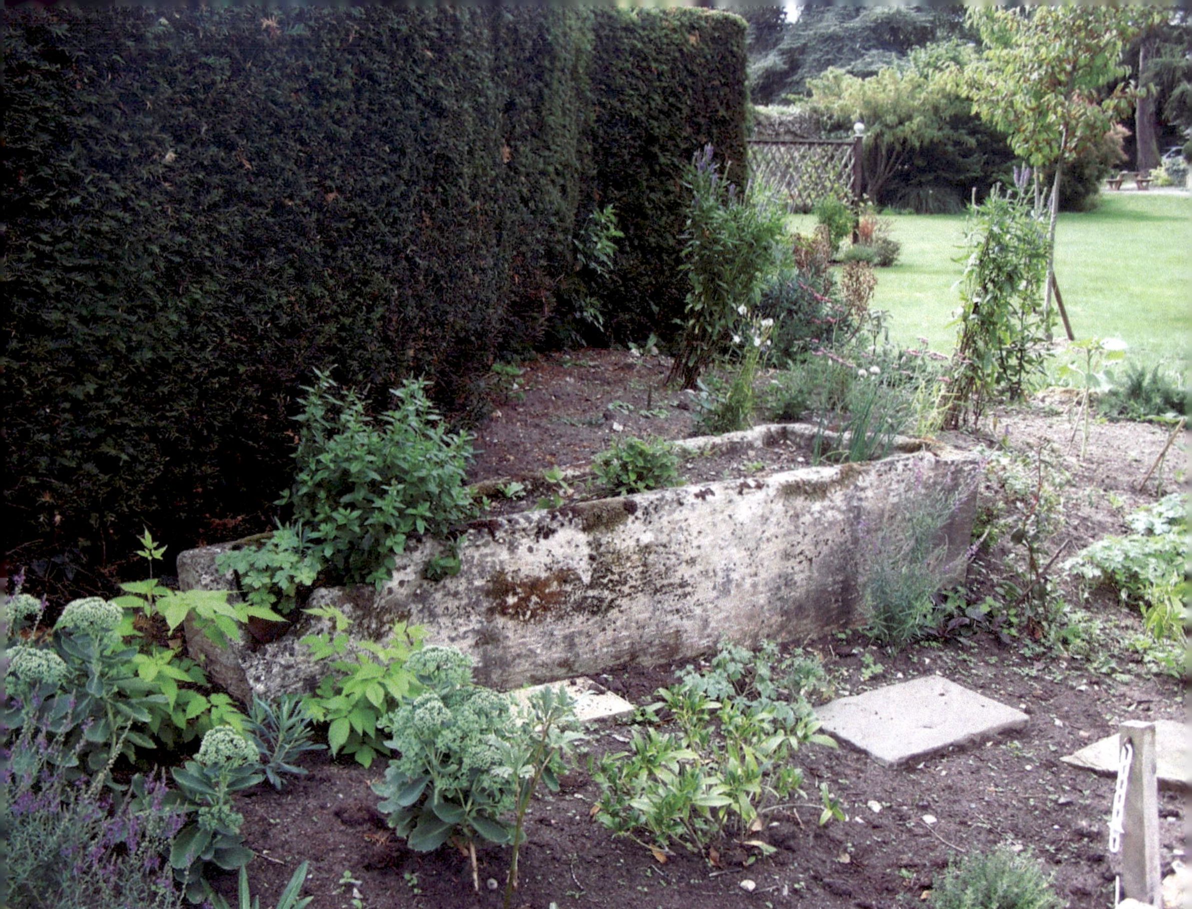

Priory Hotel burial.

Henry VIII closed the friary in 1538. It would eventually become a private house for the Boldero family. The Cullum family then owned it from the late eighteenth century until the break-up of the Cullum estate in the 1920s. Later, Alderman Olle lived here until he sold it, becoming the Priory Hotel in 1975. It is now a Best Western Hotel.

An archaeological dig in 1990 for owner Edward Cobbold's extensions to the hotel uncovered foundations of the friary church, along with twenty-three burials. One, found with a chalice and paten, probably belonged to Robert Windell, Order of Friars Minor. He was appointed on 14 January 1423 as suffragan bishop (assistant) in the dioceses of Norwich, only to be deprived of the see in 1425. He would later obtain posts at Worcester in 1433 and Salisbury from 1435 until his death in 1441. His will of 1411 requested he be buried at Babwell.

St Edmund's Church Crypt: A Notable Burial

The Catholic Relief Act of 1829 allowed Catholics more involvement in public life, emancipation, and freedom of worship. Against this background Charles Day of Worcester built a Catholic Church in Westgate Street in Ketton stone, which was consecrated on 14 December 1837. Until then services were conducted in a chapel at the rear of the adjacent presbytery.

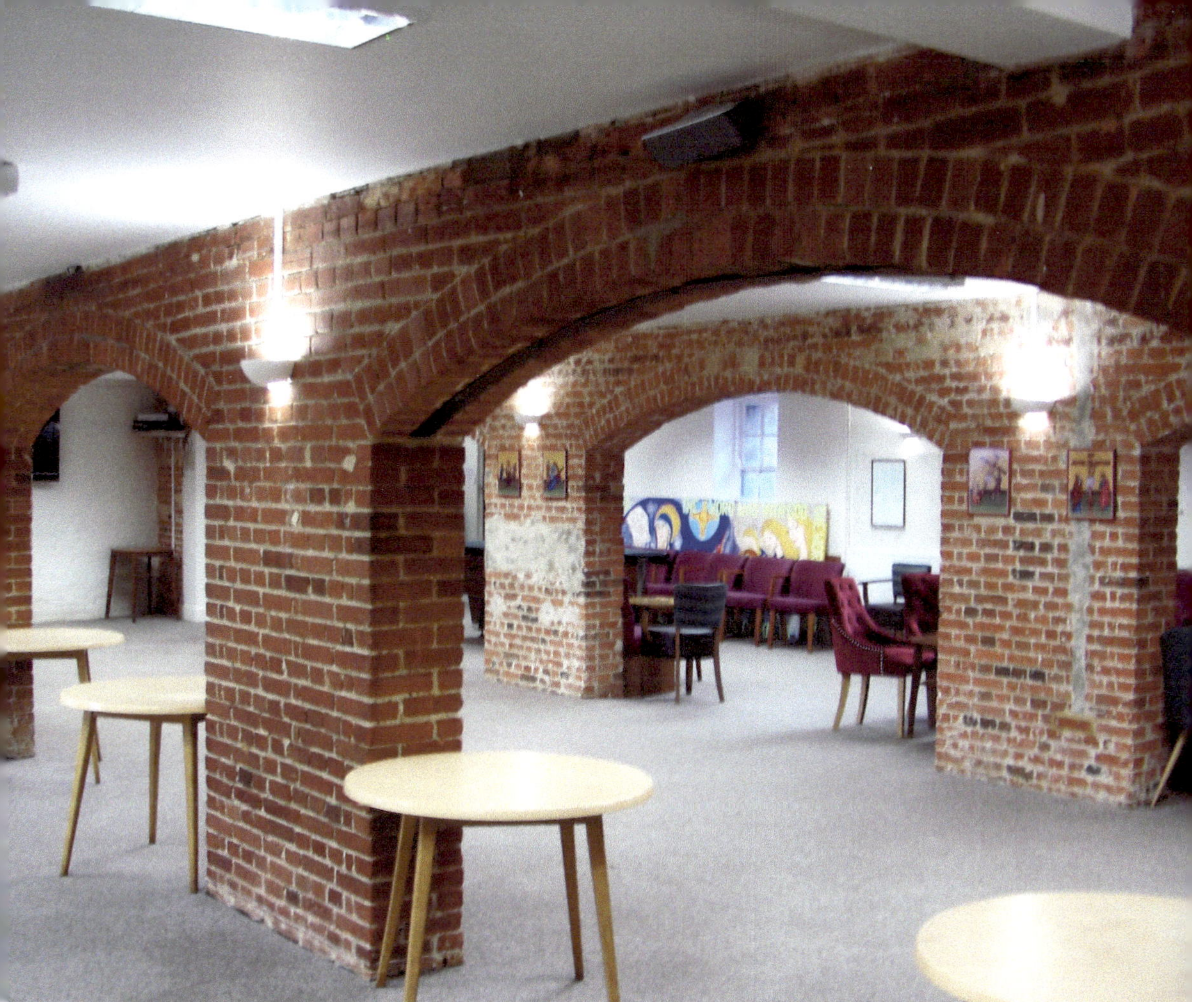

St Edmund's Church's crypt.

Burials of four priests were carried out in its garden before the church was built; whether they were exhumed and reburied in the crypt is unknown. However, it appears that a burial did take place in the crypt in 1854, that of a highly respected member of a notable local Catholic family, the Hon. Charles Berney Petre. On the day of his funeral tradesmen even shut their shops. His family subsequently installed a commemorative plaque in St Edmund's Church porch and translation of its Latin wording gives credence to the account that he is buried in the crypt. A 1920/1 receipt from George Pettit, builder and undertaker of St Andrew's Street North, supports the existence of such a burial within the crypt: 'Building new wall to cemetery, filling up deep well, laying asphalt floor, erecting stage…'

Around 1973/74 two parishioners were engaged to carry out refurbishment of the crypt. While laying a new floor a hole revealed a vault with a coffin raised on two plinths approximately 3–4 feet below floor level, apparently lead or metal with no sign of rusting, covered in material with a silver crucifix. No nameplate was visible, but it was obviously the remains of someone of nobility. They kept the matter secret, apart from informing a member of the clergy. In recent years an amazing restoration of the crypt showed no evidence of the burial.

Independent Chapel Burial Ground, Whiting Street

The earliest Nonconformist chapel in the town (from 1646), the Independent Chapel is now the United Reform Church. This came into being in 1972 when the Congregational Church and the Presbyterian Church amalgamated. It is mainly timber framed internally, though was rebuilt in 1804 at a cost of £1,200. Further work costing £600 was carried out in 1869 and a church hall for a Sunday school was added in 1887. The obelisk memorial, erected on the forecourt by Hanchets, is a smaller version of the Martyrs' Memorial in the Great Churchyard; it is to Elias Thacker and John Coping. During Elizabeth I's reign they were hanged for disseminating literature, not wanting the monarch to be head of the English Church. They follwed the teachings of Robert Browne's 'Brownist Movement', an early Nonconformist sect later to became Congregationalists.

During the eighteenth century the Independent Chapel was attended by cloth makers and wool and yarn dealers, especially the Cumberland and Corsbie families, as well as William Buck, once partner to James Oakes – he went into banking and Buck went into partnership with brewer Benjamin Greene.

This drawing of the chapel shows the view from College Lane (Hog Lane); however, the graveyard was closed for usage in 1856, a year after the opening of the Borough Cemetery. The Great Churchyard itself was closed in this year by an Act of Parliament, which decided that burials in urban areas could be detrimental and injurious to the wellbeing of residents. Allowed, though, were burials of deceased family members reunited with their departed loved ones. Today the Independent Chapel burial ground is a car park.

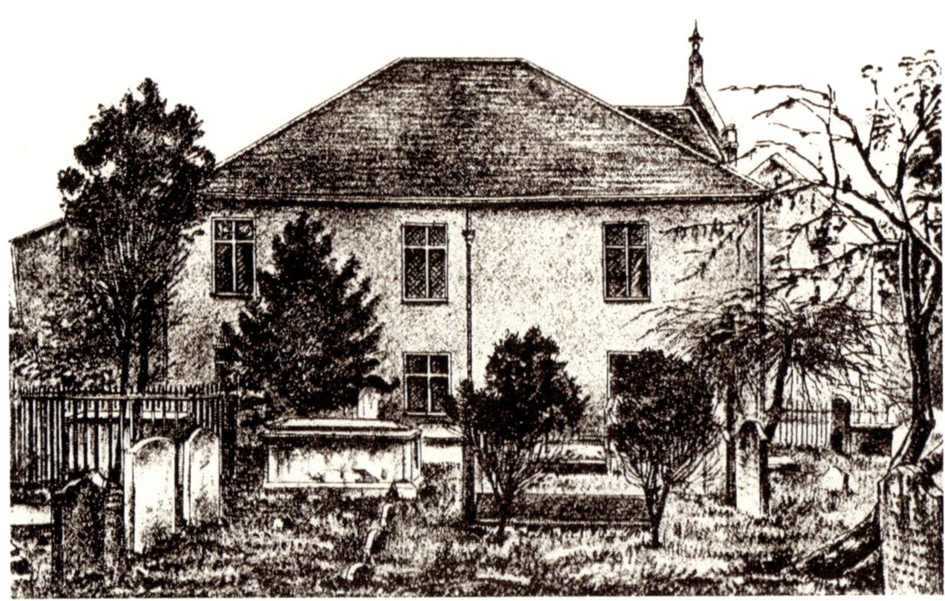

Independent Chapel.

The Borough Cemetery

The Great Churchyard closed in 1855 following an Act of Parliament:

> The Burial Act of 1853 banning burials in urban areas whereby any such Order in Council as aforesaid it is ordered that no new Burial Ground shall be opened in any City or Town, or within any limits therein mentioned, without the previous approval of one of her Majesty's Principal Secretaries of State, no new Burial Ground or Cemetery (parochial or non-parochial) shall be provided and used in such City or Town, or within such limits, without such previous approval.

The Borough Cemetery was opened in 1855 at the end of Field Lane (King's Road). The corporation had purchased 11 acres of land for £2,276 from the estate of George Brown of Tostock in 1838. Since then, other areas have been procured as in 1880 and there has been utilisation of the former allotments that led off Hospital Road. The cemetery is divided into compartments, with each grave given a designated number. It is approaching full capacity, though some family burials are still permitted; as of July 2020 there were 36,644 burials. One particular area along one of the boundary walls is very poignant: here 463 stillborn babies were buried in unmarked graves between August 1867 and March 1887.

Today access to the cemetery is from West Road (photo taken here), Hospital Road and King's Road. The caretaker's lodge is built of Kentish ragstone, as were two chapels within the cemetery, and all were designed by the architects Cooper & Peck. One Nonconformist chapel was mysteriously burnt down around 1968 and demolished several years later. With the opening of the Risby crematorium in 1989 there are obviously fewer burials these days.

The Borough Cemetery.

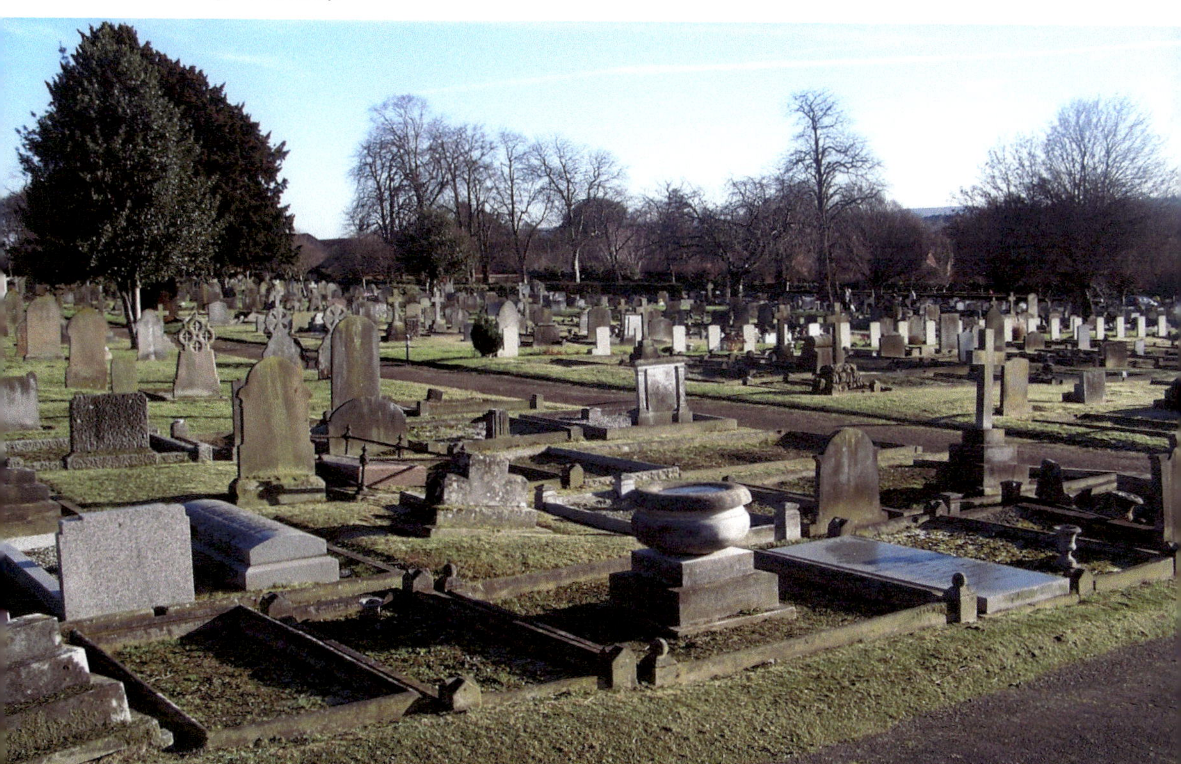

3

CHALK MINES

Chalk, known as the foundation rock of Suffolk, when excavated was important for the manufacture of lime for construction, industry and also to help farmers reduce the acidity in soil. Just after the Second World War, 5-inch lump chalk was sold at 4s a cubic yard and 100 per cent 1-inch screen chalk was sold at 8s per cubic yard. Both grades entitled farmers to government subsidies of 50 per cent. Evidentially open-cast chalk workings were here from 1540 up to around 1900. Some remaining tunnels going northwards from the pit can even be remembered by some of today's town residents. Over time, St Peter's Pit has been called 'Old Pitts' and 'Dusty Millers Pit'. Opposite the pit in medieval times stood St Peter's Hospital for Lazars (lepers), founded by Abbot Anselm. The pit was

St Peter's Pit, Out Risbygate.

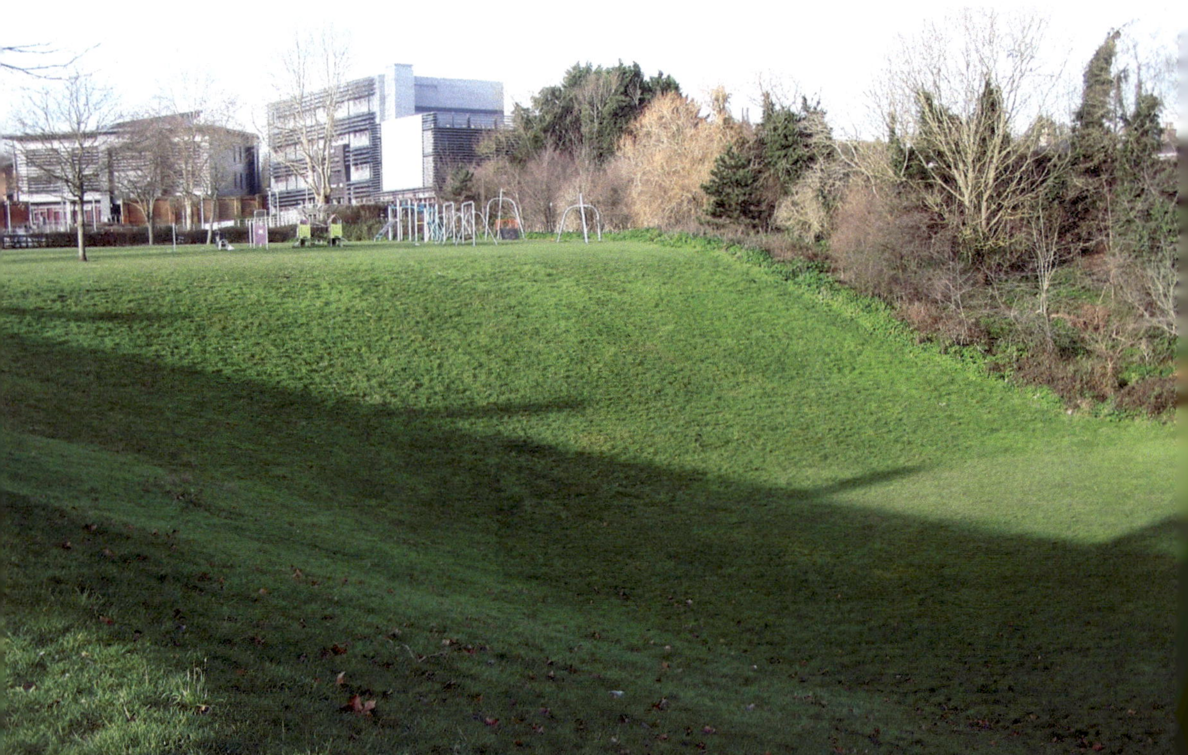

undoubtably put to good use for burials during 1637 when plague was endemic in the town. At different times when building work took place at the St Peter's residential care home, opposite, (such as in 2003), vestiges of the old hospital were discovered, including ancient, occupied graves. The much-moved Plague Stone had a hollowed-out top for disinfecting coins and is now in use as an attractive planter in front of West Suffolk College, part of University Campus, Suffolk. This was moved here from the Silver Jubilee School in Grove Road in 1959. Years later a student returning to his car after an evening's tuition at the college had a nasty surprise by the driver's door: the ground gave way and he ended up in a hole! St Peter's Pit, with its grassed-over slopes, is wonderful for tobogganing when snow is about.

Horringer Court

Horringer Court estate is a large, sprawling development that was built in the 1960s to 1980s. The estate's name is indelibly linked to Horringer Court, a large house known to many now as Clarice House and the Bannantyne Health Club and Spa. A former servant's house of the Hervey family of Ickworth was purchased by prolific Bury builder William Steggles in 1837, naming it The Red House – strangely also the name of a nearby inn on the Bury to Horringer road. Though limekilns were on site it is doubtful that Steggles was responsible for all the numerous tunnels used to extract chalk for these, as by the early 1870s the workings emanating from large pits at the rear were no longer in use. Revd Robert Fox then bought the Red House and it was later acquired by his former tenant, Edward Hawkins Esq. JP, a gentleman who demolished it, building his fine Arts and Crafts Horringer Court residence. Financially overstretching himself, he owned it up around the outbreak of the First World War. Then there were several subsequent owner occupiers/renters until a local automotive dealer, Rowland Todd, bought the property in 1947 – his wife Edith was an accomplished artist. The connection with the Todd family remained until Horringer Court was sold in 1983 and again in 1992, becoming a nursing home until 1999. After a major internal refurbishment, new owners the King family (a member collected Clarice Cliff pottery) commenced trading in 2001, advertising it as a Residential and Day Spa and Health Club until purchased by TV's *Dragons' Den* entrepreneur Duncan Bannatyne.

Around the time of the purchase by the Todds in 1947 bats were discovered hibernating in the Horringer chalk caves. The existence of Daubenton's and the rare barbastelle bat species would lead to the 500 metres of tunnels being designated a Site of Special Scientific Interest. Altogether the site covers 3.8 hectares. According to a survey carried out by Brian Francis published in *The East Anglian* magazine, February 1952, the main central tunnel in the west gallery is 60 metres long with lateral offshoots. He described the geological components of chalk deposits and that chalk is the outstanding solid formation of East Anglia, the backbone of Norfolk and Suffolk. Another theory of his is that another pit as indicated on the map as the 'East Chalk' pit is connected, albeit in a haphazard way to the West Chalk pit – perhaps an afterthought that the two of them should be joined, an idea, as he says, 'put into practice with some negligence'. To help dispel worries of those who may be perturbed that the workings are another 'Jacqueline Close' waiting to happen, chalk tunnels are not normally vertical as they are unsafe and rapidly deteriorate if dug in that manner, plus these are not thought to be directly under the Horringer Court estate.

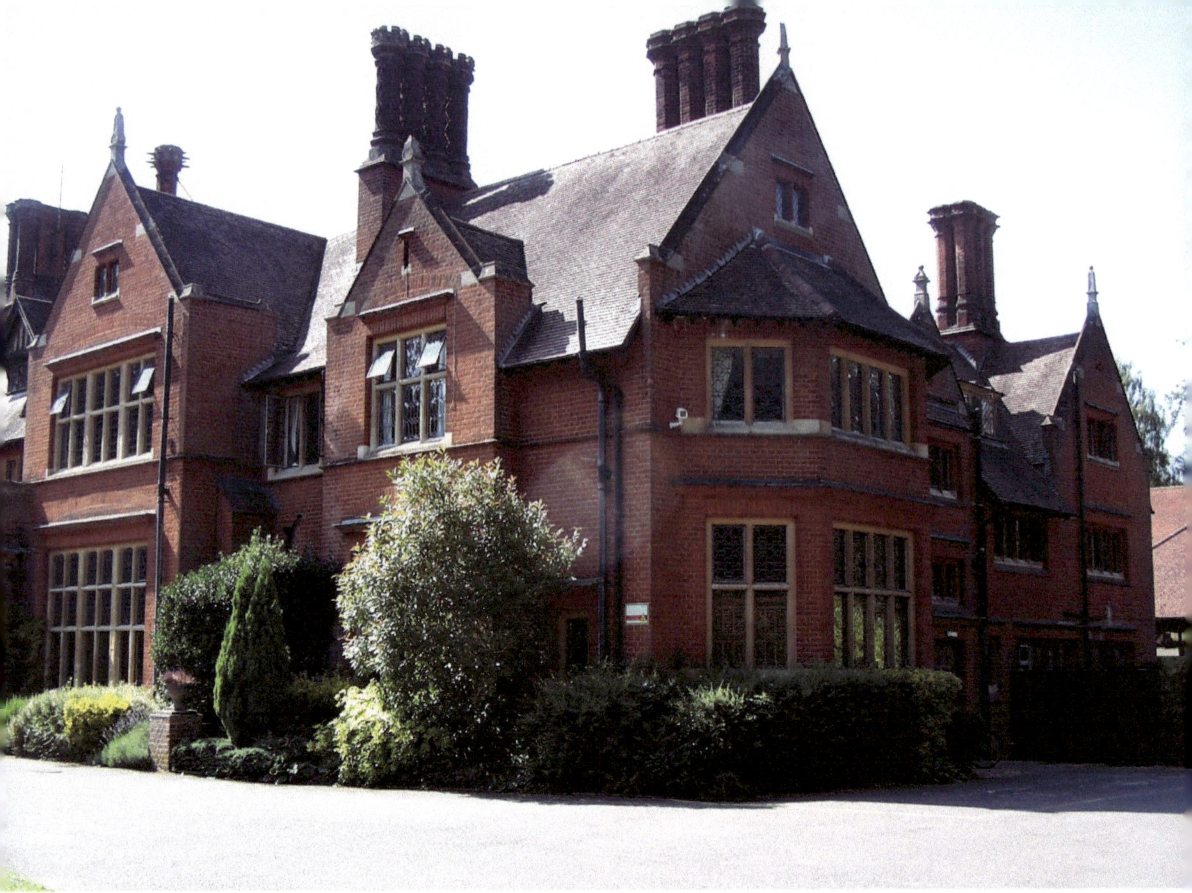

Horringer Court.

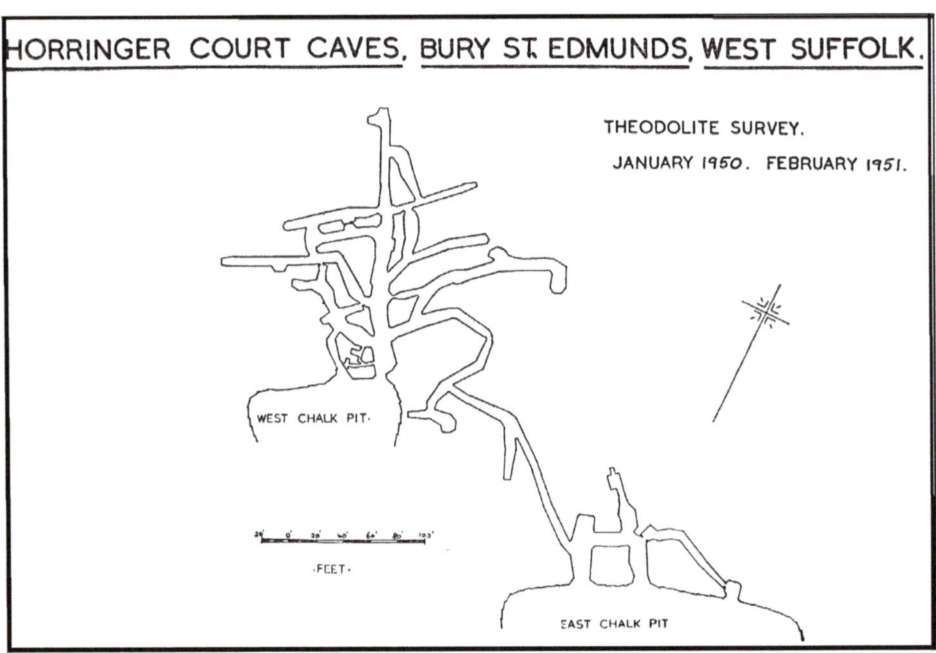

Map showing the Horringer Court chalk mines.

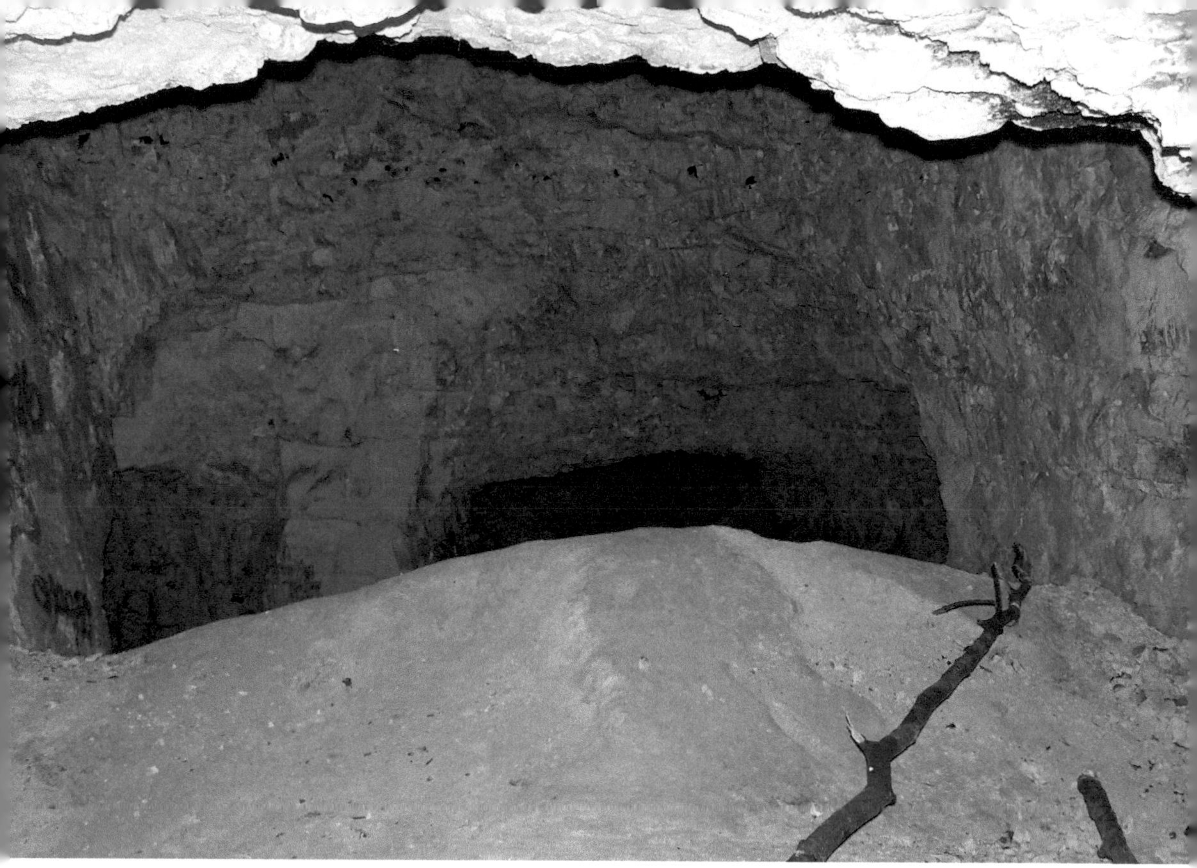

Above and below: Horringer Court chalk mines.

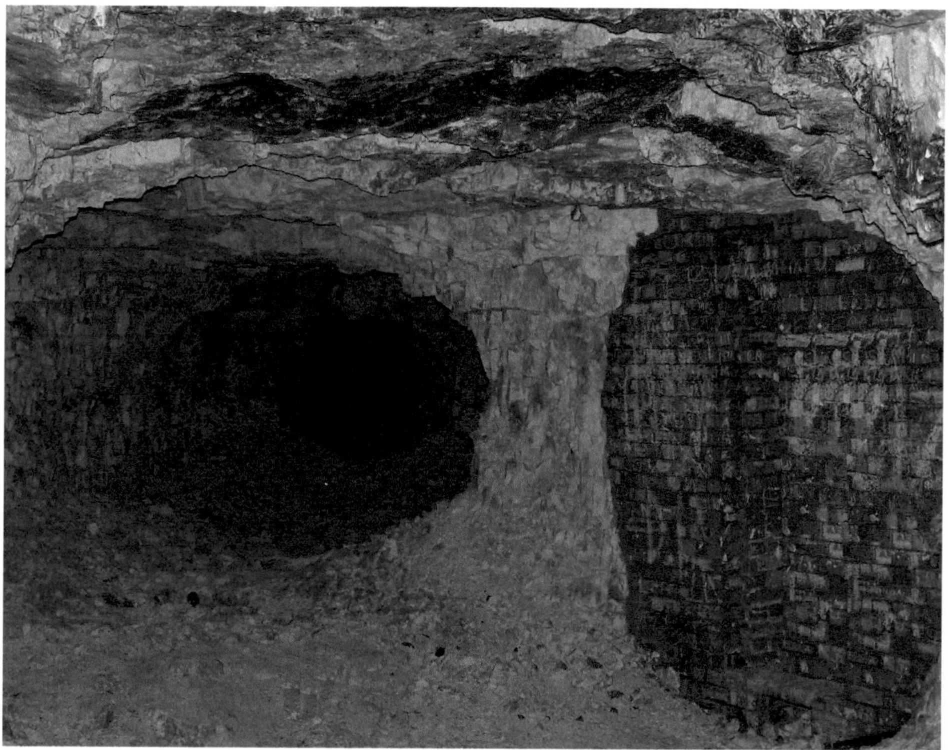

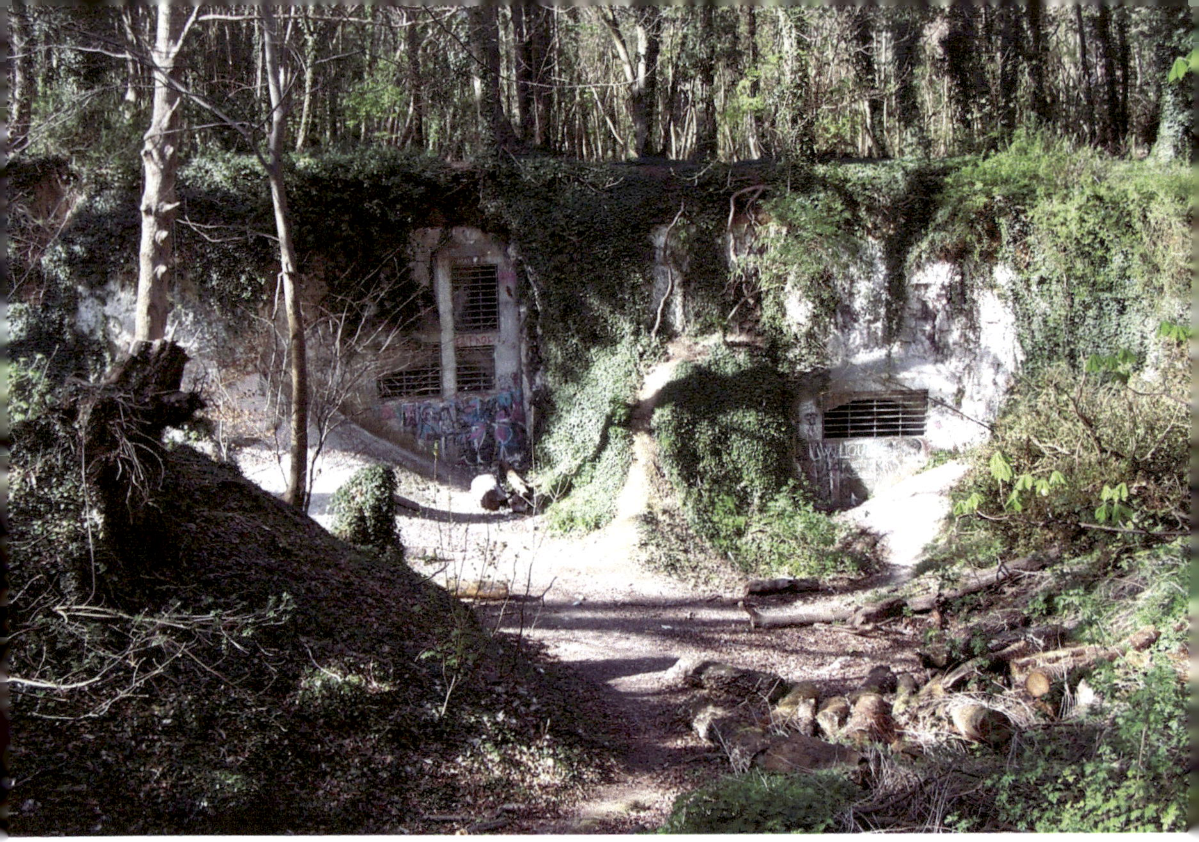

Above and below: The depth of one of the two pits at Horringer Court chalk mines can be seen here.

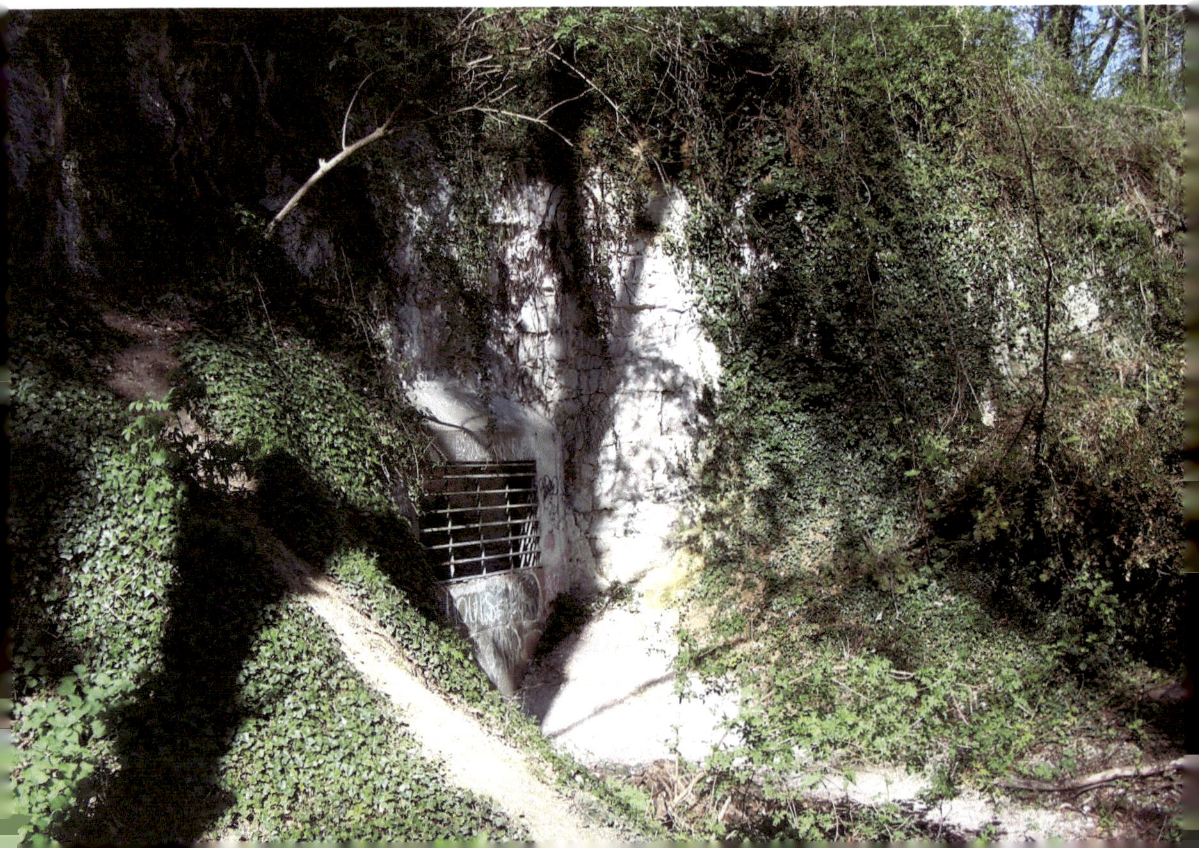

Many a child can remember exploring these 'caves', but since 1974 they have been sealed off not only to protect the bats from intrusiveness, but those commonplace words 'health and safety' are now applied to the inquisitive, which is probably a good idea – certainly for the bats!

The first photo shows how chalk was excavated – literally hewn from the hillside. Depending on the strata, the chalk was dug well below deposits of topsoil and a combination of sand and gravel. A benefit of the mining were flints, which could be used in construction. The other photo shows a tunnel that used to go off to one side but has been bricked up for whatever reason; you can still make out the soot from the miners' candles on the ceiling. Before the protection grids were put up, youths unfortunately used to get in, the entrances having been blighted over the years by graffiti.

These photographs, set in private woodland, remnants of the landscaped gardens of the Revd Robert Fox, show the depth of one of the two pits and tunnels leading off. Rumours that there are other access points to the mines amid the large expanse of chalk workings are probably apocryphal. These mine workings, along with others in the town, are definite commercial enterprises and nothing at all to do with tunnels used as boltholes for the monks.

Chalk Mines, Rear of No. 84 Eastgate Street

This house, known as The Glen, on the top of Eastgate Street, dates from the eighteenth and nineteenth centuries and was owned at different times in the twentieth century by Geoffrey Oliver and builder John Boughton, who built a bungalow to the rear aptly named

Tunnel behind The Glen, Eastgate Street.

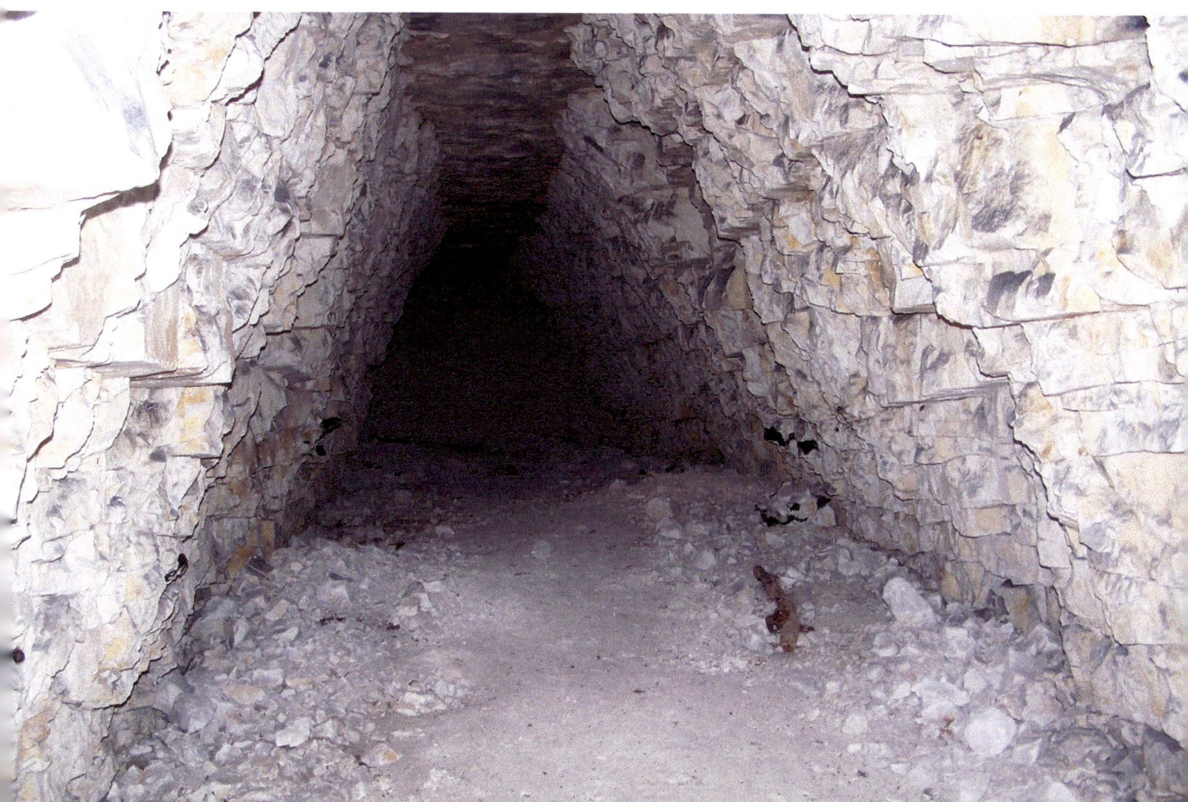

Quarrymans Cottage. Nearby chalk workings extend east up Mount Road and north up Barton Road, past the junction with Hollow Road. The horizontal dark tunnels are over 200 metres long and the workings themselves cover 1.6 hectares (nearly 4 acres). Within these, the floors may suddenly slope down, and loose scree will cause you to lose your footing, which I can unfortunately vouch for! Over the years erosion and anti-social goings-on within caused John to put in place civil engineering works to protect them for future generations but still allowing some of the other inhabitants of the caves – bats – to come and go. It is a Site of Special Scientific Interest (SSSI), notified under Section 28 of the Wildlife and Countryside Act 1981. Five species of bats regularly use them, especially during their hibernation period between September and April. Natterer's Wood, further up Mount Road, is named after the Natterer's bat and another species, the Daubenton's, has lent its name to a recent development off nearby East Close. Incredibly, a Daubenton's bat that was ringed in 1961 was recaptured in 1983, making it twenty-two years old and one of the oldest recorded ages for a bat. As these mammals have been regularly observed since 1947 there has been a steady increase in numbers, possibly due to the local ecological environment, the micro-climate within the caves themselves and an abundance of insects attracted to the diverse habitat.

Mount Road Chalk Mines

The Glen, now a Grade II property, was put up for sale in 1920 with Miss Ledward a sitting tenant, paying £35 per annum. Surprisingly, there was no mention in the sales particulars of chalk workings being in the grounds. The tunnels to these emanate from a very large pit, which has a brick limekiln. The town's oldest documented limekiln is in St Andrew's Street South, dating from 1489. Limekilns are recorded on this site with the Warren map of 1791 when the Durrant family were in residence. This limekiln, now possibly the only one in Suffolk, was used as an air-raid shelter during the Second World War and carefully restored by owner John Boughton over the past forty years. The town sits on a layer of flint and chalk, calcium carbonate, the process that turns this into calcium oxide, quicklime, requires heat. Chalk is fed into a conical chamber above and combustible material such as charcoal offered up into a fireplace or hearth. Temperatures between 954 and 1,066 °C are required for a chemical reaction to take place. After this you have quicklime. This is mixed thoroughly with water to give 'slaked' or hydrated lime, which is left to rest for a period of time, depending on what use you have for it; this lapsed time results in a putty. Generally, one part putty to three parts of sharp sand makes a mortar mix. For hundreds of years lime mortar has been used in the building trade until the advent of Portland cement, although it is still crucial for lime mortar to be used on buildings where stonework is in place as it can accommodate stresses caused by building movement without excessive cracking.

The actual age of these workings with several tunnels off is hard to determine. The enormous pit had solid chalk hewn out over centuries, possibly for the nearby abbey. Vestiges of times gone by have also been found here. There are gravestones to Gurth (buried 17 February 1867) and Fanny (buried 16 May 1873) – probably donkeys or pit ponies. Their headstones have been mounted on a flint and mortar base. Incidentally, more animal graves, family pets, belonging to the Cullum family are to be found near the St Nicholas Hospice, Hardwick Lane.

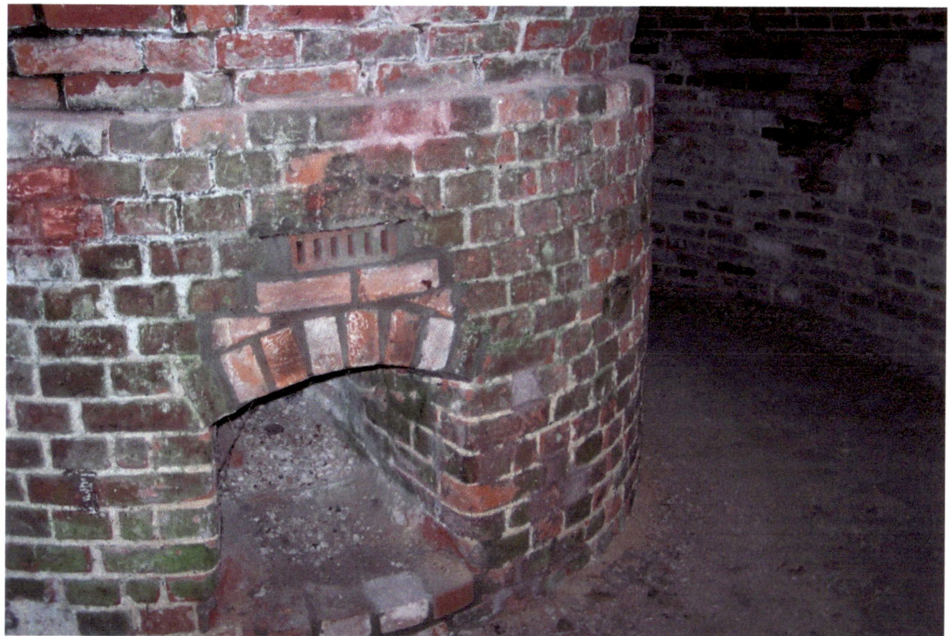

Limekiln, Mount Road chalk mines.

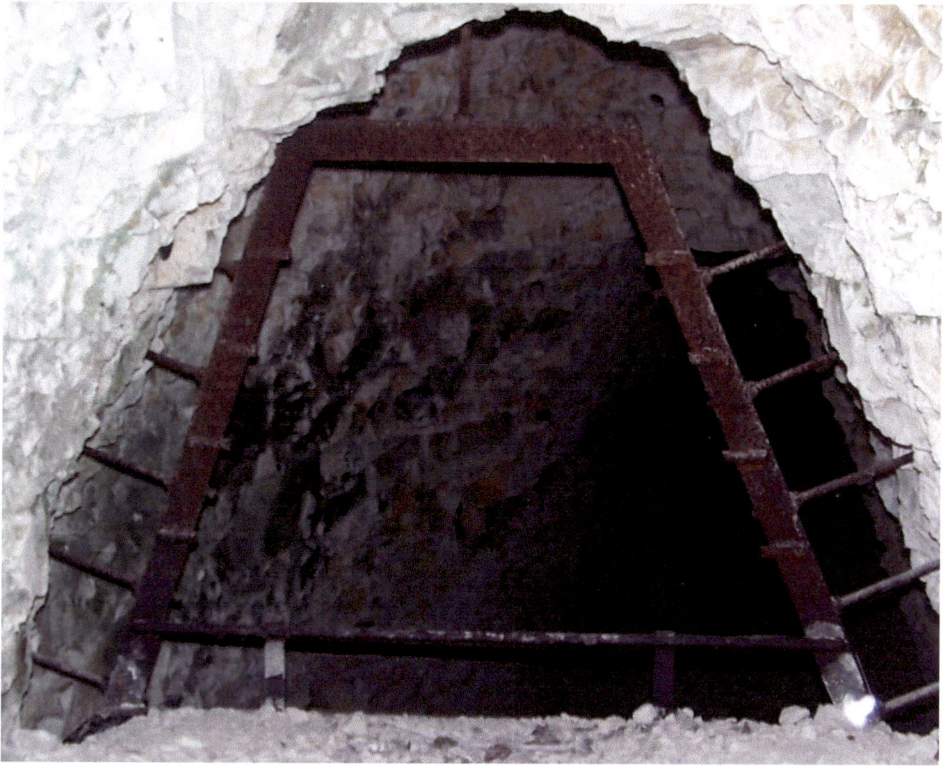

Mount Road tunnel entrance.

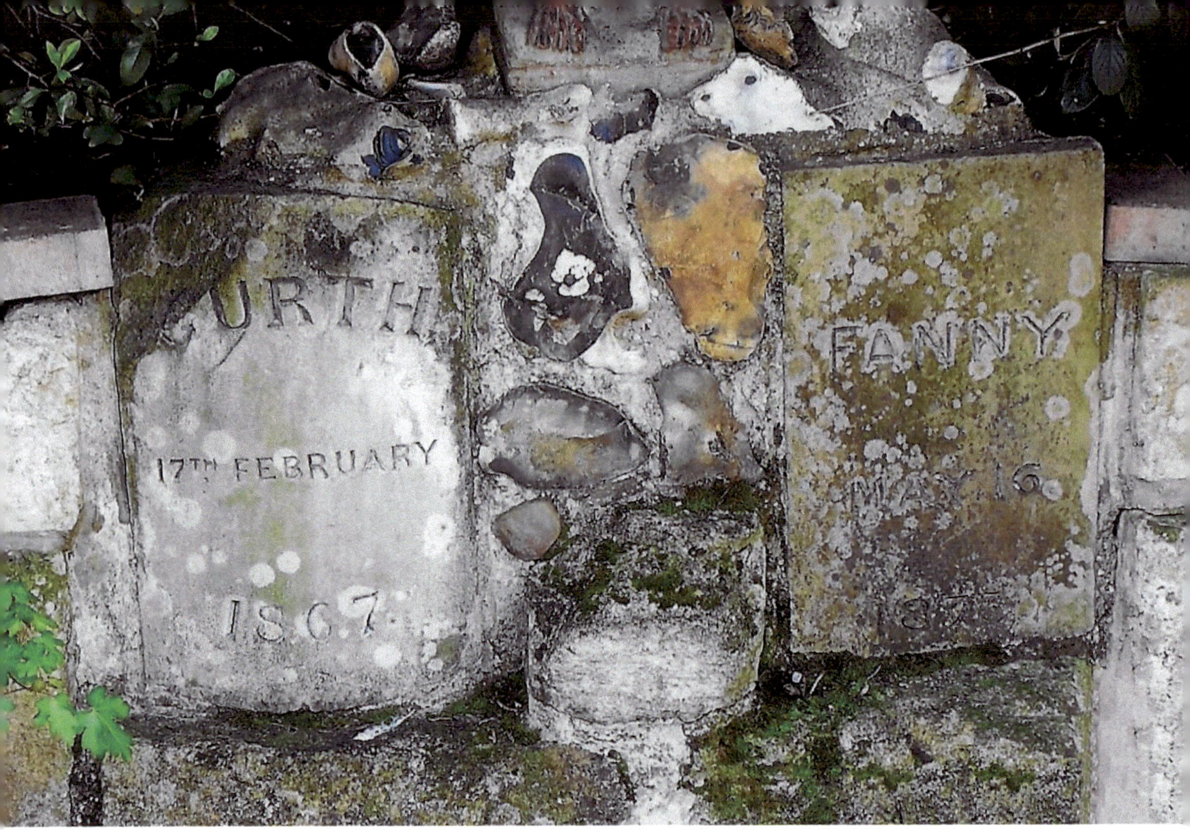

Animal graves, Mount Road chalk mines.

Jacqueline Close Chalk Mines

Jacqueline Close holds bitter memories for many people. Just two properties remain from this development of thirty at the top of Mill Road. The Hospital Management Board considered purchasing the site for expansion of their nearby hospital laundry. Fortunately for them a knowledgeable local surveyor advised them not to touch it with the proverbial barge pole. The land, put up for auction in 1960, held dark secrets beneath – a chalk mine. These had been in use throughout the nineteenth and early twentieth centuries, and locals knew of them. However, a London-based firm, Tricord Developments, bought the land and in 1964 desirable three-storey town houses were built with a price range starting from £4,250. A survey of the site had supposedly given the all-clear and the home owners, most with mortgages, moved in. During 1967 a large hole appeared, causing a gas main to rupture, which was dealt with, but in December 1968, following weeks of torrential rain, there was a major collapse in front of No. 9. The houses had conventional rainwater disposal systems: guttering into downpipes and into soakaways. Normally this was more than adequate, but the chalk below was slowly being liquified and washed away. The foundations were compromised, and houses could collapse. Emergency housing in the form of newly built council houses on the Howard Estate was eventually given to the residents on a temporary basis. Then the post-mortem began. Fortunately, the Chelsea Speleological Society (study of caves) stepped in and offered their services, laying out a subterranean map. Beneath, they found Victorian graffiti – 'E Long 1857 and W Calton 1861' – 50 feet below the surface tunnels and huge caverns spread over 2 acres. The original survey had not gone down deep enough.

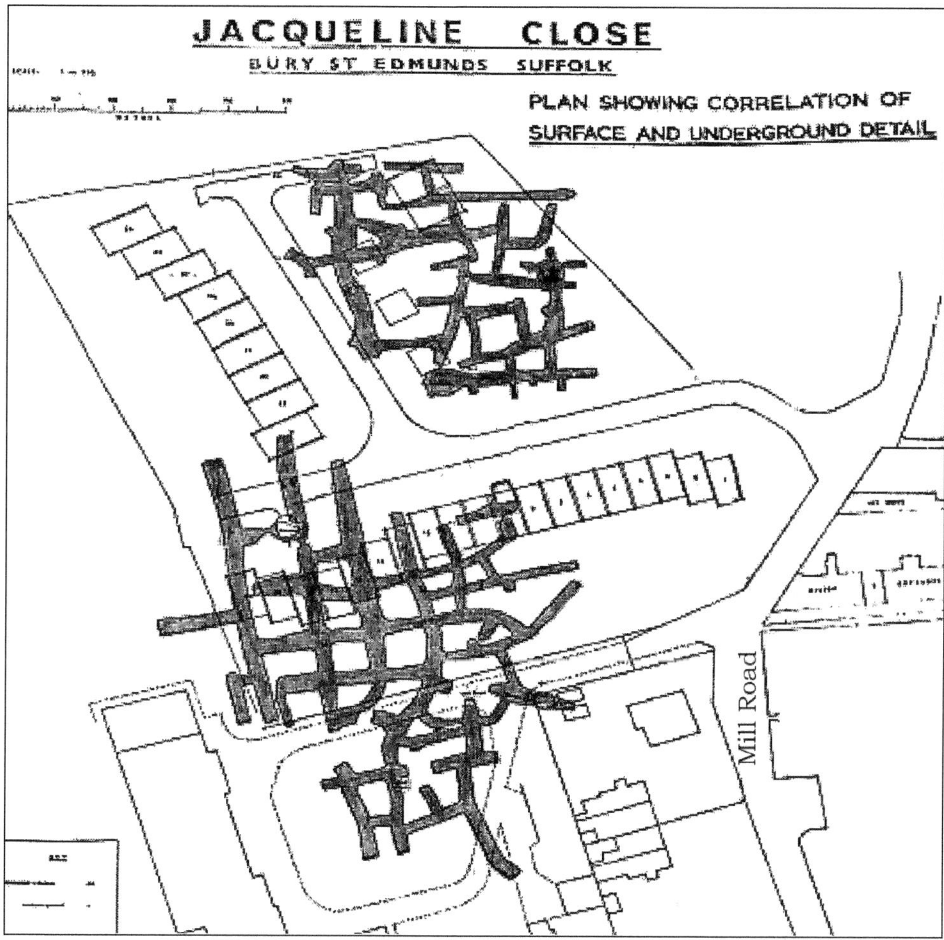

Jacqueline Close chalk mines.

Questions were then asked: Surely someone knew? Why so deep? Well, someone probably did know, but for various reasons kept a tight lip. Fingers of suspicion pointed in different directions. Deep extraction of chalk from these mines was necessary to ensure impurities were kept to a minimum – the cleaner the chalk so much the better. As for the depth of the workings themselves, hindsight is a wonderful thing. Had the survey bore holes gone deeper the land might not have been sold 'caveat emptor', buyer beware, but what of the poor house owners left severely out of pocket? Supported by local MP Eldon Griffiths the public enquiry of 1976 unbelievably could not attach blame to anyone. A residents' association for Jacqueline Close took Queen's Counsel advice as to whom might be responsible and could they be sued. The answer was no. The recriminations that followed fell on deaf ears, despite the enquiry – many of those in office were akin to Pontius Pilate. Only two owners had subsidence insurance and fortunately for them it paid out. It later emerged that some mortgage lenders had looked upon the owners with sympathy, either setting aside payments or cancelling the debt completely. A resident of Jacqueline Close, Brian Cross, whose family owns the two remaining houses, wrote a narrative in 2005 of the debacle called *A Blight at the End of the Tunnel* under the pseudonym D. Pole;

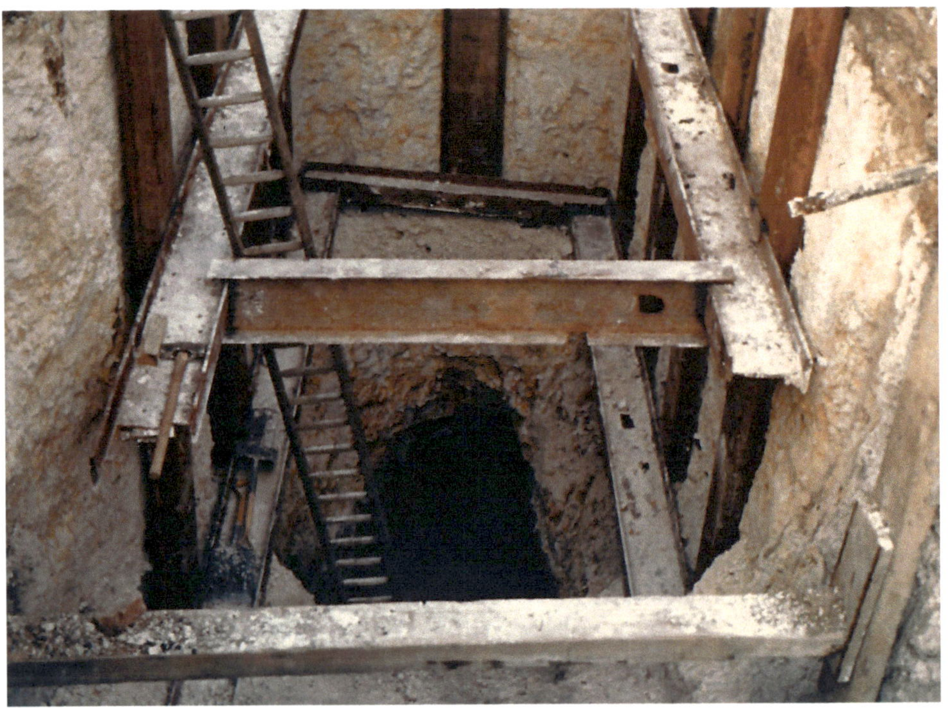

Shoring up of a tunnel shaft.

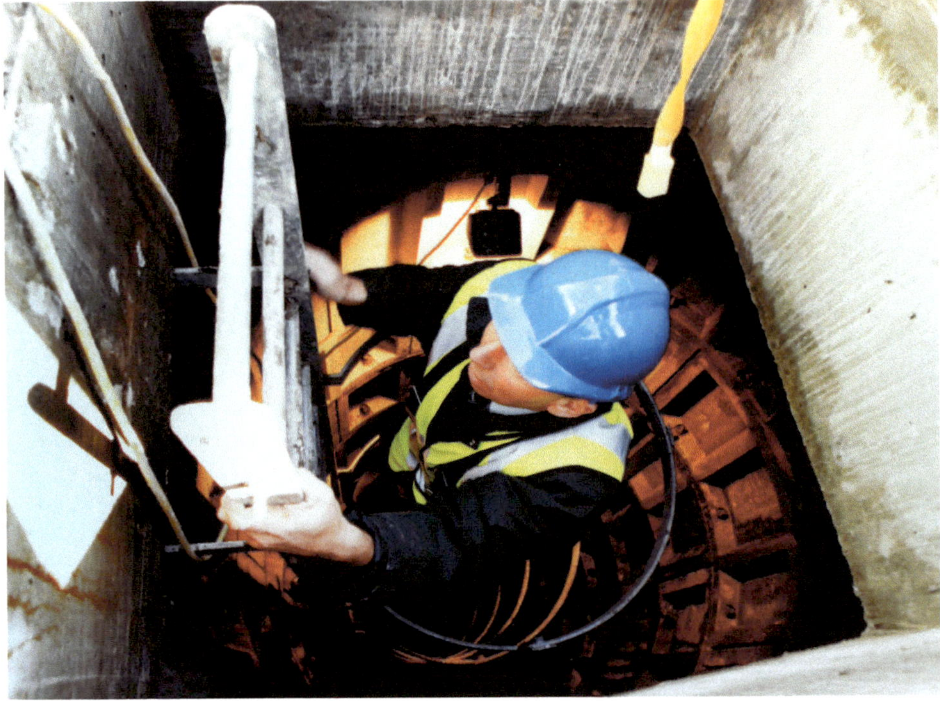

Descending into the tunnels.

it has since reprinted under his real name. He appeared on a Channel 5 TV documentary called *Sinkholes* in 2017, retelling the sad events of fifty years earlier. Sadly, Brian died in July 2019 without managing to get the whole truth of this debacle out.

Clues in the surrounding area might have given an inkling that something was not right here, such as the nearby names of Limekiln Cottages and Chalk Road. Thomas George Bullen, a local lime burner, even has his initials and the date of 1848 on a plaque in Mill Road. He had purchased nearby land called Pinners Folly in 1845 where the ill-fated

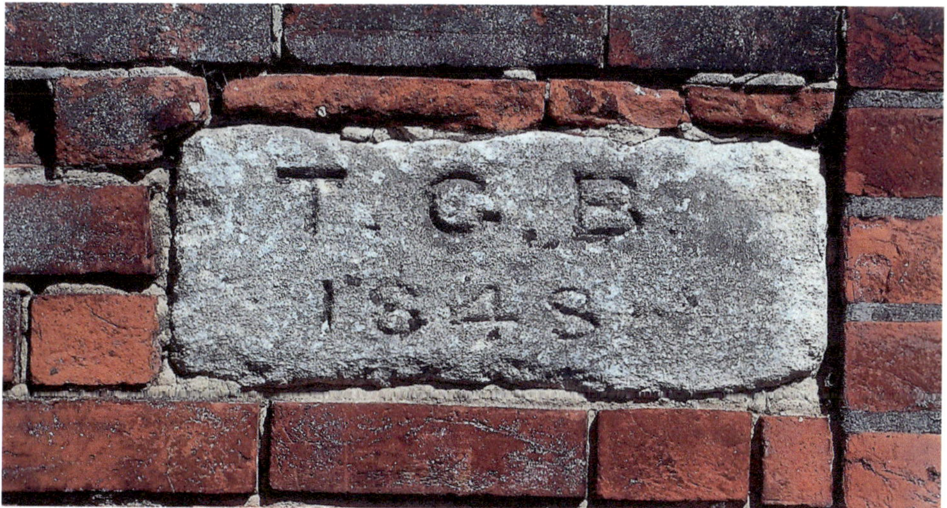

Thomas George Bullen, 'TGB', was a local lime burner.

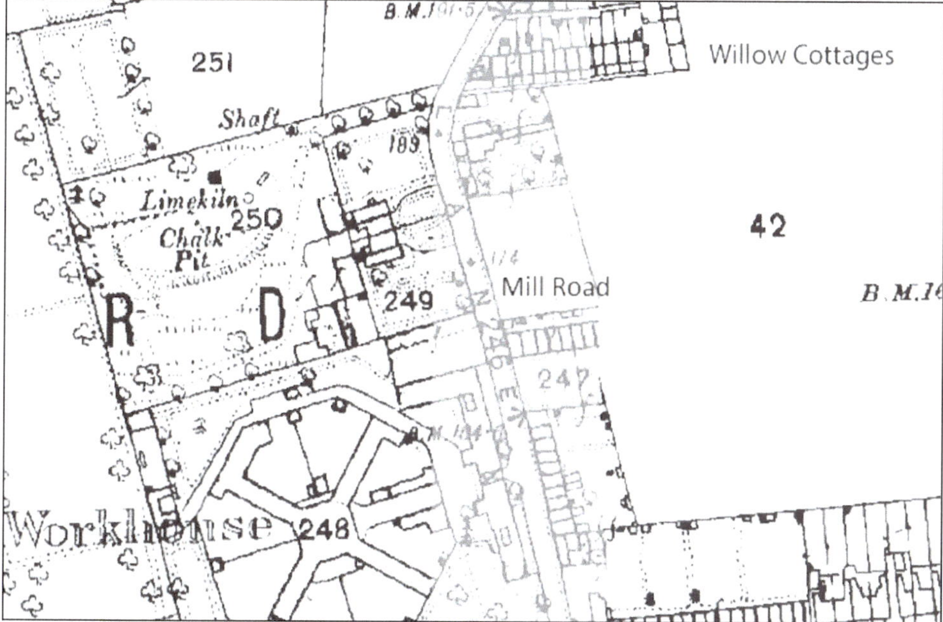

Map of Bury (1844) showing the limekilns, a chalk pit and a shaft to the mines.

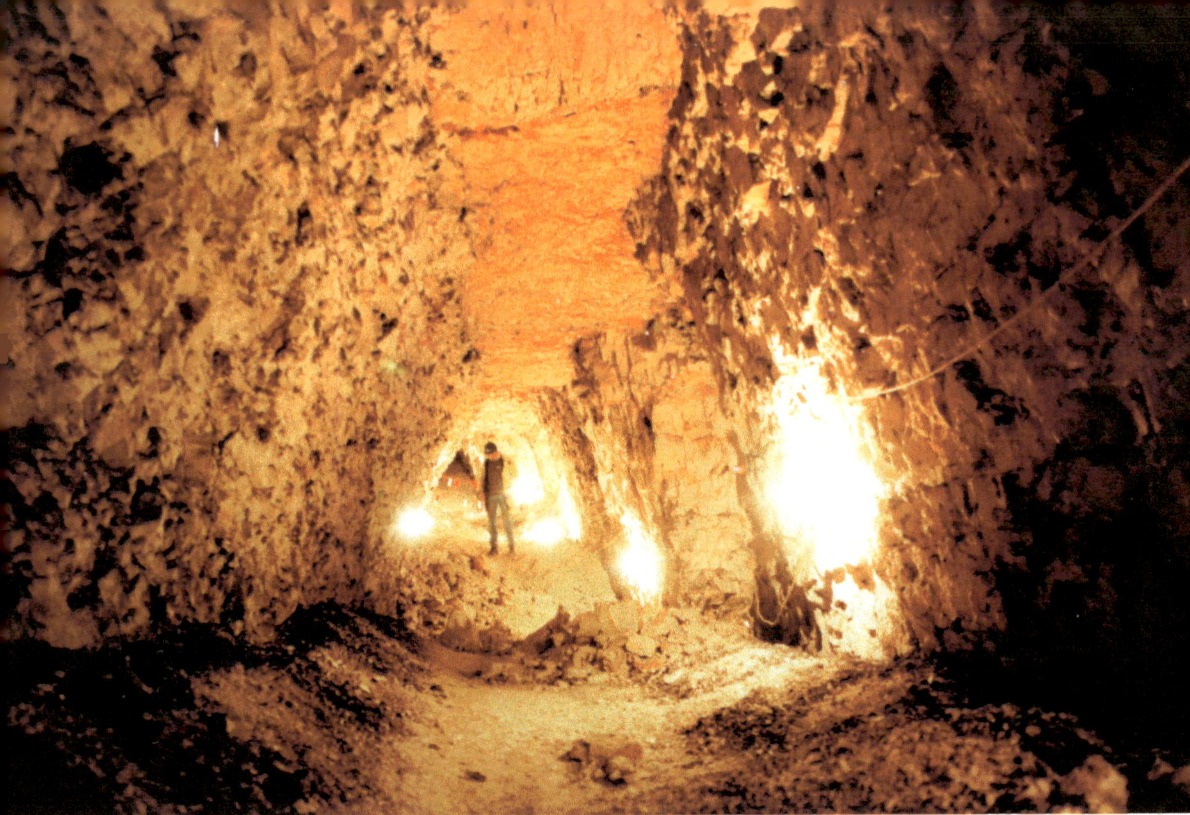

The mines lit up. (Photo courtesy of Andy Abbott)

Jacquelin Close came to be. A Bury map of 1884 shows not only limekilns and a chalk pit, but also a shaft to the mines. At the time of the properties being built a local could even remember chalk-laden carts pulled by donkeys just before the First World War, but his protestations were ignored.

Some ceilings of the tunnels below had been washed away. Formerly 45 to 50 feet away from the surface, the voids were a lot closer now. A solution to fill the caverns was put forward, utilising fly ash from the Cliff Quay Power Station at Ipswich, FOC, but the residents would have to pay for labour and transportation costs, akin to filling a perforated bucket with water. Just two of the houses remain and the site is fenced off with noticeable depressions in the ground. Incredibly, Jacqueline Close is included as a brownfield site in the document *Vision 31*, which shows the expansion of the town.

4

MUNICIPAL WORKS

Watercourses

A medieval town, Bury had little need for real structural defences as most of the surrounding areas were water meadows. The town is bound to the south by the River Linnet and to the east by the River Lark. The Tay Fen Water to the north fed marshy, inhospitable wetlands. When the last gasholder in Tayfen Road was demolished in 2016, a survey to ascertain the contamination of the soil there identified peat deposits 3 to 4 metres down – food for thought for any future development. There are other interesting areas of 'water run-offs' in the town, such as the ditch coming down from Hardwick Heath, diagonally crossing under a culvert in Vinery Road then via the rear of Holywell Close, going under Rembrandt Way. Interestingly, the name Holywell has nothing to do

Watercourse going under Rembrandt Way.

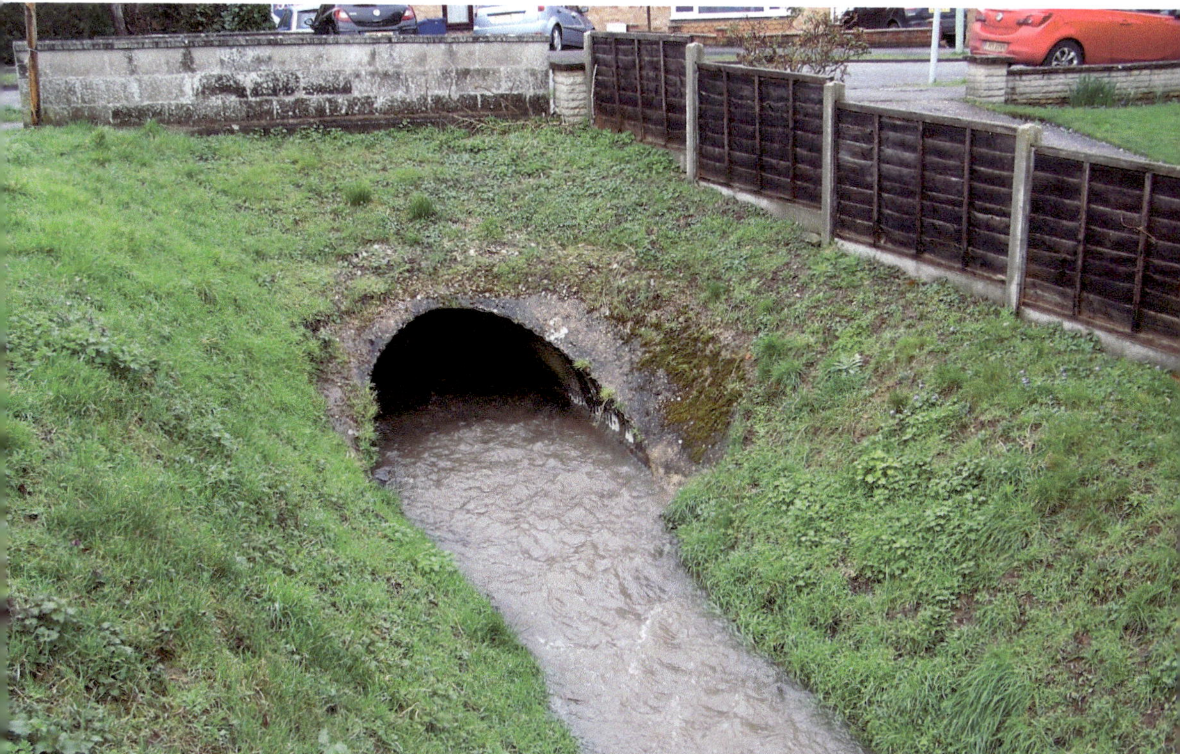

with religion, but is thought to come from 'Holewell', a spring in the area of Holywater Meadows. The Linnet, which rises in Ickworth Park, flows under the Spread Eagle junction bridge (known in medieval times as Stanwerpbrigg). From here it eventually goes under Cullum Road via a culvert. When this road was built in 1973 it had to be raised to prevent flooding. Running parallel with Cullum Road is another watercourse that emanates from springs near the Grindle, once thought to be part of the southern medieval defences of the town. All the water from the extensive Butts area feeds into the Linnet. Meanwhile, the Lark rises south of Bury, near Bradfield Combust, and entering Bury goes under Rougham Hill. Once the Lark and Linnet conjoined in the abbey's grounds, with the Linnet diverted to turn the abbot's water mill. Today the rivers meet not far from the Premier Inn hotel's car park.

Underpasses

The definition of an underpass or a subway is a short road or pedestrian tunnel passing under a road or railway line. If the underpass in Beetons Way, constructed in 1972 and costing £106,000, is considered then we have four in the town. Another on the Moreton Hall estate near the Coffee House café officially opened in April 1987 and goes under Orttewell Road by Lawson Place. A recent tribute has been put there for Kaine Williams, a DJ who sadly died at a young age. A third underpass goes under the town's inner relief

Volunteers who cleaned up the underpass.

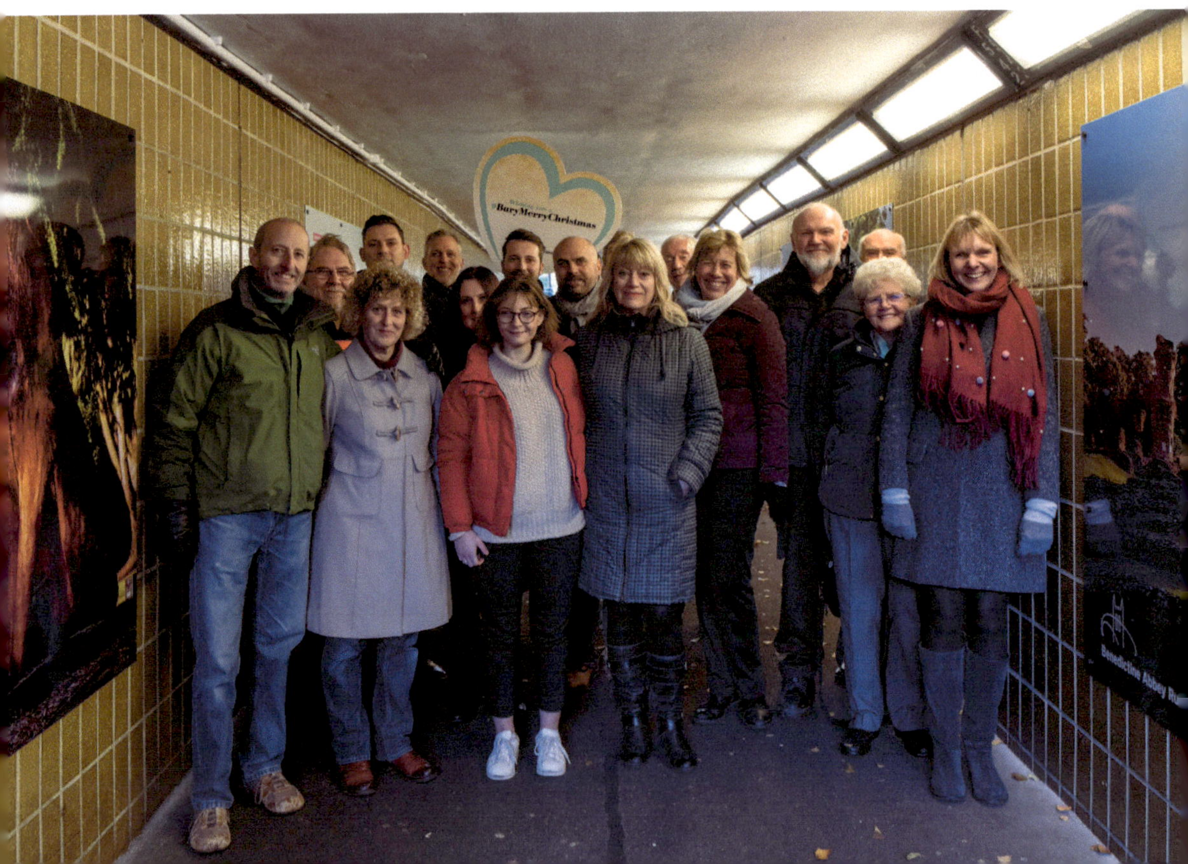

road, Parkway, which was completed in 1978. Never a salubrious thoroughfare, this underpass runs from Cineworld to the cattle market car park by the arc. As time went by local resident Sarah Ruczaj approached the then Bury in Bloom co-ordinator Melanie Lesser to see if a clean-up and improvement of this subway could be implemented. Sure enough, willing volunteers supported by various organisations carried out a major overhaul, with weeding, painting and wonderful artwork by Coastline Graphics, which came to fruition in December 2017. Our last underpass is under the busy A14 (former A45), which was opened in 1973. The approaches to this via Rougham Hill have also seen a £150,000 improvement to reconstruct the bridleway/cycle route completed in 2019 by contractor Stabilised Pavements Ltd utilising recycled materials from road resurfacing work. Walkers also enjoy this route towards the Moreton Hall Industrial Estate, the Sybil Andrews Academy and the Suffolk Business Park.

The subway under the A14, near the Suffolk Business Park, was made before the road was completed. Unfortunately, as the photo shows, it has been blighted by graffiti. On the approaches to the underpass, Suffolk County Council gave some thought in providing mounting blocks for horse riders – a nice touch. Once, only by using the unmanned railway crossing could get you from Tollgate Lane to Newmarket Road, until the Beetons Way A14 underpass finally allowed vehicular traffic via Western Way.

The subway under the A14, near the Suffolk Business Park.

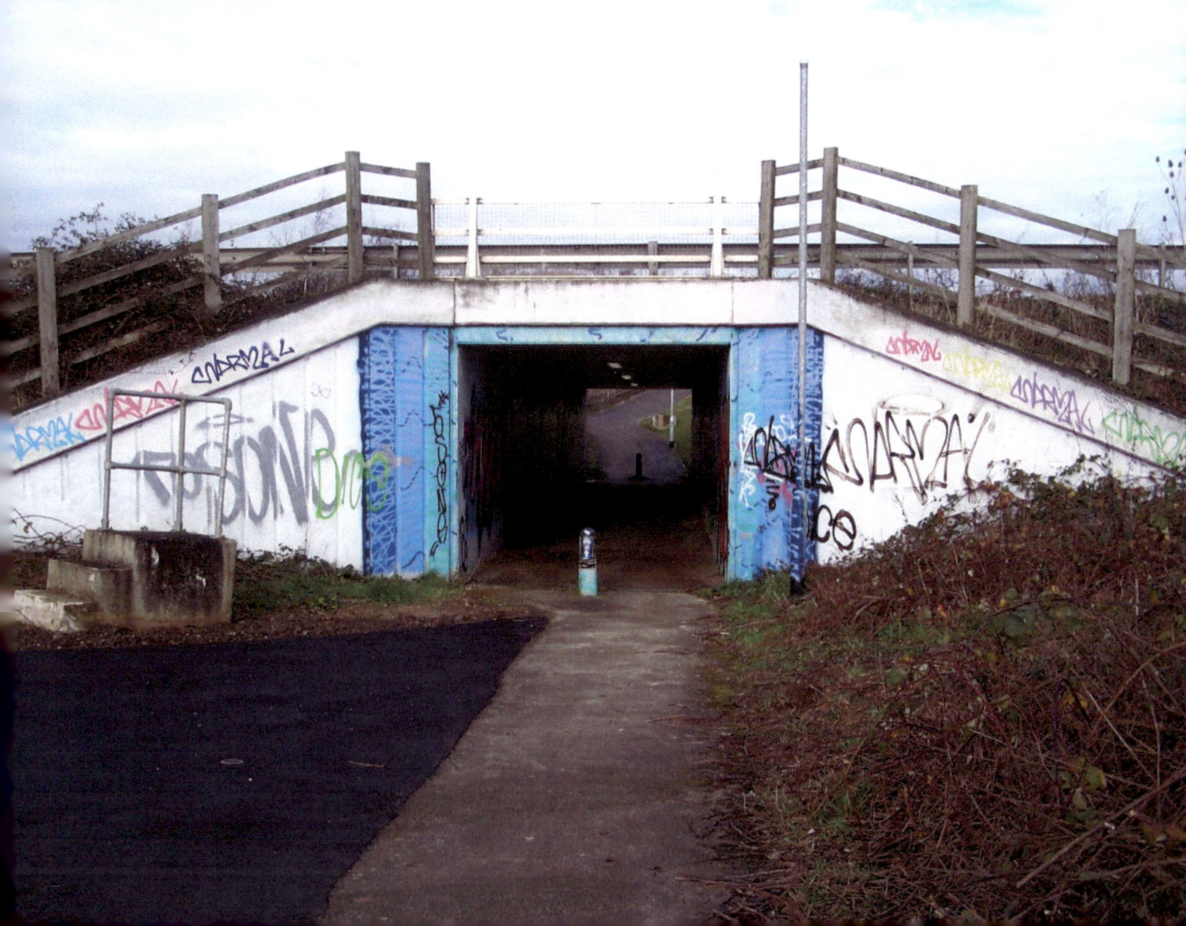

Sewers

Right up to the middle of the nineteenth century some people were still having their 'night soil' collected by cart for farmers to fertilise their fields. It was left to the Bury St Edmunds Paving and Improvement Commissioners to formulate a proper way of sewage disposal. With new powers under the Public Health Act of 1848 and the Local Government Act of 1858 new properties within the town had to be built with drains and WCs. By 1858 there were sewage pipes in the town leading to the Tayfen, near the town's gasworks; however, this was unsatisfactory because of smells emanating there. Five years later a new filtration plant opened at Bell Meadow, near the River Lark, but complaints still came in. In 1885/7 a purpose-built sewage farm opened at West Stow, but there was still the old problem of the smell. It was against this background that a solution was sought: stench pipes, not only to ventilate the sewers so smells dissipated up high, but allowing in air prevented a vacuum being created, thus allowing the sewer to work efficiently. William Edward Farrer of Solihull, who had a background in metal design, formed Farrer Sewage in 1898, which manufactured the pipes; some of his pipes were used in Bury. Stench pipes are to be found in Mustow Street (shown), Raingate Street, Friar's Lane, by Northgate station railway bridge and by The Greengage public house at around 22 feet tall and topped by a metal crown; they have served the test of time. Some people actually believe that many of the town's culverts and sewers are subterranean walkways. After all, is it possible after seeing these Victorian civic works to be mistaken?

Stench pipe on Mustow Street.

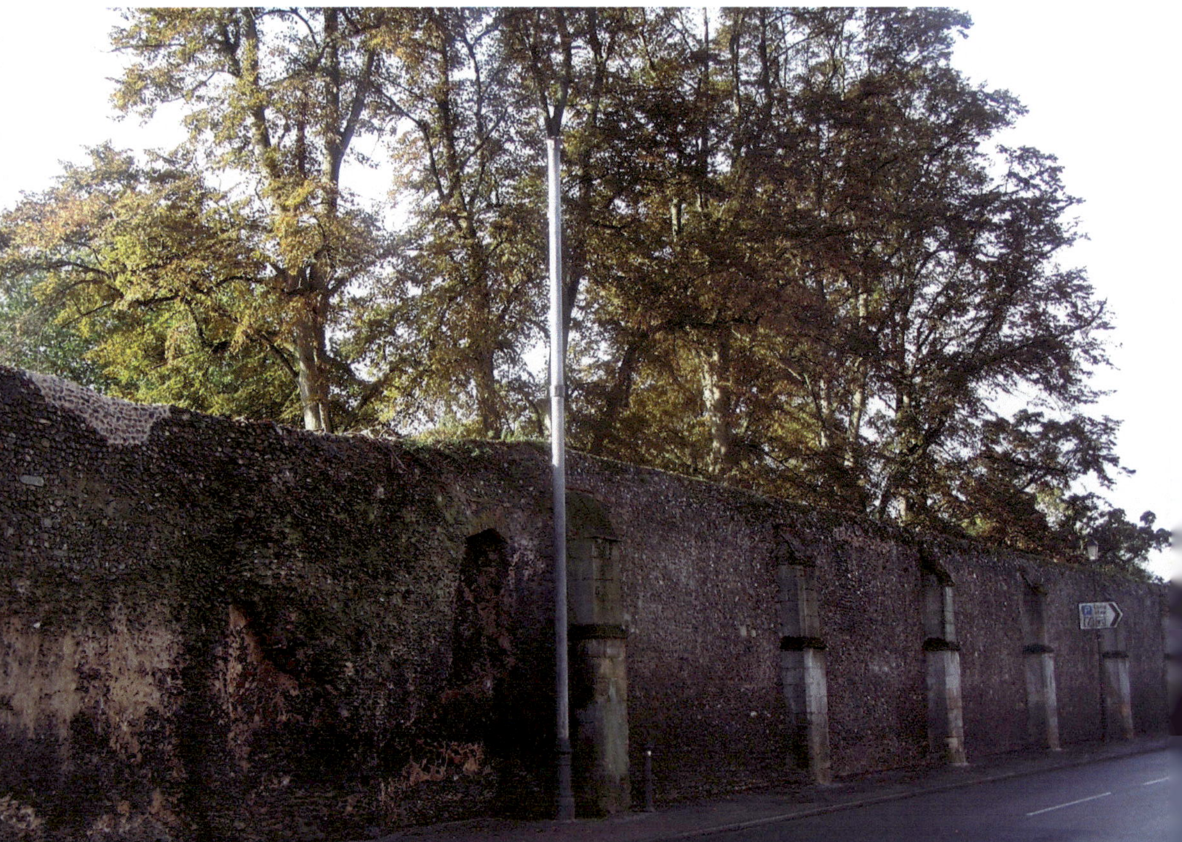

One person tried to convince me there were brick-lined tunnels going up Eastgate Street. I tried to let him down gently: 'Show me a photo and I will believe you.' As to be expected, he could not; for tunnels, read sewers. Over the years mains sewer pipes have been laid throughout the town. In the early 1960s Fornham Road residents were almost prisoners in their own homes, as civil engineering contractors Thomas Stewart of Western Way dug deep trenches before setting in the huge pipes. In 1961, sewer pipes were laid parallel to the River Lark, as shown, in the abbey gardens. In the same year the Fornham Park works opened to replace the old West Stow sewage farm to receive and treat the waste from Bury St Edmunds. To cope with the town's expanding population an extension to these treatment works opened in July 1971. With the creation of the Anglian Water Authority in 1973, higher standards had to be met for the final discharge of water that had been treated. This involved the installation of what is known as a 'polishing plant', whereby granular media filters removed any additional suspended solids before the effluent could be finally released into the river. The year 1974 saw local councils no longer accountable for sewage, rivers and supplying drinking water, Anglian Water now being responsible. In 1985 work commenced on the construction of an 850-metre-long, 1.5-metre-diameter tunnel in Barton Road to take surface and foul water from the northern part of Moreton Hall, the second phase of the estate, which was completed in 1986.

Sewer trenches in the abbey gardens.

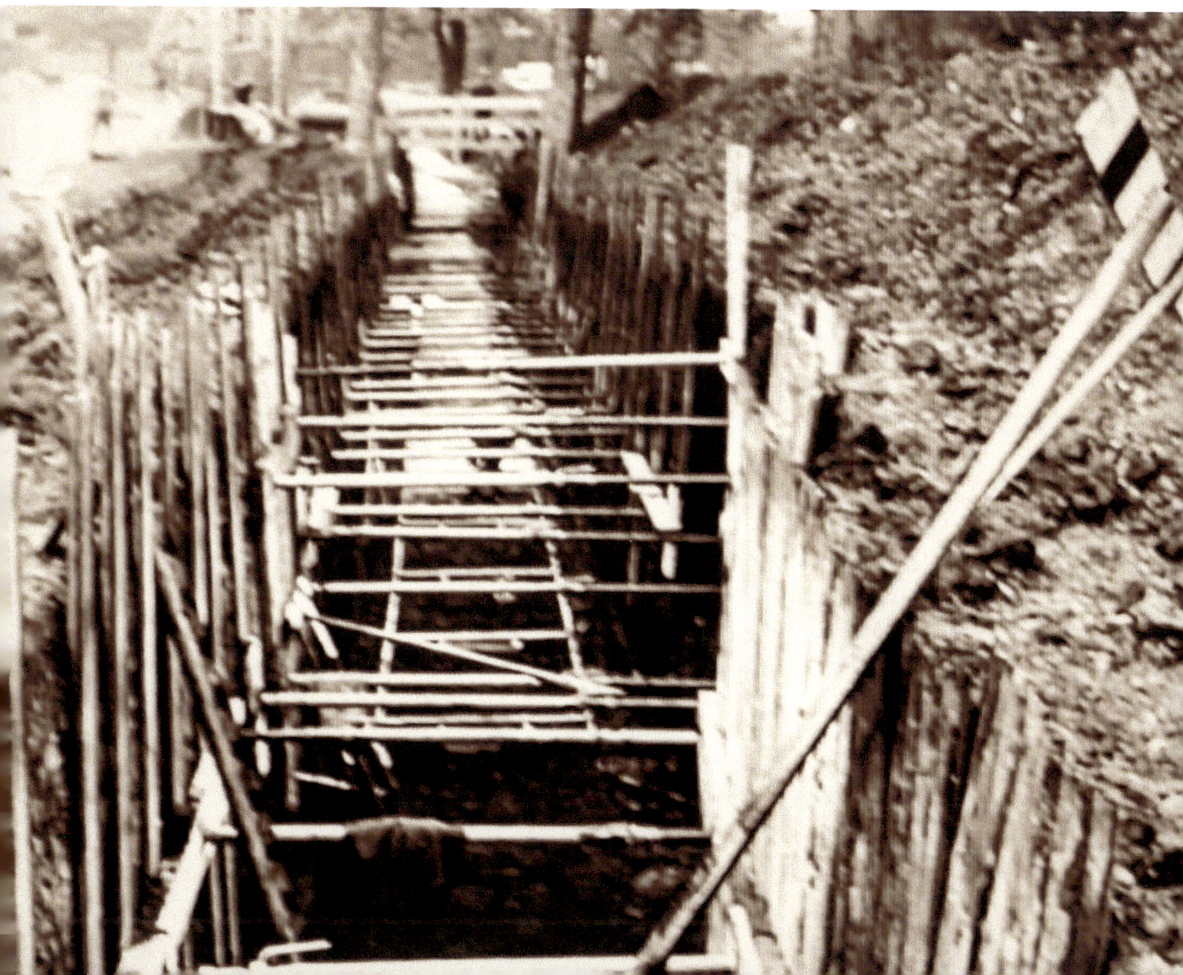

Utility Works

The installation of new services or repairs are a necessary evil, but to onlookers the roadworks always seem to take an inordinately length of time, causing upheaval and inconvenience. The older the cables or pipes, the more likely it is they need replacing or repair work, particularly burst water mains and gas mains, which receive the utmost priority as you would expect. In January 2002, contractors on Moreton Hall punctured a gas main while working on it, causing no end of aggravation as people had to be evacuated to the Moreton Hall Community Centre. Only well into the evening was the all-clear given and people returned home after the leak was successfully repaired. In April 2011, the Gas National Grid began a programme of gas mains replacement across Bury St Edmunds. These works were supposed to last until the spring of 2012. Traffic flow across town was severely disrupted, but finally the work was completed in 2013. During 2019–20 work to replace the existing gas pipes with the distinctive new yellow plastic mains in the south-west area of the town was carried out by Cadent Gas. They own, operate and maintain the largest natural gas distribution network in the United Kingdom, transporting gas to 11 million homes and businesses across the West Midlands, North West England, East of England and North London. The company works with Skanska and Morrison Utilities and it is anticipated work should now be completed by 2021. As the town continues to expand further disruptions will occur with new services being laid, especially the fibre optic cables – the old adage 'grinning and bearing' seems to be all that can be done.

Rembrandt Way, 2020.

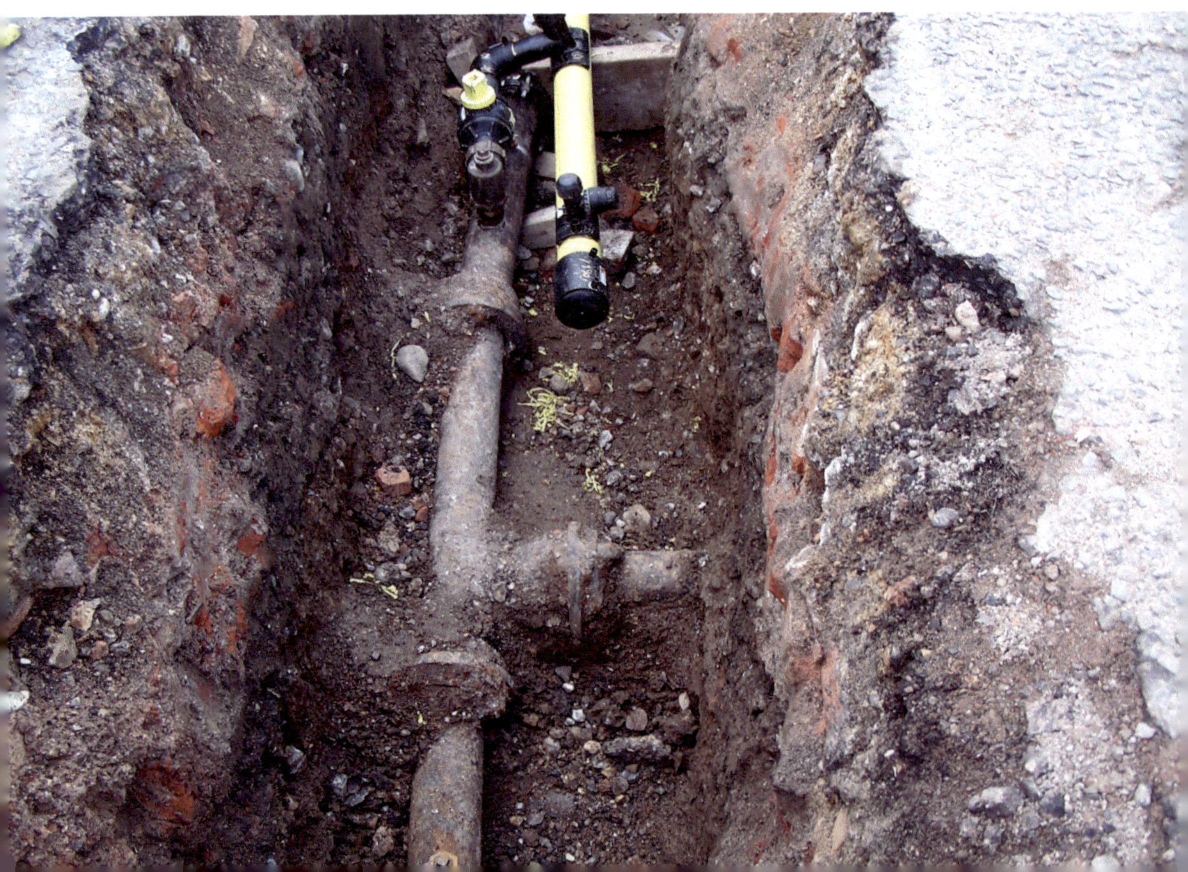

Gasworks Site, Tayfen Road

This, a place of execution in the distant past, was always a wet area of the town – hence the Tay Fen. Osier beds were once here, the young, coppiced, flexible willow shoots invaluable for basket weaving. The Tay Water, a stream once emanating from springs in the area off Spring Lane, is no longer visible, though a watercourse goes via a culvert adjacent to Turners Garage (2020) all the way to the Lark by Tesco. In 1834 Hull-based company, Malam & Peckston were contracted by the Bury Paving and Lighting commissioners to provide gas for street lighting and housing. After only a few months the firm folded, but a consortium of local interested businesspeople known as the Bury St Edmunds Gas Light Company took over. Four telescopic gasholders were erected in the nineteenth and twentieth centuries, the last in 1952. The workers were issued with strict rules and regulations as to their conduct for obvious reasons – this was the town's industrial district peppered with numerous public houses. With the discovery of natural gas in the 1960s the gasworks days were numbered; the cost to produce coal gas through heating became unviable. In 1964 the gasworks closed and the remaining gasholder on the north side of Tayfen Road stored the imported natural gas. This was demolished in 2016 for the National Grid by KDC, specialist decommissioning and demolition contractors. Situated between Ipswich Street and St Andrew's Street North, where one of the other gasometers stood, a controversial development of forty-six apartments started in 2019. The topsoil had to be removed and taken away as it was contaminated, then followed piling for foundations. It was known initially as The Gaslight with a subsequent name change to The Lantern.

Site of former gasworks, Tayfen Road.

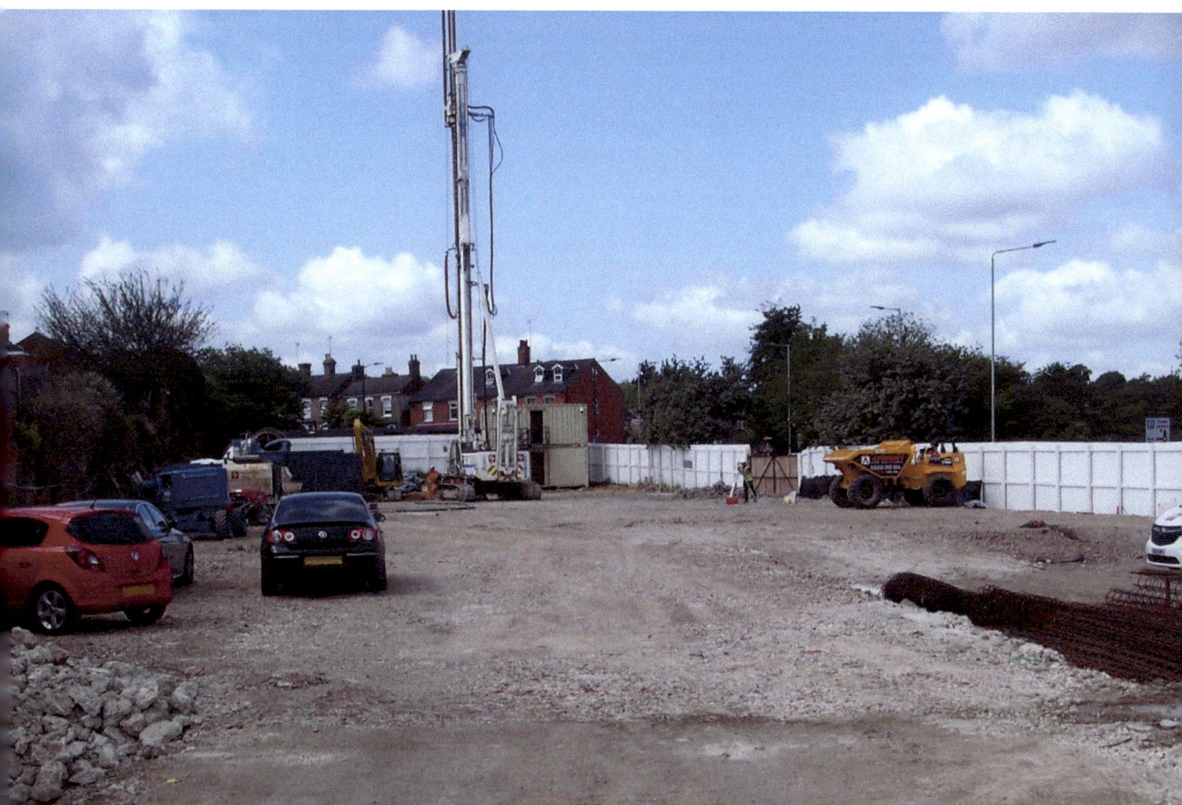

Abbeygate Street Blocks

Once, perceived criminals were sent to serve their sentences in the colonies. But the end of the American War of Independence in 1783 saw the newly created USA refusing to accept any more transportees, so a new strategy came into being: send them to Australia! Thus, the ship *The Guardian* left for New South Wales in July 1789 carrying a ragbag of miscreants to serve sentences from seven years to life. Those who completed their allocated terms very rarely returned. Enforced oceanic crossings ceased in 1867. Devoid of human cargo to make the return journey to 'Old Blighty' safely, it was necessary to take on ballast – if profitable, so much the better. This is how jarrah wood (eucalyptus marginata), a high-density wood from Western Australia, came to Britain. Jarrah's natural properties, being fire and water resistant, led to it being used in construction work and road surfacing during the nineteenth century. Abbeygate Street was at one time overlaid with jarrah wood blocks (as shown). The 8 × 4 × 3-inch tar-soaked blocks were laid on their side with the idea of muffling the noise of tradesmen's horses and carts in this, the town's principal shopping street. Heavier modern-day traffic would see the street closed and the blocks removed in 1952 then resurfaced with tarmac. These days, the street is now surfaced with herringbone, rustic, coloured brick pavers and is subject to certain closure times, in effect pedestrianised.

One of Abbeygate Street's blocks.

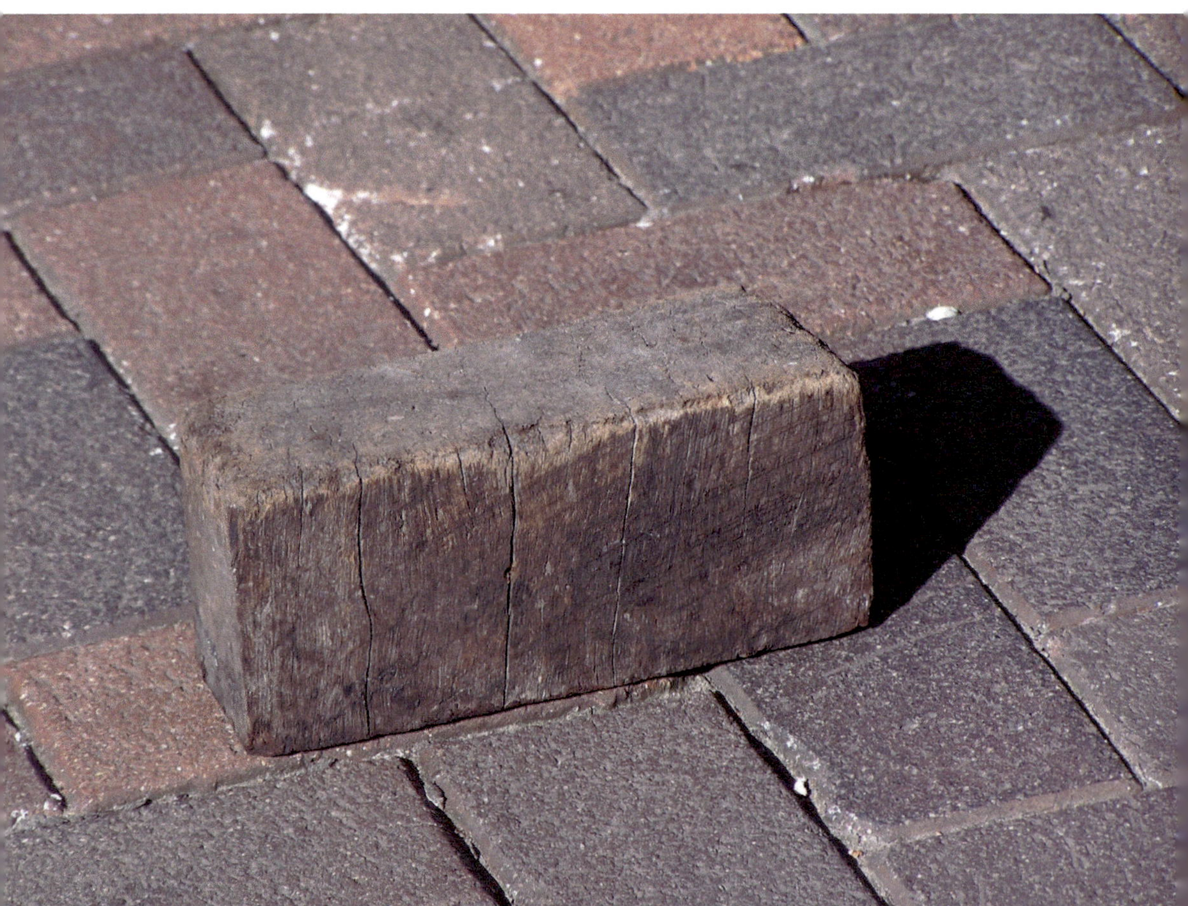

Spread Eagle Crossroads Road Blocks

During the Second World War the major roads in and out of the town were designated as 'green enforcement' roads where road blocks could be set up. Concrete pyramidal blocks known as 'dragons' teeth' or 'pimples' were also used. In 2018, when protracted roadworks were being carried out to improve this junction, four unwelcome vestiges of those times were discovered: buried were massive concrete cubes that could be used in the event of an invasion. Too heavy to be moved, they were broken up using jackhammers.

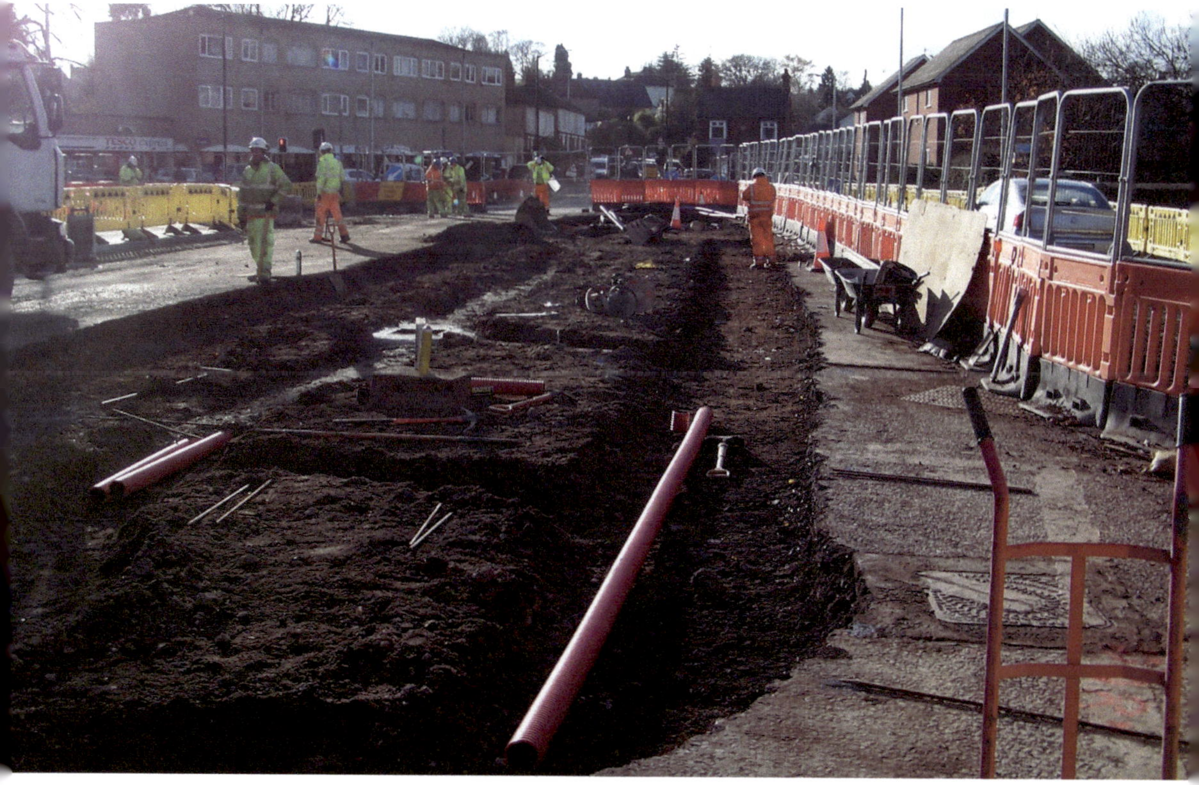

Above and right: Road blocks.

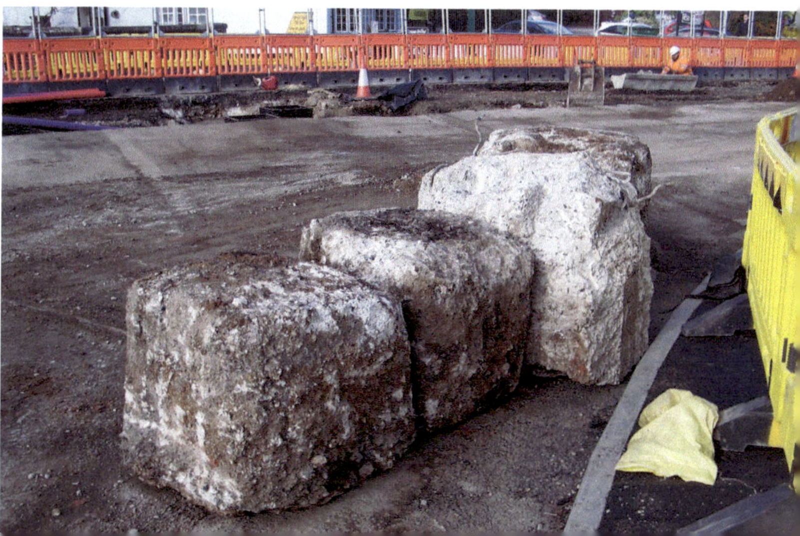

Water Tower, West Road

After the Second World War, more hygiene facilities were required for Bury's growing population so a new water tower in West Road was decided on. The lineage of chosen local builder Harvey George Frost, based in Out Westgate, went back to 1834, himself taking over in 1920. His portfolio of public works executed in the town made very impressive reading: work for the West Suffolk Hospital Board, Priors Inn, apprentice master for houses on the burgeoning Mildenhall Estate and the subsequent Theatre Royal restoration. His company had a strong reputation locally and across the UK.

Work started in 1951 at this, the highest point in the borough, with a large, excavated pit several metres deep. A steel cage was infilled with concrete to create a collar foundation onto which the 'legs' of the 100-foot-high tower were supported. After completion, the water was pumped here via 5 miles of new mains from boreholes sunk on the Playfields in King's Road to the 4,546,091-litre underground reservoir. The tower would hold 100,000 gallons at a water level of 300 feet above datum. From here the whole town could be supplied. The entire new system was completed in 1952. Nowadays there is a twin compartment service reservoir with a capacity of 6,818,997 litres. Booster pumps situated under the tower lifts water from the reservoir to the tower, which has a capacity of 454,000 litres. From here it gravitates into the Bury St Edmunds supply system. Today the water is drawn from boreholes at Barrow Heath and Risby via Little Saxham and supplies about half the towns current needs. The other half comes from boreholes at Nowton, Rushbrooke and (still) King's Road via booster pumps.

Water Tower foundations, West Road.

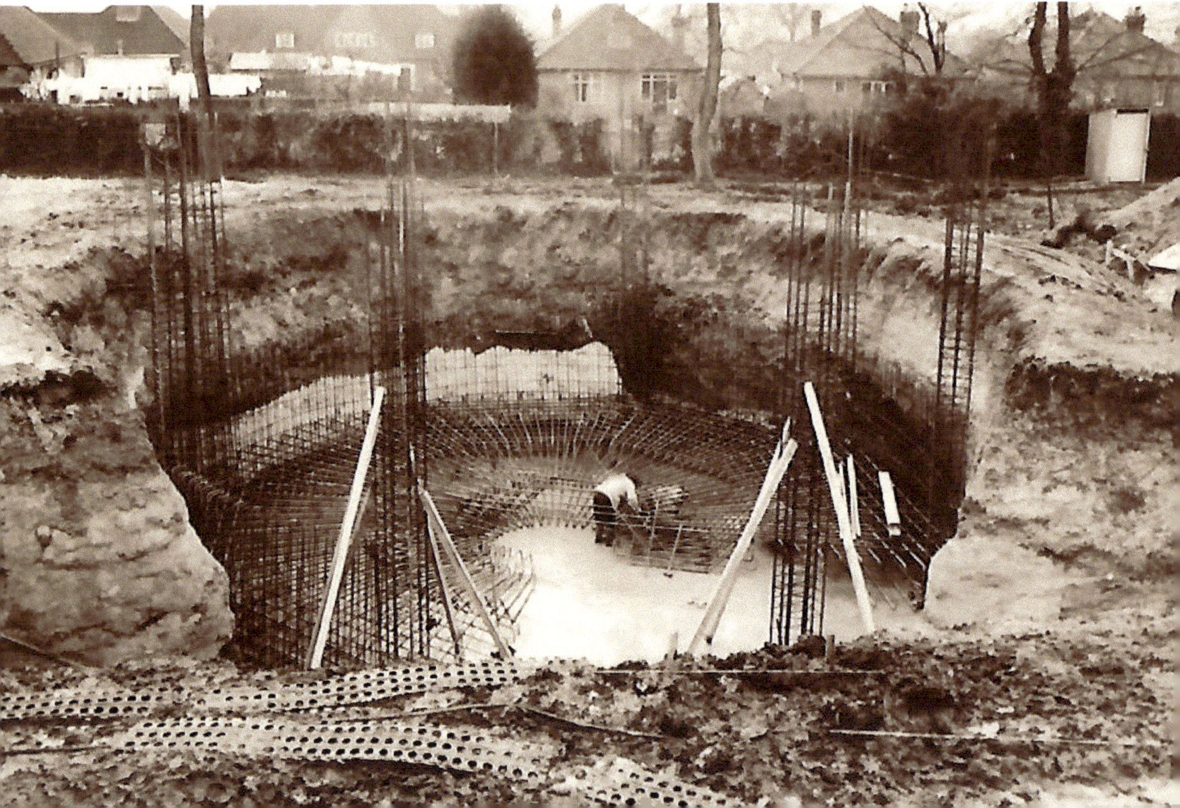

Royal Observer Corps Bunker, 1962–91

After the end of the Second World War, a stand-off between two superpowers – the USA and USSR – came into being, known to history as the Cold War. Britain, as a member of NATO, could be considered a viable target for a nuclear attack, so in this age of uncertainty it was decided to construct Royal Observer Corps listening posts across the country, to give an early warning of such a strike. In the Bury St Edmunds area a site near the Westley grass landing strip, once used by the West Suffolk Aero Club, was chosen by the Air Ministry of Works. The year 1962 saw a bunker costing around £1,000 built, in what is now a playing field off Westley Middle School. This standard design consisted of a large hole roughly 9 feet deep with thick reinforced concrete walls, ceiling, floors and 'tanked' with bitumen to make it damp-proof. The access mound shaft doubled as a ventilation shaft, with another internally opposite with downward sloping louvres, which controlled airflow. The bunker, staffed by up to four operatives, had bedding, a chemical toilet/store and rations, though these were for an indeterminable period of time as no-one knew how long any possible radioactive fallout would be around. Earth was ramped up over the whole structure save for the access point. With the collapse of the Soviet Union/ bloc in December 1991 following five years of glasnost or openness, the ROC bunkers were superfluous to requirements and our bunker was decommissioned. All surface features were removed and the entry shaft sealed, a slightly raised area in the playing field being the only visible evidence.

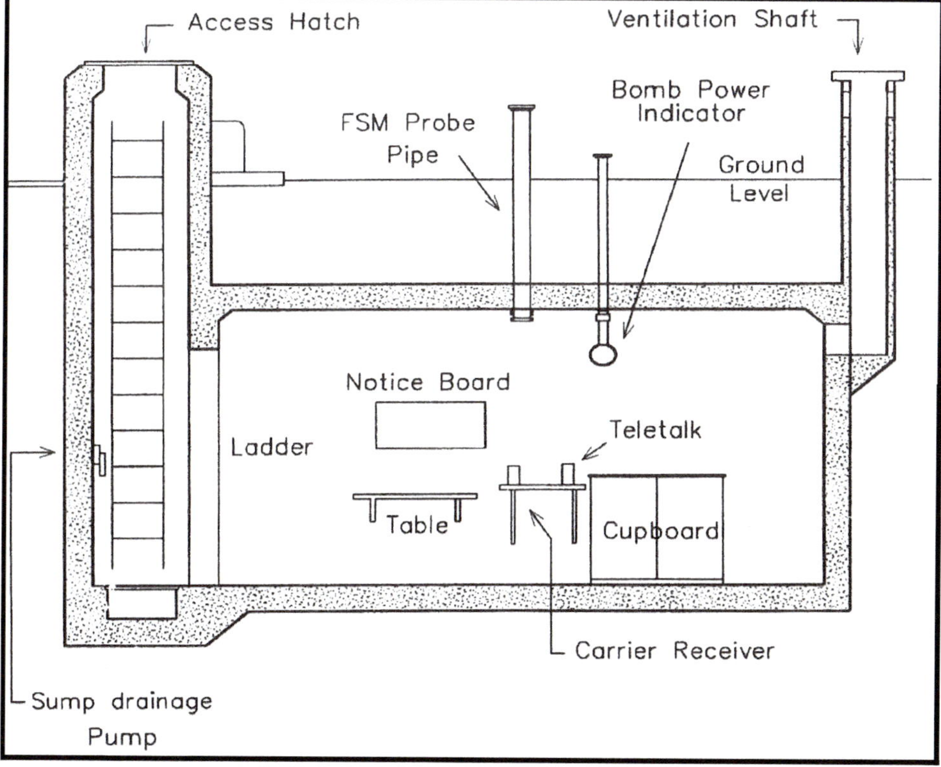

Royal Observer Corps bunker.

Second World War Air-raid Shelters

During the First World War, Zeppelins bombed the town, with some tragic loss of life. Therefore with the improvement of aircraft and their bombing capabilities it was anticipated there could be more casualties in the event of another conflict. With war declared in September 1939, large cities and towns were targeted and, with an estimated population of 22,000, there was no guarantee Bury would escape unscathed. Because of this a concerted effort by the authorities, namely the Combined Military and Civil Defence Scheme, was published on 1 May 1942, to put in place adequate provision for air-raid shelters. For private use there were three types available. The first, the ubiquitous Anderson shelter, used six sheets of corrugated iron that were half-buried in the ground then bolted at the top with steel plates either end. Another, the Morrison, was basically a steel cage or box that you assembled and used in the home. Finally, above ground, a brick shelter with a reinforced concrete dome. According to records there were twenty-five individual shelters, 259 surface shelters with a housing capability of 3,005 and 160 private dug outs, enough for 1,695. These did not take into consideration military shelters as at the Gibraltar Barracks. Altogether private accommodation catered for 7,090 persons and 1,100 in public shelters. These were spread across town, however, as we did not have the large housing estates as we have now – the Priors

APPENDIX G.

AIR RAID SHELTERS.

PUBLIC SHELTERS.

Location.	No. of Shelters.	Accommodation of each.	Total.
King's Road (opposite Prospect Row)	1	50	50
St. Andrew's Street, South	4	50	200
Junction of Hospital Road—St. Andrew's Street, South ..	1	50	50
St. Martin's Street	1	50	50
Angel Hill	4	50	200
Short Brackland	1	50	50
Risbygate Street	5	50	250
Play Field	4	50	200
Playhouse Car Park, Butter Market	1	50	50
			1,100

Bury's air-raid shelters.

Estate, built from 1927, was Bury's first. If you scrutinise the public air-raid shelters table with the nine locations, you will note that shelters on Angel Hill could take 200 people, but no trace remains today as it seems public toilets were built over these underground bunkers.

The Arc

In January 2007, main contractors Taylor Woodrow started building the arc shopping development on the site of the old Bury St Edmunds cattle market. The clients were Centros Miller, the arc developer, with architects Hopkins and Associates on behalf of St Edmundsbury Council. The arc was opened in March 2009 to the tune of £100 million. Multinational retailer Debenhams (went into administration in 2020) who left the town in 1998 were enticed to come back with a promise of a prime site, much to the chagrin of the two Palmers shops in the town that would close in 2018. Debenhams' avant garde building was constructed by Execa, the architectural division of the CA Group Ltd of Evenwood, County Durham. It has two floors with a very large basement excavated out of the chalk. An initial fear that there may be cavities did not materialise, after all nearby Chalk Road in 1979 revealed a 15 × 42-foot-deep hole, which is now filled in. This same fear might have been expressed when, finally, a multipurpose entertainment centre that had been proposed to take pride of place with the working title of 'The Venue' started. The building shell was finally fitted out by August 2010; however, costs had rocketed out of proportion to the initial estimate, eventually finishing over £18 million. More indignation was raised when it was announced that the chosen name was to be the Apex, but to be fair it is a wonderful events venue – not big enough, agreed, but auditorium seating can be lowered into a basement to give added standing room. Adjacent to the Apex is a large underground car park with 217 spaces. I wonder if any voids were avoided in its construction?

The large underground car park adjacent to the Apex.

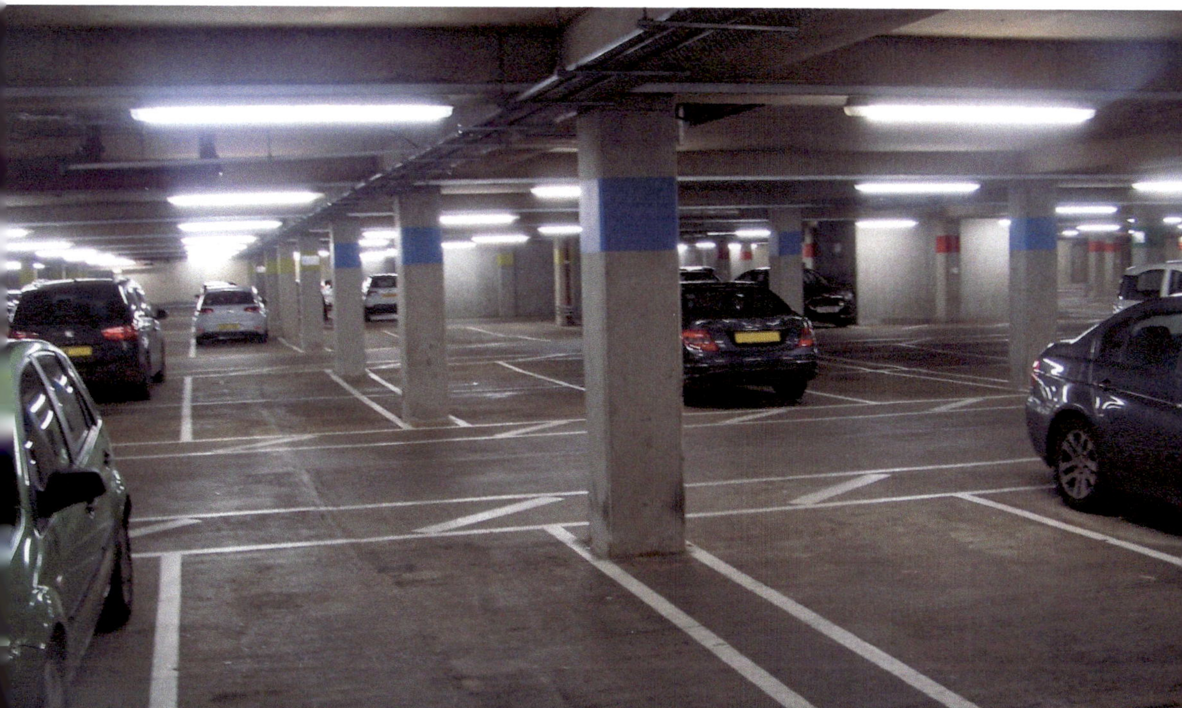

Wells

The town is peppered with wells. Whenever building works are carried out, one or more might be found. A survey of Suffolk in 1906 identified 571 wells, though many others were not recorded. When Tools & Things, a corner shop at No. 21 Churchgate Street, had a refurbishment following the closure of W. Pryke & Son (a hardware shop), a very deep internal well was discovered. In Finsbury Place, just off Whiting Street, set in a random rubble wall is a curious plaque that states, 'The well is directly in front under this stone.' It isn't, however, because the plaque was relocated from behind Peatlings in Westgate Street where there were wells. After Everards Hotel closed, site clearance at the rear uncovered seventeen wells – probably a vestige of when it was the short-lived Buckley and Garness brewery of 1792.

One important aspect of the success of Greene King's beer is attributable to their potable water obtained from deep artesian aquifer wells beneath the brewery. An aquifer is a geological layer of porous and permeable material, such as sand and gravel, limestone or sandstone, through which water flows and is stored. An artesian aquifer contains groundwater under positive pressure. When an artesian well is bored pressure forces the water to the surface without any sort of assistance. Once drawn, the water is de-mineralised, removing nitrates and other undesirable ingredients, although some valuable minerals are subsequently added, including gypsum, to make the water hard as softened water does not make good beer. Modern techniques enable Greene King to create different 'varieties' of water, in order to match the original waters from the several breweries that Greene King bought in the twentieth century. The water is identical to the original, which means that the historic regionality of beers no longer applies.

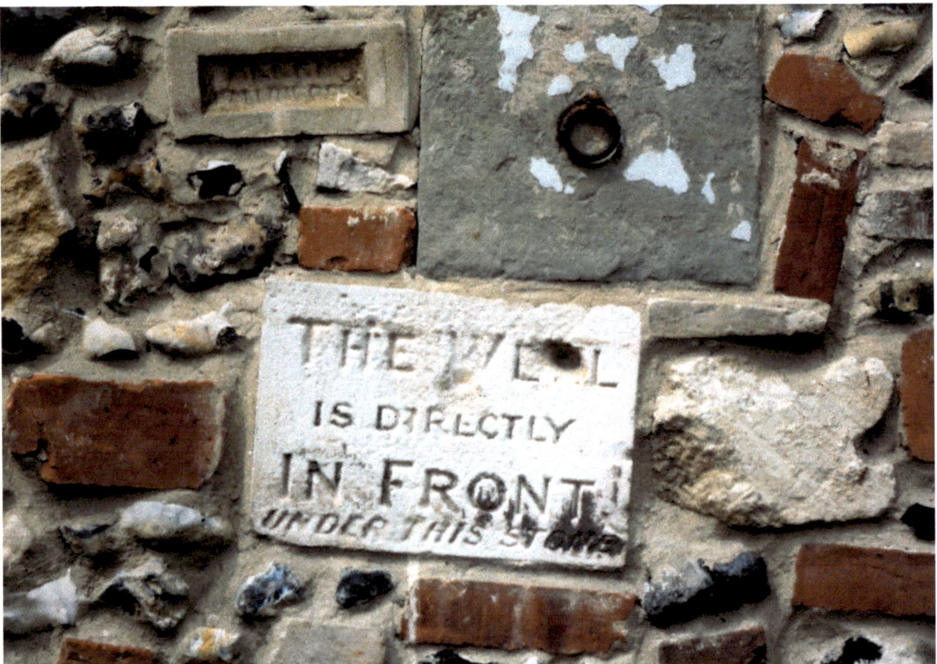

'The well is directly in front under this stone.'

No. 25 Abbeygate Street Well

Phase Eight, a leading women's fashion retailer, currently occupies No. 25 Abbeygate Street. The company was established in 1979 by Patsy Seddon when she opened its first store in Wandsworth Common, London, in order to design and sell clothes that satisfied a sophisticated taste but were affordable and practical. To date, Phase Eight has in excess of 100 shops and many more concessions within well-known department stores, including several abroad. Previous businesses at these Abbeygate Street premises have been Oddbins, Rack Stack and Store, Ridleys Paints and, probably having the longest tenure, Bulling's high-class draper's shop, which was there from 1886 until 1961. This was also, as Phase Eight is today, a ladies' fashion shop. John Bulling had purchased the shop from the estate of Thomas Day, who had been running Taylors Music Warehouse, founded in 1849 by James Last. Previously, Samuel Ridley was listed as a brazier and tinplate worker here. The Ridley name was synonymous with other businesses in Abbeygate Street, with grocers and gent's outfitters represented at different times. Though Grade II listed, the interior of No. 25 has been much altered over time and little of its origins remain evident. The cellar has twentieth-century timber ceilings with walls, a conglomeration of flint and limestone blocks, which obviously

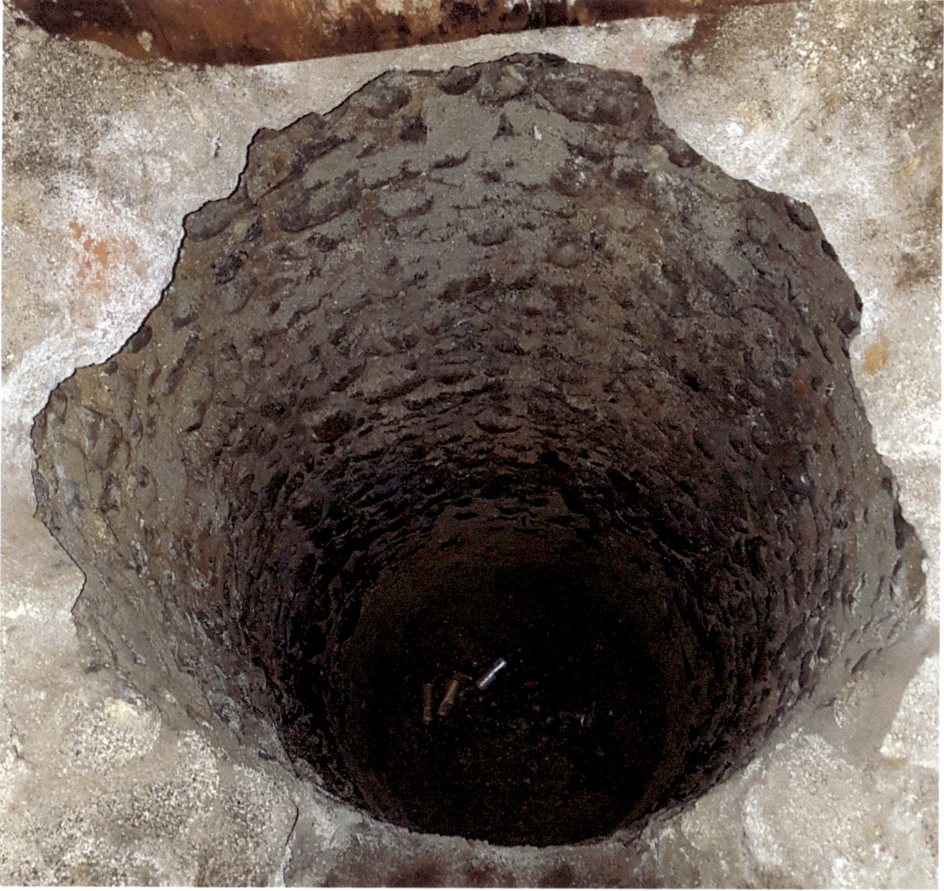

Abbeygate Street's well.

gives rise to an association with the nearby abbey. In places there are shallow retaining arches of old brick. The medieval well in the photo, as you can see, has a very coarse rubble lining, 3 feet in diameter and lying very close to Lower Baxter Street. At one time it would have sunk down to the water table, but has been partially filled in over the years.

Cupola House Well, The Traverse

During the Cupola rebuild some vinyl flooring was removed in the kitchen in one of the cellars, subsequently revealing a well cover. Beneath this was a deep well, cut out of solid chalk. This is probably medieval and predates the Thomas and Susan Macro build of 1693. David Clarke, project engineer of Richard Jackson Ltd, engineering consultants for the Cupola rebuild, said, 'It is certainly something we have never discovered before. No-one we had spoken to that had been advising us during this rebuilding process had told us about it, so it was completely unexpected.' Mr Clarke said they only realised what they had found in the cellar when they lowered a lamp through the hatch. The well, which is 9 metres deep and 12 metres below street level, is said to be structurally sound but does not contain any water. He added, 'We removed some slurry from the bottom but there was no water due to abstraction of water in Bury over many years, the water table now below the bottom of the well.' The concealed well, combined with the third small unknown cellar, extended the fluid contractual time from the original proposed date – the finishing time 'went out of the window'. On completion, upmarket surf 'n' turf restaurant Bourgee was opened in May 2017, but only lasted a year, going into administration. June 2019 saw Cupola House downgraded from Grade I to Grade II status. Though looking the part, the workmanship superb, it is not the building it once was. In 2020 it became a Japanese restaurant, Sakura, specialising in sushi.

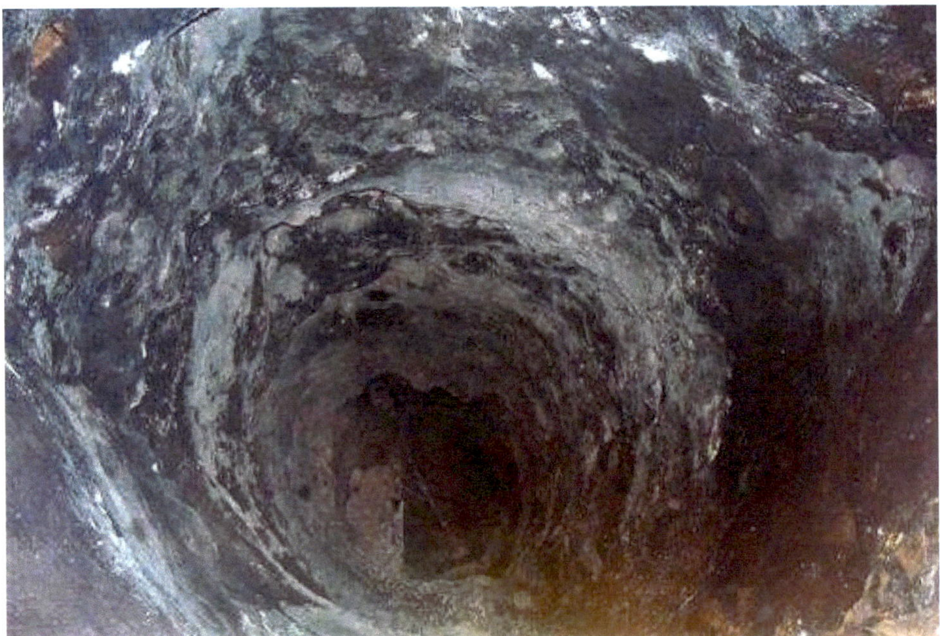

Cupola House well.

Cathedral Treasury

The expansion of the cathedral continued from 1990 onwards when it had a Cathedral Centre built, consisting of a refectory, toilets, offices, song school, meeting room and treasury. The latter, temporarily upstairs in the room, that is now the Discovery Centre is funded by the Yorktown/Jamestown Foundation. As part of the Millennium Project the cathedral treasury closed for a while until a new space in the crypt was built. This was opened in 2009 and is approached from a descending stone staircase at the end of the cloisters. In a controlled secure environment, it houses a fine display of Communion plate, flagons, etc., belonging to the many diocesan parishes. Of note is a pair of silver gilt flagons given by Dorothy Buckenham in 1685. Surely, though, the prize exhibit is a replica of the 'Cloister Cross', a laser copy in resin of a wonderful twelfth-century walrus ivory (aka morse) Romanesque altar cross that is now in the Metropolitan Museum, New York, but originally hailed from St Edmundsbury Abbey. Accredited to Master Hugo, an accomplished medieval artist, it is also known as the Bury Cross. With the 800-year anniversary of the barons of England meeting in the abbey in 1214 to compel King John to agree to Magna Carta, part of the celebrations in the town were to have an original Magna Carta exhibited in Bury. With much security in the treasury, the Lincoln Magna Carta, one of only four left in the country, was able to be viewed via a FOC ticket system. Thousands were able to see this 18-inch square historic document with its abbreviated Latin text on sheepskin parchment, formative of the common law of this land.

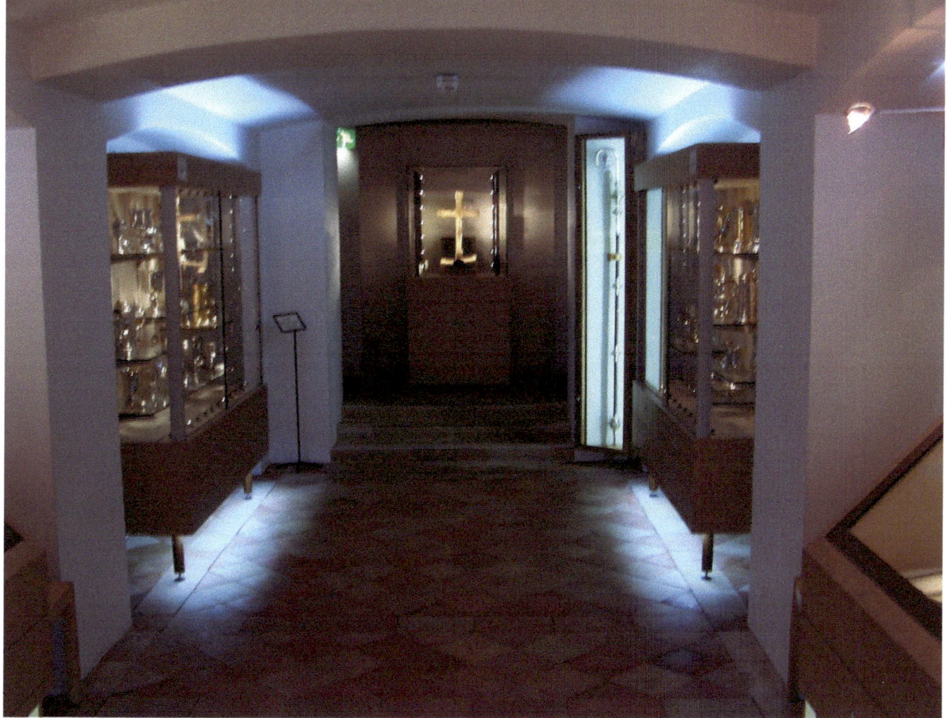

The cathedral's treasury.

Other Accounts of Voids

A long-lost icehouse was discovered in July 1969 off Westley Road, near Fleming Road, part of the estate where Luton builder H. C. Janes (Homes) Ltd were building. It was brick-lined and once filled with ice, and kept at a constant temperature for preserving food, most probably for the Hervey mansion at Ickworth. Alas, it is no longer with us, having been filled in.

In 1955, plumber Percy Cook fell into a 42-foot hole while working in the external privy of No. 5 Willow Cottages, off Mill Road. Fortunately, he was pulled out, though somewhat flushed! The row of fourteen cottages was demolished by 1972, with Baker Builders later building twelve houses here called St Mary's Court. A licence was given on the understanding that the development could not proceed until underground investigations had taken place.

In 1979 a 42-foot-deep hole suddenly appeared behind what is now the Cineworld car park, opposite No. 67 Chalk Road – hence why that space is what it is. But the ultimate story has to be that reported in the *Bury Free Press* in 1988: the abbey's cellars were to become an underground car park – the date was 1 April.

Nearby, the town's inner relief road, Parkway, was opened in 1974 cutting through former open chalk workings.

The rear of St Peter's Church, off St Andrew's Street South, at the end of the nineteenth century was used as a rubbish tip. Bottle and pot lid collectors descended on the former dump in droves! William Warren, the last lime burner recorded in Bury St Edmunds at the end of nineteenth century, lived at No. 26 St Andrew's Street, which backed onto the chalk workings. His limekilns were nearby.

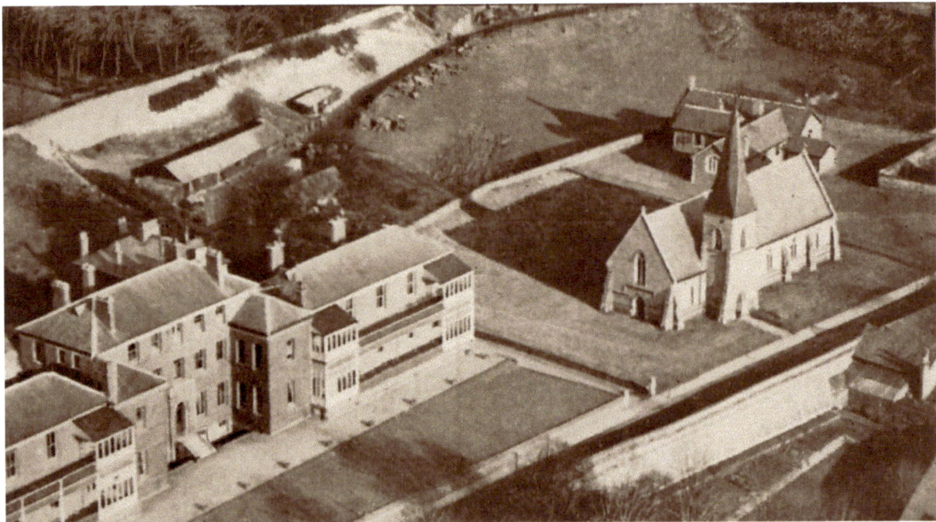

Chalk workings to the rear of St Peter's Church.

5

CELLARS

No. 44 College Street, The Old Angel

No. 44 College Street was once two properties, but is now separated by a yard that is accessed through a large, gated entrance. Jettied and sixteenth century in origin, it is a Grade II listed former public house with a rich history. Starting life in the early eighteenth century as The Angel and Crown, the building of the Angel Hotel meant a change of name from the Old Angel to avoid confusion. Thomas Jennings was one of its early, more colourful, landlords. Another name change, to The Oddfellows Arms, occurred in the mid-nineteenth century. With it advertising itself as a 'comfortable place to stay', which was quite strange as around this time the street had a reputation as being the red-light district of the town.

On 25 March 1807, forty-year-old Robert Clarke was found guilty at Bury Spring Assizes for passing a forged £1 note in the Old Angel. He was hanged for this capital crime on 8 April.

Numbers 44–46 have combined cellars and they are quite extraordinary. They have a variety of finishes to the walls, brick, flint and stone, including circular pieces from former

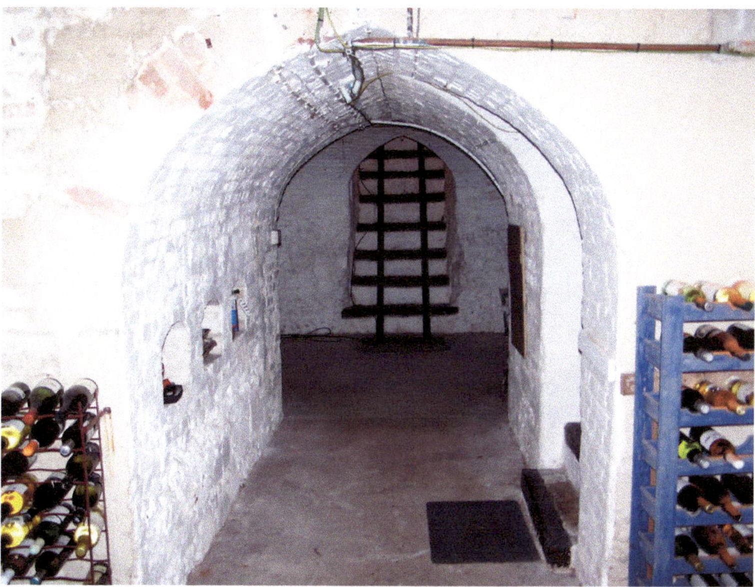

The Old Angel's cellars.

columns – possibly ex-abbey. The barrel chute, aka the skid, at the rear (west side) is in situ, as the photograph shows.

Once a popular hostelry with home-brewed beer and much used by carriers and locals throughout its life, the closure of the Old Angel on 14 April 1975 saw the town lose one of its 'community pubs'. The last landlord, the popular John Ward, would go around the corner to pull pints in the Rose & Crown in Westgate Street. The Old Angel was purchased from Greene King by Philip Greenwood before passing onto John Lacy Scott and eventually to David Rees, a retired doctor.

Between Nos 79 and 80, Whiting Street

No. 79 Whiting Street was once the Guildhall Keepers premises (the Guildhall is to the rear). Today's No. 80 was an early nineteenth-century inn, the Heart in Hand, aka the Fountain Inn, which was closed in 1906. It is currently funeral director L. Fulcher. Between these two properties and before the houses were numbered, a house once stood – what the Americans would now call 'a vacant lot'. During the latter part of 2018 work carried out in the Guildhall garden revealed a small void with an interesting feature that was just visible.

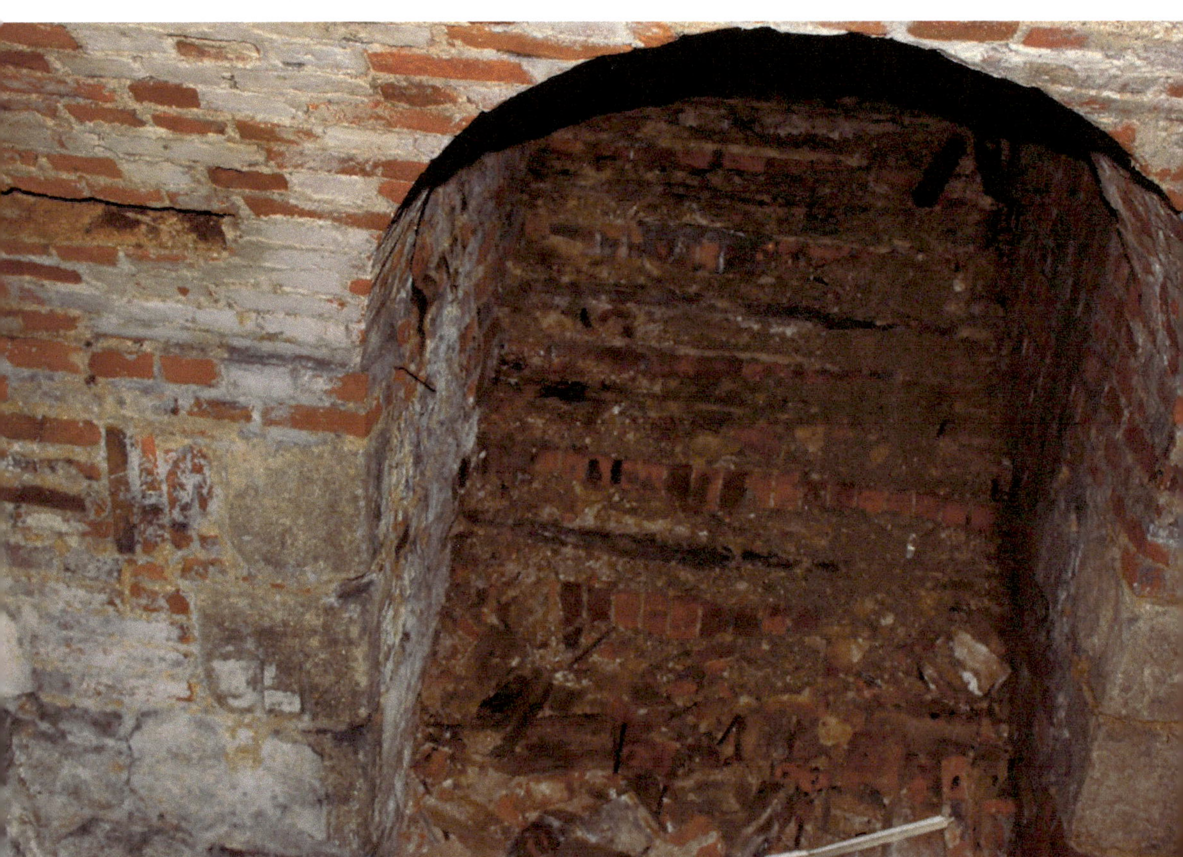

Between Nos 79 and 80 Whiting Street.

David Gill, a renowned archaeologist, attended, and in his own words: 'I put my camera down the hole at Whiting Street and did some press and hope photography.' The 'chamber' is a real beauty, a barrel-vaulted cellar dating back at least to the sixteenth century with a nice mix of choice bits of abbey stone and brick.

No. 79 is built across what was once two medieval plots and its barrel-vaulted cellar extends partly beneath the north end and under about half of the width of what is now a driveway. The north wall of No. 79 is built off the vaulting and over the void of the cellar, showing how strong the arch is. At the rear of the cellar is a flight of stairs reckoned to have come up in the path between the back wall of No. 79 and the garden. The 'lost house' relating to this cellar appears on the 1776 Warren map. No.79's cellar is possibly the same age as the barrel-vaulted one, but includes some reused timber that is probably from the timber-framed house that was knocked down to make way for No. 79 in the early nineteenth century. Access to the chamber is now via a manhole cover.

No. 27 Churchgate Street

This Grade II house with a seventeenth-century core was 'modernised' around 1690 according to records, and again during the early eighteenth century. The cellar is rendered on three walls, with abbey stone rubble on the west wall. Three niches rest here with arched heads in a cusped or curved projection, in a fourteenth-century Gothic style. As they do not match up it is obvious they have been taken from the abbey after it was dissolved.

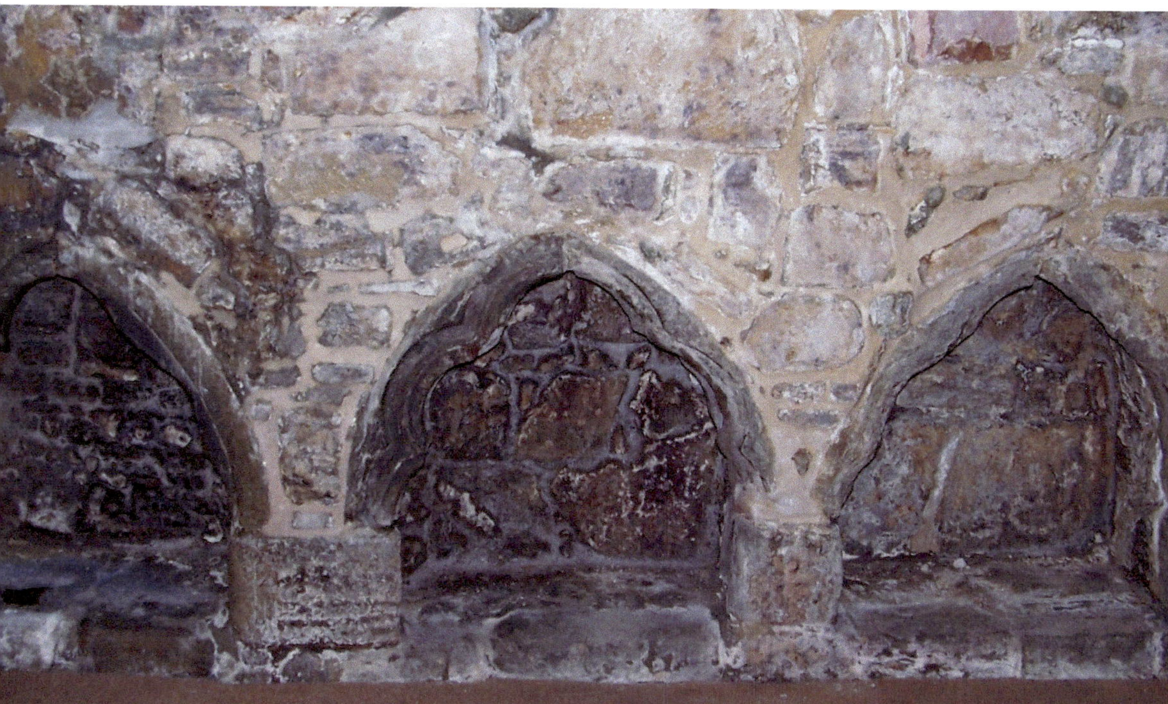

The cellar of No. 27 Churchgate Street.

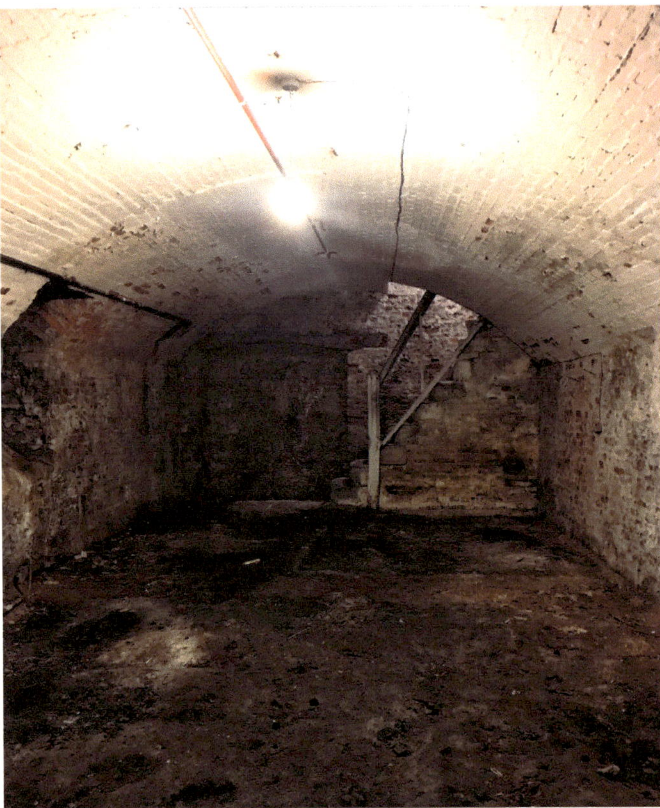

The barrel-vaulted cellar of No. 10 Honey Hill.

No. 10 Honey Hill

Once two properties, this Grade II listed building has an incredible barrel-vaulted cellar underneath the left-hand section, which probably predates the official listing date of the early eighteenth century. The extant dimensions are 10.7 × 4.45 meters and 2.6 meters high to the brick ceiling. To the right of the bottom of the stairs is a classic blocked-up doorway, possibly with a lintel. The property was sympathetically restored by Thurston-based builders Seamans in 2019, including the cellar.

No. 56 Abbeygate Street

'This shop must be one of the most beautiful in England,' a quote used by Alec Clifton-Taylor in his TV series *Another Six English Towns*, first shown on BBC 2 in 1984. Quite extraordinarily, it was a pharmacy for over 200 years, with the most recent occupants being Smalleys Ltd, Savoury & Moore Ltd and Lloyds. It is now occupied by Cotswolds, retailers of outdoor clothing, etc. It shares premises with Nos 1 and 2 Whiting Street.

Inside, there are wonderful beams and a diagonal dragon beam leading to an ornate, carved corner post of a male and female in sixteenth-century garb. Do they represent

Henry VIII and one of his wives, possibly Anne of Cleves? The Grade II* listing of the combined properties states that the interior is from the fifteenth and seventeenth centuries, with refronting carried out in the early nineteenth.

During the ownership of the business by Smalleys from 1956, much restoration was carried out by the very reputable local firm Warren Builders. It included a complete overhaul of a neo-Jacobean staircase and fine ceiling/roof timbers on the first floor. During this work a young Ernie Warren discovered a very rare vestige of the past sitting on top of a beam: a hearth tax book from 1662 to 1689, when tax was levied according to the number of hearths in your home.

It goes without saying that a building such as this and with this much history would have ancient cellars, and you would not be wrong. A foundation wall in the part under Abbeygate Street (once Cook Row) has been dated to the thirteenth century and may well have once been part of a Guildhall belonging to the Candlemas Guild, Bury's premier guild.

The medieval cellars under No. 56 are quite special. One of the niches here may have contained a piscina (now removed), a stone basin used in religious services to wash Communion vessels. It was found in the cellar, re-enforcing the Candlemas Guild theory. The walls are lined with the obligatory limestone and part flint that is so prevalent in town centre cellars. A heavy chamfered main ceiling beam is supported on abbey stone columns with the joists of the floor above sitting on these. The nineteenth-century, brick-lined section between No. 56 and Nos 1–2 Whiting Street links the two cellars, which nowadays are used for storing equipment.

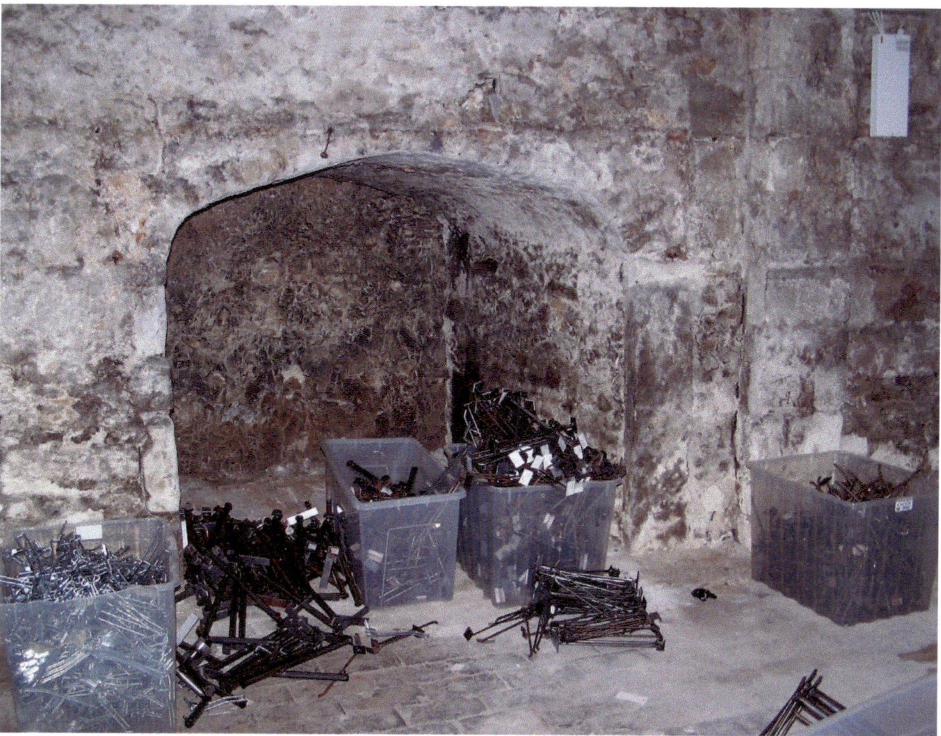

Beneath No. 56 Abbeygate Street.

Hatter Street

This is one of the oldest streets in Bury St Edmunds and it has ancient cellars. It was known as Heathenmens Street in medieval times and was the town's Jewish quarter. A terrible incident started here on Palm Sunday in 1190 when Jewish residents fled from townspeople to the abbey seeking sanctuary. Abbot Samson shut the then Abbeygate and fifty-seven Jews, 'not St Edmunds men', as stated by Samson, were killed – supposedly in revenge for crucifying a young boy called Robert years earlier. However, later theories abounded that Abbot Samson manipulated the incident to renege on debts that Abbot Hugh, his predecessor, had incurred.

No. 4 Hatter Street, York House, was at one time owned by auctioneer Henry Stanley, but was demolished to make way for the Central Cinema, which was opened in 1924 and was owned by cinema entrepreneur Douglas Bostock. As a 650-seater it attracted large audiences. It rebranded in 1959 as the Abbeygate, followed by several name changes before becoming the Picture House in 2010. In 2014, the Competition Commission ruled that new owners Cineworld had to sell it as it was unfair to consumers (a Cineworld cinema is also on Parkway). Picture House manager Pat Church, who has worked here for well over fifty years, was delighted when an independent company purchased it, saving the cinema for the future as the Abbeygate.

In 2019, extensive works were carried out that revealed cellar details – part of the two buildings that once included York House. They have several arched, brick recesses, the most interesting faces onto Hatter Street itself and has a double soldier course (upright bricks). One cannot help but wonder why, dare I say, there is a possible entrance to a tunnel that led across the road, though this is pure speculation.

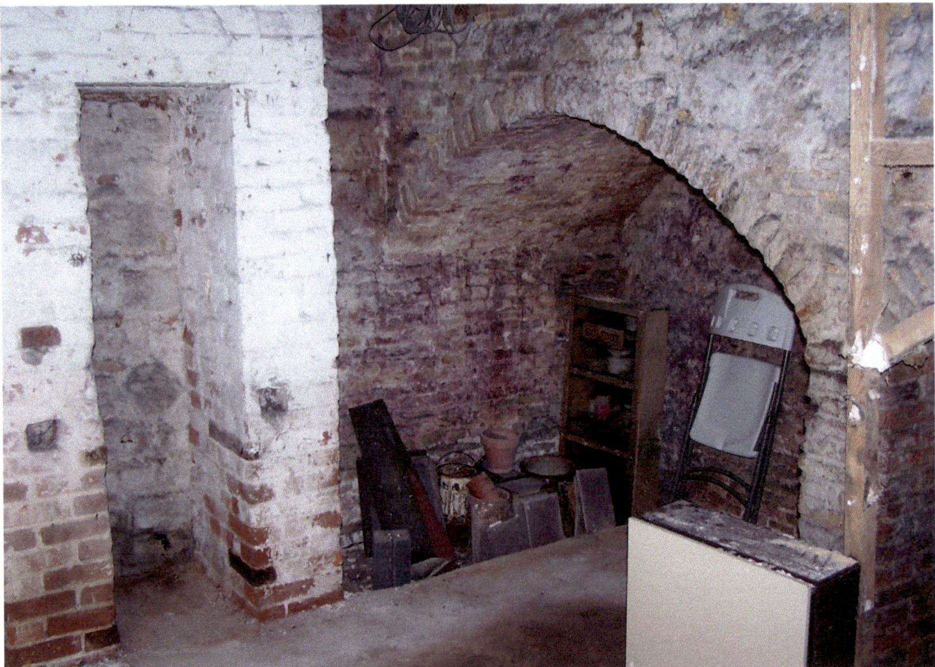

The cellar beneath No. 23 Hatter Street.

Opposite the Abbeygate cinema is a shop at No. 23 (Sew Much to Do in 2020) with interesting features within. Its cellar (possibly late fifteenth century) is Grade II listed, as is the adjacent property at Nos 25–26. This was once thought to be where Bury benefactor the grocer John Nottingham lived. Many years later it was also the premises of Peter Gedge, editor of the *Bury & Norwich Post* as well as notable Bury printers FG Pawsey & Co. Ltd, who produced a fine postcard series of the 1907 pageant. There is some probable Norman stonework at the rear, in situ, which may even be contemporary with the cellar, where a laver (a receptacle used in religious ceremonies to wash oneself) possibly once used to be. The connection to the Jewish faith via this object has led to conjecture that a synagogue occupied Hatter Street, which was also once the Jewish quarter of the town. Another hypothesis is that a mikvah was here (a Jewish immersion well), which was possibly fed by a running watercourse that may have even led to St Margaret's Well in the crypt of the abbey.

The entrance off Hatter Street to Langton Place has stonework that is thought to be part of a fireplace relating to Jewish activity. The likelihood is then that houses built of stone for security reasons were here; their stone-lined cellars are all that remain. Nos 7 and 8 Hatter Street are particularly old. One of the gable ends is built of wide flint construction as per the east side of the Guildhall, making this Norman part of the house one of the oldest in Bury. Both have limestone in their cellars.

Cupola House, The Traverse

Thomas and Susan Macro, important members of Bury society, were the owners of this fine Stuart-era, timber-framed apothecary from 1693. It looked upon a very different market place, devoid of buildings obscuring the view. Internally, there were many fine features, such as fireplaces, a magnificent oak staircase and a ground-floor room with oak panelling par excellence.

Over time the usage changed. During the nineteenth century the Jennings family held it as grocers, then it was a public house from around 1861 when it was renamed The Victoria. From 1901, Clarks Brewery of Risbygate Street owned it until 1917, when Greene King bought them out; the Cupola's cellars were much used by them during the Second World War for the bottling of wine. The building would subsequently be put on the at-risk register until it was lovingly restored in 2003 by owner Paul Romaine, assisted by local historian Dr Pat Murrell. The restoration led to the discovery of a mummified cat under the floorboards, which was placed there to ward off evil spirits (alas, not fire – more on that later). OMC Investments Ltd then acquired Cupola, with it becoming part of the national restaurant chain Strada, famed for their Italian cuisine.

The brick-lined cellars would be instrumental in the disaster that unfolded on the evening of Saturday 16 June 2012 when Cupola House was devastated by fire. That fateful Saturday evening saw the restaurant busy as usual. Staff were already well underway with the preparation of meals in the subterranean kitchen located in one of the cellars. What happened next is shrouded in mystery, though it was possibly down to a lack of understanding by a staff member. It would seem this person was instructed that in the event of any flames flickering on the main oven hob they were to put a fire blanket over them and leave it a while. However, the employee removed the blanket too soon and somehow the flames shot up the dumb waiter and eventually through into the roof space. Here, unknown

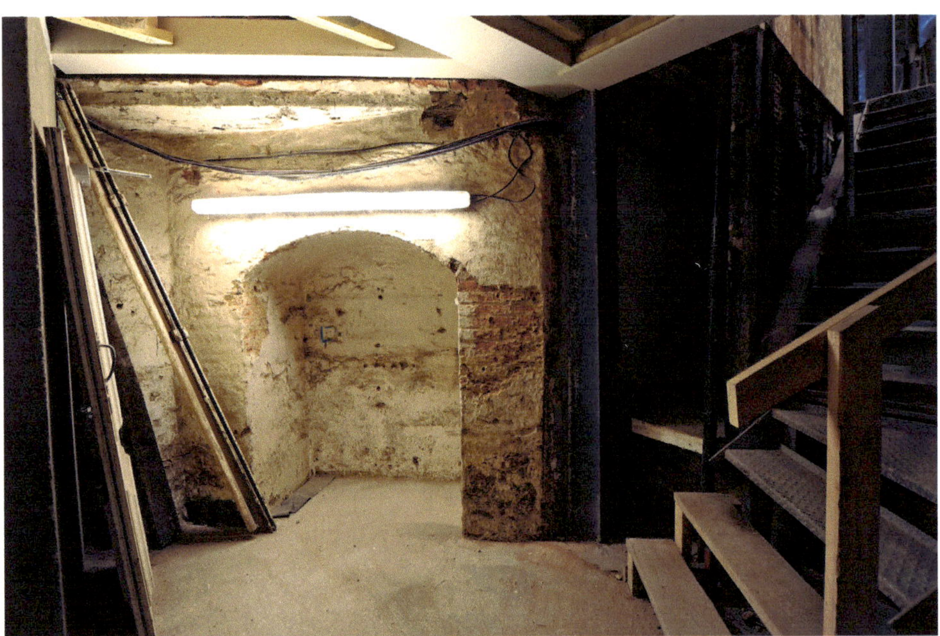

Above and below: Cupola House. (Courtesy of Bury Free Press)

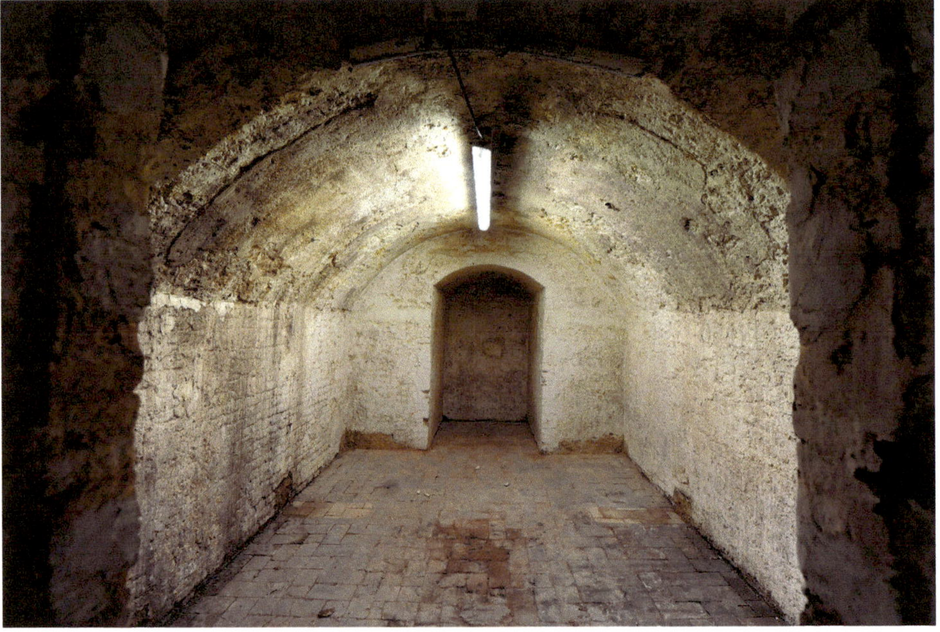

to everyone, the flames took hold in the upper reaches of this timber-framed building until fire alarms were set off, leading to the evacuation of all staff and customers – thankfully no-one was injured. Over eighty firefighters attended.

It was one of the biggest fires in the town for many a long year. Only the façade and one ground-floor room could be saved, but the fire service did a wonderful job to prevent the fire spreading. So, what was to be done? A rebuild was the answer. Many architectural elements were salvaged from the rubble and historical photographs were utilised as well. Norwich-based architects Purcell were used, as was engineering consultant Richard Jackson Ltd and builders Seamans, achieving a notable award-winning 'phoenix' from the ashes. It was not without hiccups, though. The timescale for the rebuild went well beyond what was envisaged due to the discovery of a hidden cellar, adding to the other two large cellars that went under Traverse and Skinner Street. An unknown feature in the south-east corner of the basement had previously shown up in surveys and historic plans as solid masonry, but upon investigation, to allow for a new concrete beam, the top of an arched brick structure was revealed. Following further exploration this arched structure appeared to be part of a further small cellar parallel to Skinner Street. Deemed to be of no architectural merit and structurally unsound, it was documented then infilled with concrete, ready to take the beam.

Zen Noodle Bar, Angel Lane

An unpretentious, industrial-looking building from the outside has within it a fine East Asian restaurant at ground-floor level and in the basement. This is quite remarkable as it has an amazing barrel-vaulted ceiling constructed in red brick. It makes you wonder what

Zen Noodle Bar Restaurant cellar.

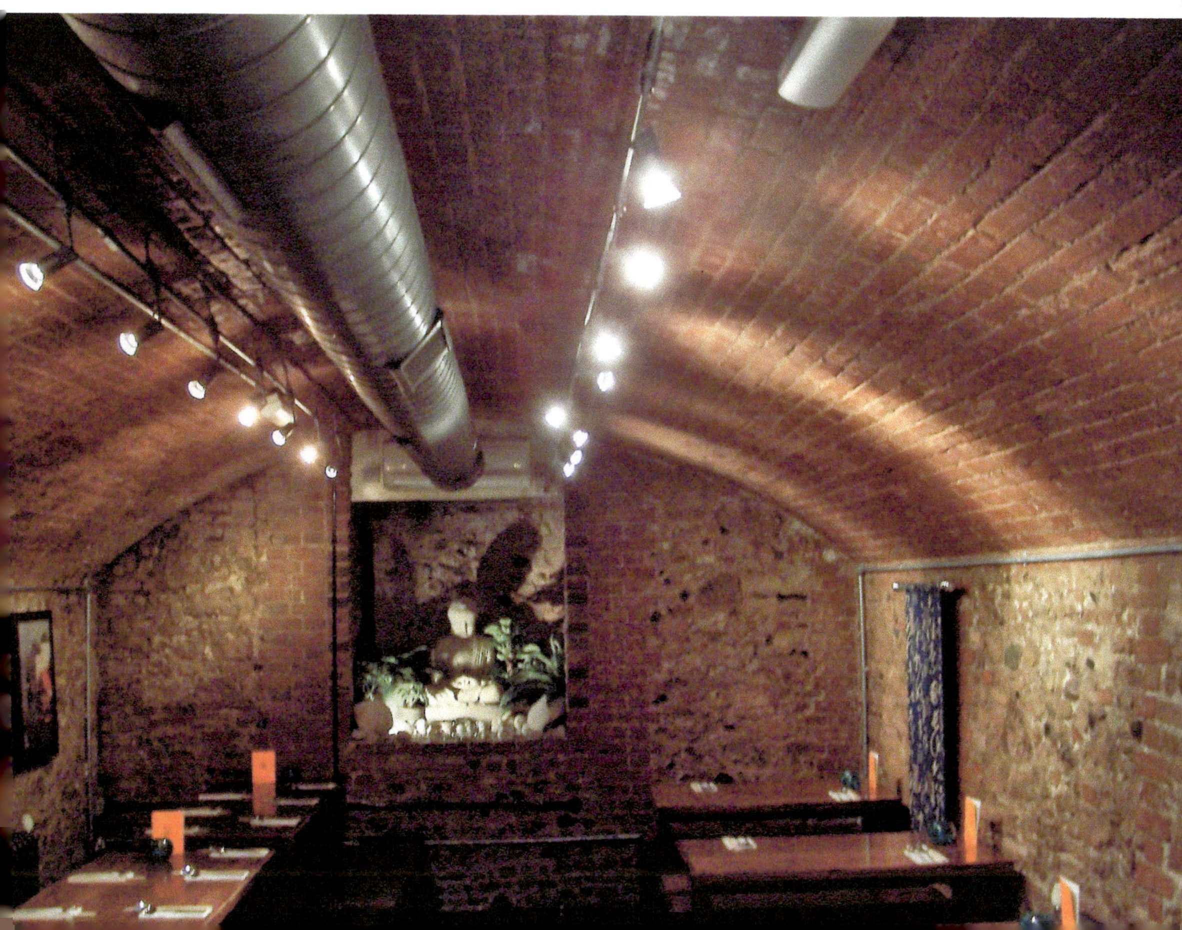

was here before the present structure above ground. Well, before Zen it had been the Red Onion and also The Brasserie restaurants, but this cellar is something special. A clue may be in the north side random rubble wall where there is a plaque with the initials 'J S' and the date '1876'. There is another plaque, though somewhat worn, on the other side of the lane with 'James Sparke' and the date '187?'. James used to live at No. 7 Hatter Street, a house not too far away from the Zen building. A well-known figure in Victorian times, James was the son of Ezekiel Sparke, the attorney to prominent local banker and one-time wool merchant of the town James Oakes. For a man with only one head James wore several hats, earning his living as a solicitor, a commissioner in all courts, a clerk of the peace and to the Thingoe Union Workhouse, acting sheriff, borough coroner and finally a clerk to the Guildhall feoffees – phew! He died at the age of seventy-seven in January 1884 and is buried in Risby Churchyard, though there is a brass lectern in his memory in St Mary's Church. If, indeed, James Sparke did own this building, what could the cellar have been used for? A man who moved around in such exalted circles may have kept a well-stocked wine cellar, which is as good a guess as you could make.

No. 18 Whiting Street

Nos 17–19 Whiting Street was once a hall house with origins from the sixteenth century. It is now split into three properties, with No. 19 being the original centre part of that building. As you might expect from a multi-layered house of this age and in the town's 'Medieval Grid', it has many interesting features within. No. 19's cellar is under No. 18's sitting room, though

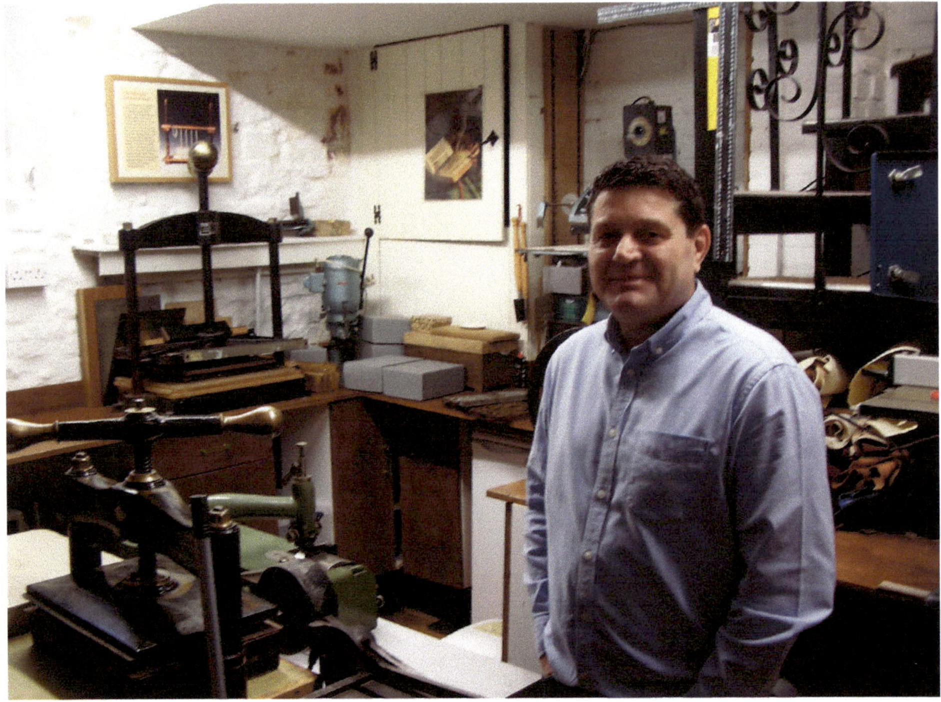

Shaun Thompson and his private workshop.

it is the property of No. 19; No. 18's smaller cellar is underneath No. 17; and the very small cellar for No. 17 is tucked away under that property – complicated, isn't it?! No. 17 is the only cellar to sit under its own property. A metal spiral staircase leads to the deep cellar of No. 18, which has a small window on the north side facing the former Rogers brothers' garage – now replaced by a pair of semi-detached houses. However, the cellar is not used for conventional purposes. It is the private workshop of a very talented man, Shaun Thompson. Still utilising traditional working methods and tools, he undertakes work for Cambridge University as a bookbinder-cum-conservator. In his spare time, he takes commissions for the repair of antiquarian books, spines and covers as well as making up very fine folders for magazines, etc. In 2020, as part of the abbey's millennium celebrations he was going to supervise abbey manuscripts from Pembroke College to the cathedral treasury, but Covid-19 prevented this. Being a conservator, he appreciates the original bindings, the commonest form consisting of plain white vellum over wooden boards. The boards themselves are usually quite flat and the chain mark, used to prevent pilfering, is almost always on the front cover, with the commonest form of fastening being a strap with a metal loop.

Adie's Barber Shop, No. 2b St Andrew's Street North

On entering the premises, you descend a narrow staircase into the cellar of No. 2b, which has a flying freehold with the adjacent cellars of No. 2c. A flying freehold is an English legal term to describe a freehold that overhangs or underlies another freehold. Six working stations are kept busy by the large number of loyal customers coming in for their haircuts. As individual

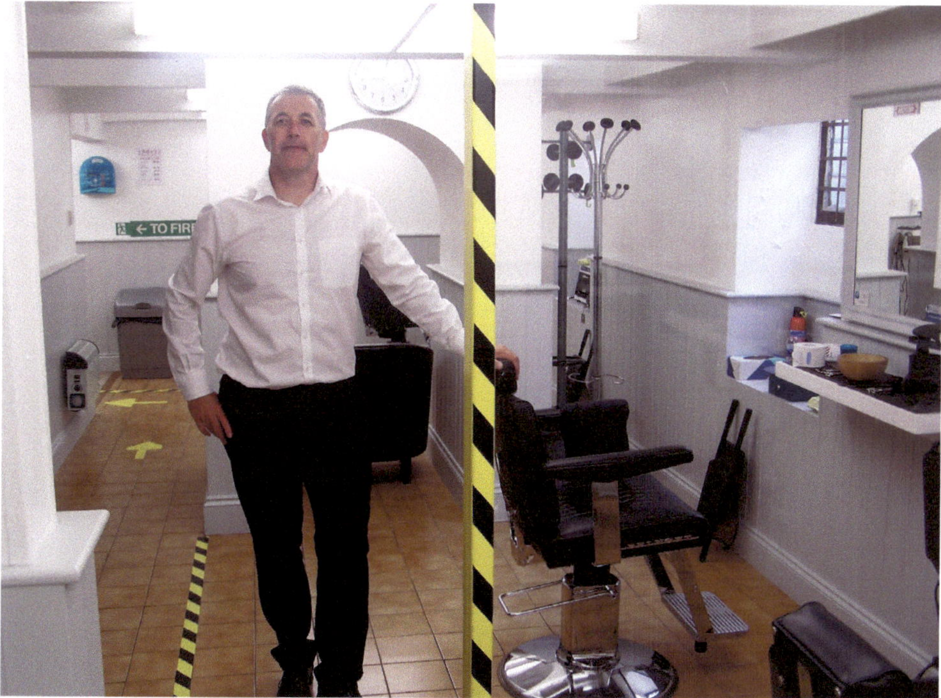

Adie's Barber Shop, No. 2b St Andrew's Street North.

cellars they were part of a Victorian terrace but now have had their internal walls removed, completely transforming their origins. This refurbishment was carried out years ago by Jimmy Mitchell for his business Burnett James, which sold soft furnishings, such as curtains, cushions and furniture coverings. Experienced in his job, Jimmy used to work for the Bury Linen Shop on Cornhill. His claim to fame was being goalkeeper for the England roller hockey team.

Tony's popular barber business started above ground in the former card shop adjacent to Roger Avis letting agents before descending in 1986/7. Tony ran the business for twenty-eight years until his son Adrian successfully took over a few years ago. Adrian, who goes by the name Adie, is a keen Ipswich Town football supporter and is also a regular blood donor. This caring side of Adie is well known because he took part in an amazing three-way exchange with three donors and three recipients in 2019 so that his sister, Lynn, could have a new kidney – she was born with only one. Adie's son, Liam, has now joined what is a true family business. The photo of Adie shows Covid-19 protocol in place in July 2020 after lockdown and redecoration.

No. 43 Crown Street

Parts of the end of this three-house terrace in a street once known as Churchgovel Street are probably from the sixteenth century, but its fine cellar is older. One wall is lined with

No. 43 Crown Street.

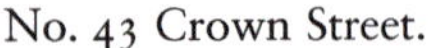

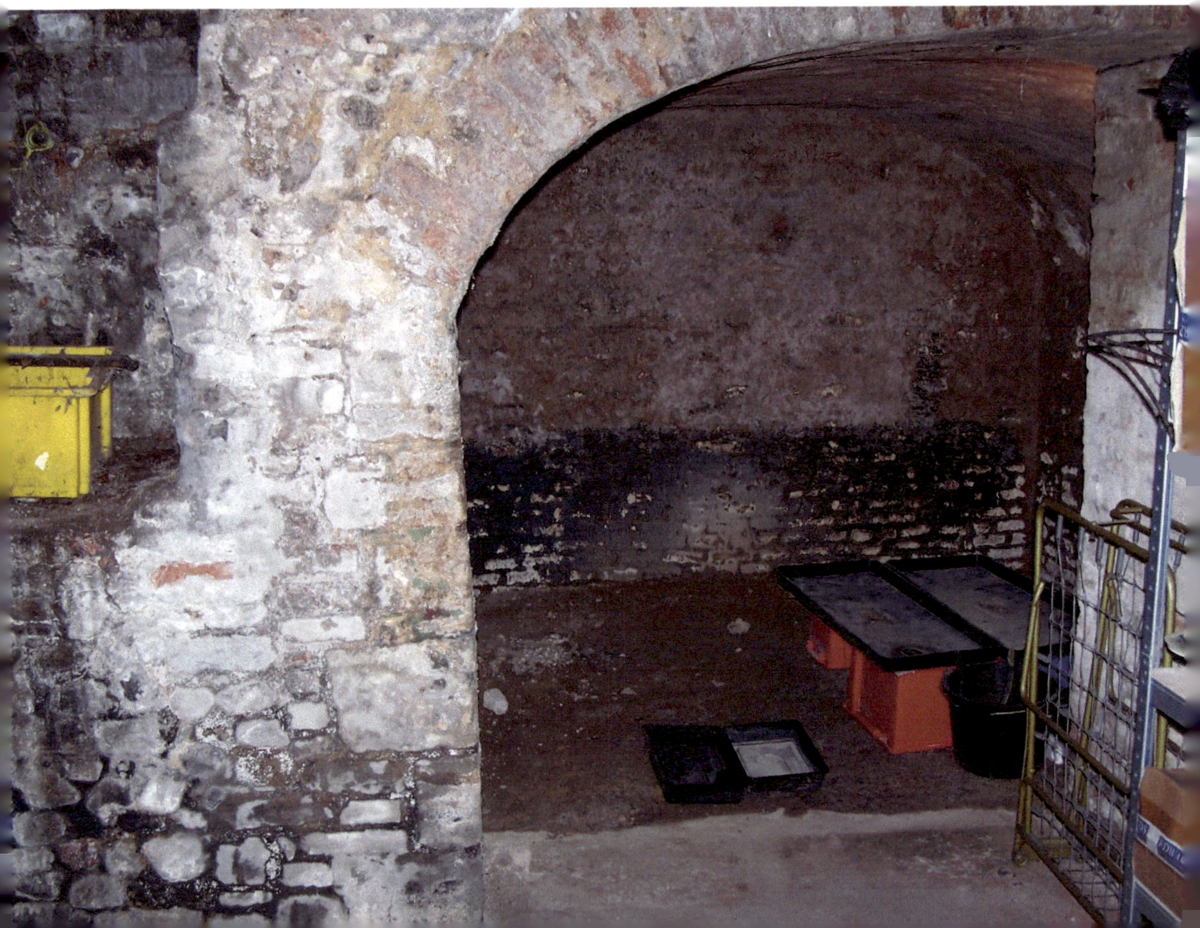

ashlar (limestone blocks), and it has a Tudor brick archway over a recess that goes under the Crown Street pavement. Curiously, during the summer months the cellar is damp, but in winter it is dry. Is this due to condensation?

Palmers, Abbeygate Street

Plumptons, a draper shop, was here from the late nineteenth century up to 1961 when it was taken over by Palmers department store. This independent company, whose main business was ladieswear, fragrances and luggage, had originated in Great Yarmouth. In 2017, chairman Bruce Sturrock announced that Palmers, on this prominent corner, would close by January 2018, with all stock removed, as can be seen in the empty storage areas in the cellars.

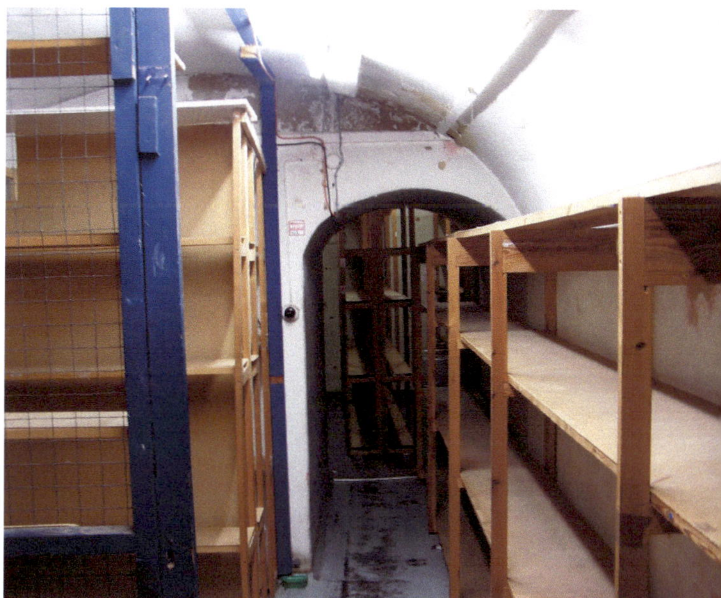

Palmers, Abbeygate Street.

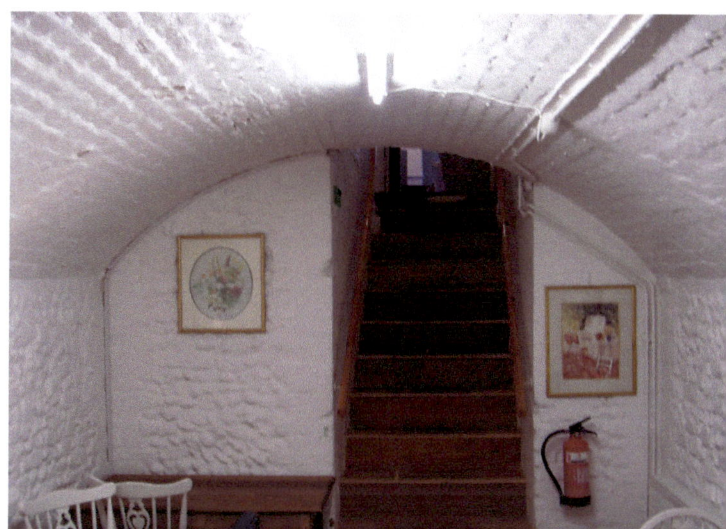

Abbey Hotel.

The Olde White Hart, No. 35, Southgate Street

One of six public houses in Southgate Street that are all now gone. It has a long history, its interior stretching back to the fifteenth century. Owned by Henry Braddock during the nineteenth century, on Henry's death in 1868 Edward Greene immediately purchased this, along with Henry's nearby Southgate Brewery, to stop them falling into the hands of his arch-rival, Fred King. Now the Abbey Hotel, it has an excellent barrel-vaulted cellar.

No. 63, College Street

Sharing the corner with Churchgate Street, this building was the Golden Fleece pub, dating from at least 1737. It was one of the last pubs in the town to brew its own beer. It closed upon the retirement of landlord Frank Taylor in 1933. The builders H. G. Frost gave it a complete makeover in 2000 on the cessation of Foto Fayre, its last commercial owner. Shown is an unusual, vaulted ceiling in the cellar, which is now used as an attractive sitting room.

No. 63 College Street.

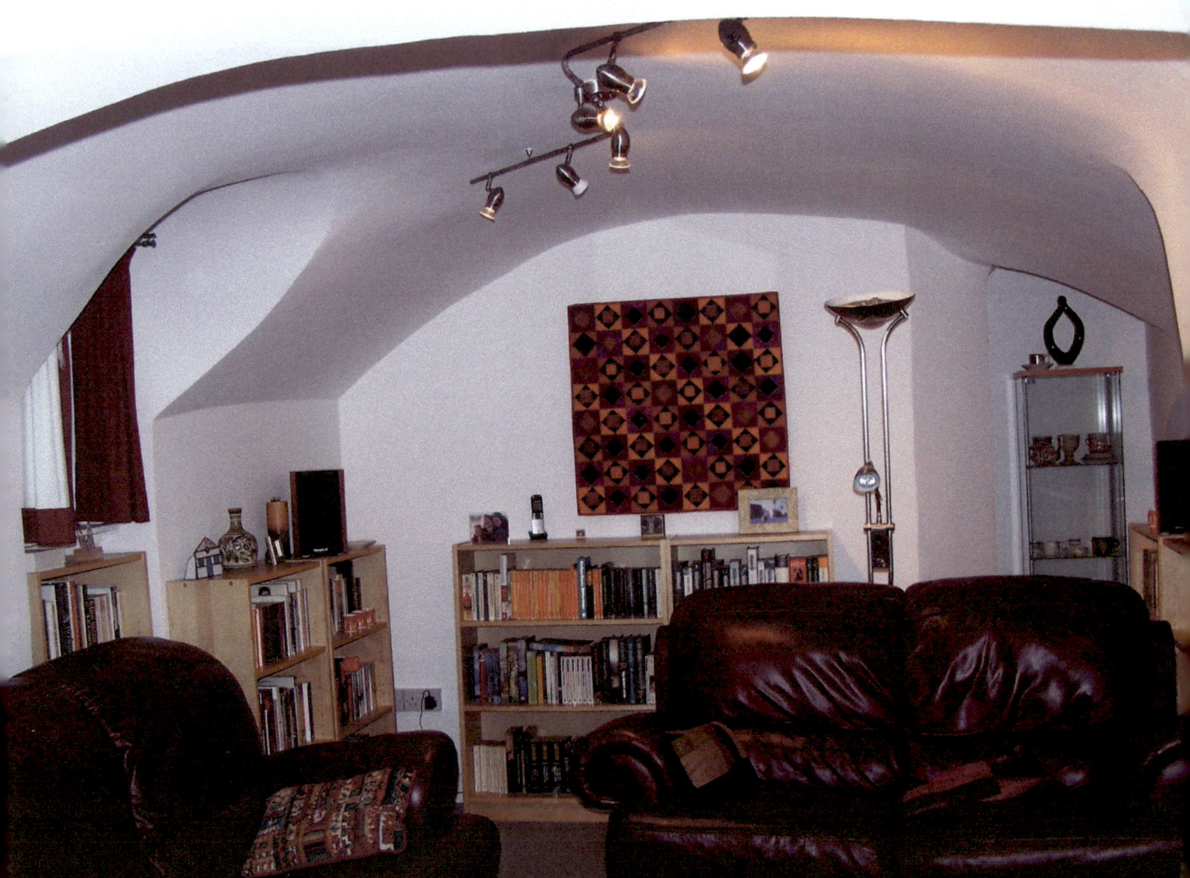

Javelin, Nos 37–38, Abbeygate Street

It is no surprise that lurking in the shop cellars in Abbeygate Street are hidden architectural gems going back hundreds of years. Some of these became evident when Jeremy Clayton, the owner of Javelin, a boutique shop selling top quality designer men's and women's clothing, decided to open the late fifteenth- and sixteenth-century extensive cellars under his shop. The results of this makeover, after months of hard work, were amazing: exposed beams, a limestone doorway and brick vaulting, obviously synonymous with days gone by when Abbeygate Street was known as Cook Row.

In the nineteenth century Waite Gates, tailors and drapers, were trading at No. 37 before moving up to No. 23 Buttermarket. During the twentieth century Westgate Seeds had a horticultural business here, their seed potatoes de rigueur for the keen gardener. With Westgate Seeds closing, Cramphorns pet and garden shop opened where an African grey parrot with a remarkable vocabulary was the star attraction. The origins of Javelin are from when Robert and Violet Clayton purchased Hodgson's Gun and Sports Shop in The Traverse in 1953 until retiring in 1976. It would later become Clayton Sports when it was run by their son, also called Robert, with his son Jeremy continuing the family name in a partnership. When No. 37, a prime site at the corner of Angel Lane, became available the business moved there. Further growth saw expansion into the adjacent shop at No. 38,

The fifteenth/sixteenth century cellars beneath Javelin.

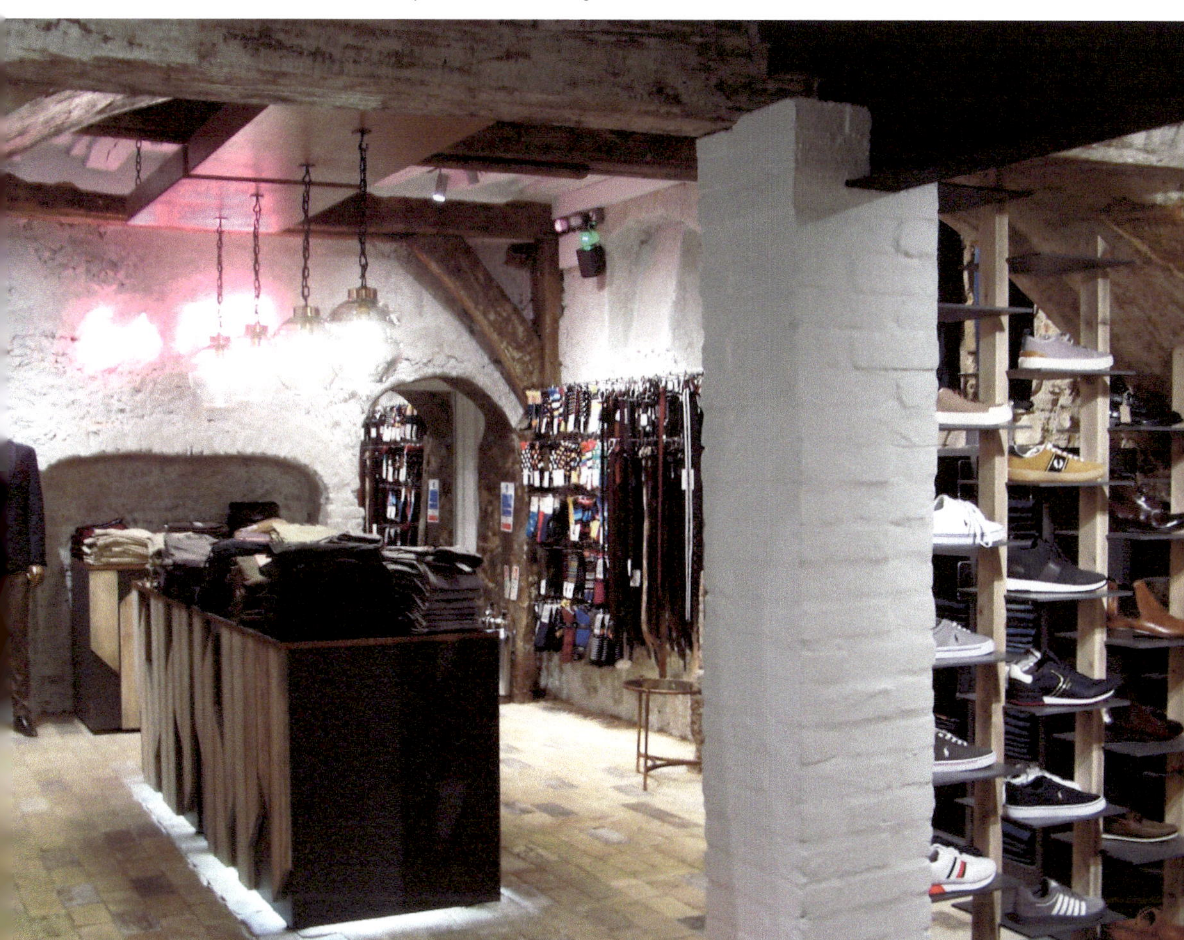

once Payne's China and then Carousel Fashions. In 2012, Javelin won a Drapers award for 'Independent Womenswear Retailer of the Year'. It celebrated its thirty-year anniversary in 2019.

Greene King

An amazing warren of mainly now unused brick-built cellars with barrel-vaulted ceilings from Edward Greene's nineteenth century Westgate Brewery are hidden from view. The up-to-date machinery of today's modern brewery carries out the many tasks once undertaken manually. A fact not often appreciated is that from here Greene King sends its effluent from production after initial treatment to the Anglian Water processing plant at Fornham.

Edward VIII's coronation (1937) never happened, so beer bottled for that event was not sold and some is kept locked away below ground. When I asked Greene King's Quality

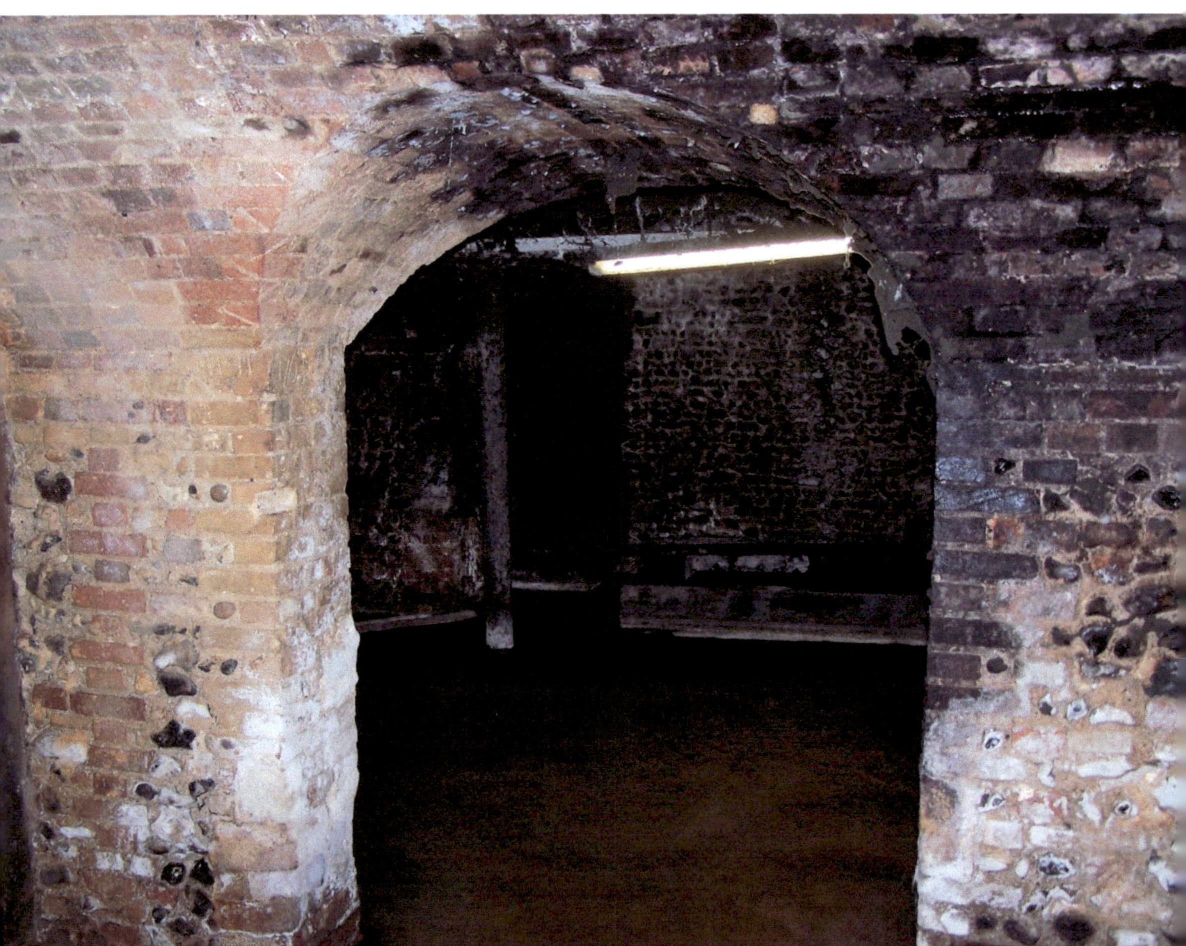

Above and opposite: Greene King's Victorian cellars in the Westgate Brewery.

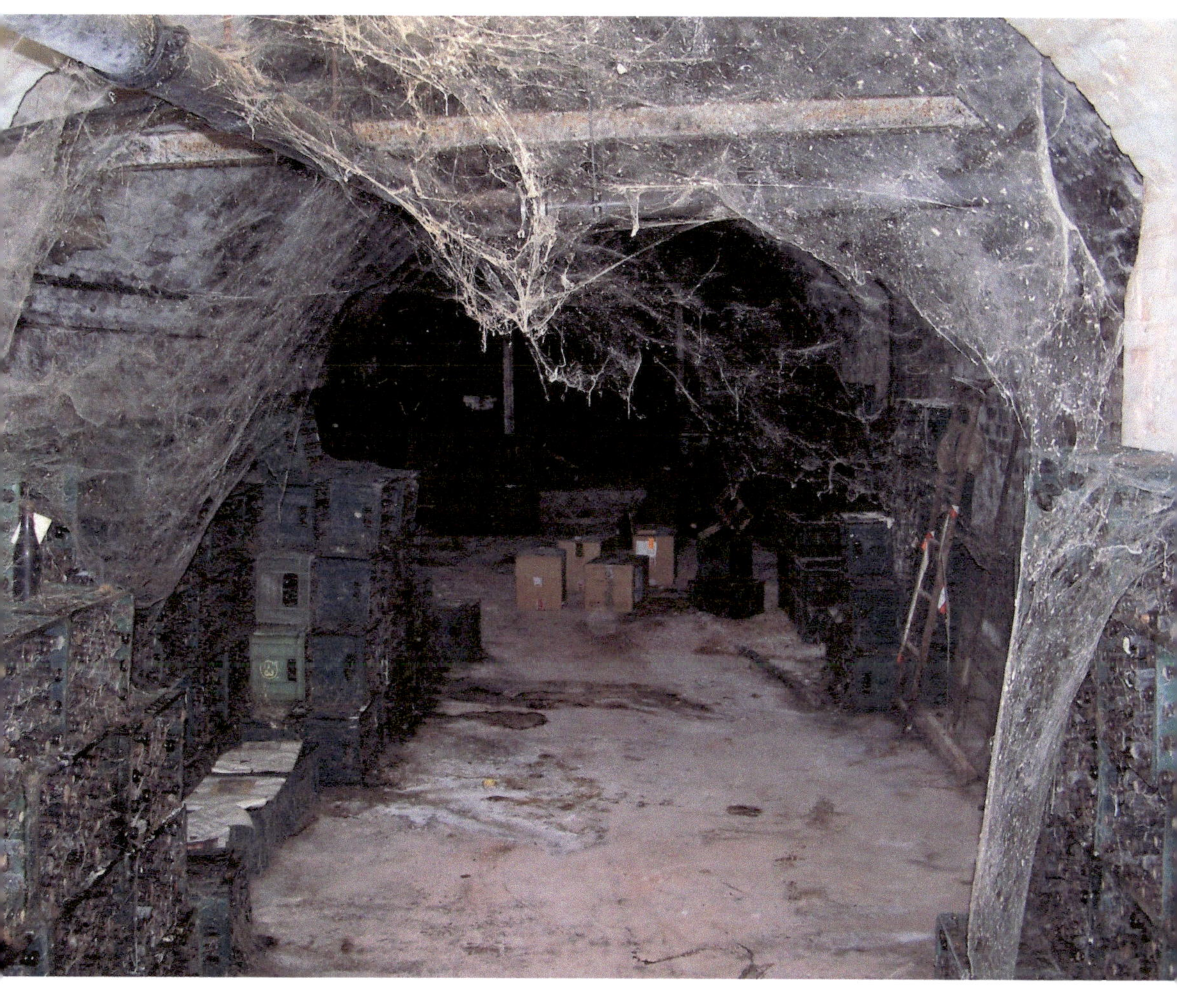

Control Manager Susan Chisholm, whose knowledge of the company is exceptional, as to its drinkability, she said: 'At first it tastes like Madeira, then of rusty nails!'

Barley wine that was brewed by the Cambridge Panton Brewery, taken over by Greene King in 1925, is also one of five different tipples kept here.

6
EXCAVATIONS

Abbey Parch Marks

Following the abbey's dissolution in 1539 the buildings were systematically demolished, stone by stone, brick by brick. It is said that limestone can be found all over the town, particularly in cellars and walls, such as in Pump Lane and Barn Lane. However, you most probably will not find it much further than 6 miles from town – the distance a cart would get out of town and back in a day. All that is left of the once magnificent abbey church and its ancillary buildings are flint cores – mere glimpses of what was once there. The wonderful abbey painting by William Hardy in 1883 gives you a comparison to the surviving impressive elements of the abbey – the Abbeygate and Norman Tower. The Abbey of St Edmund Heritage Partnership commissioned in 2018 a thorough assessment

Parch marks, Bury St Edmunds Abbey.

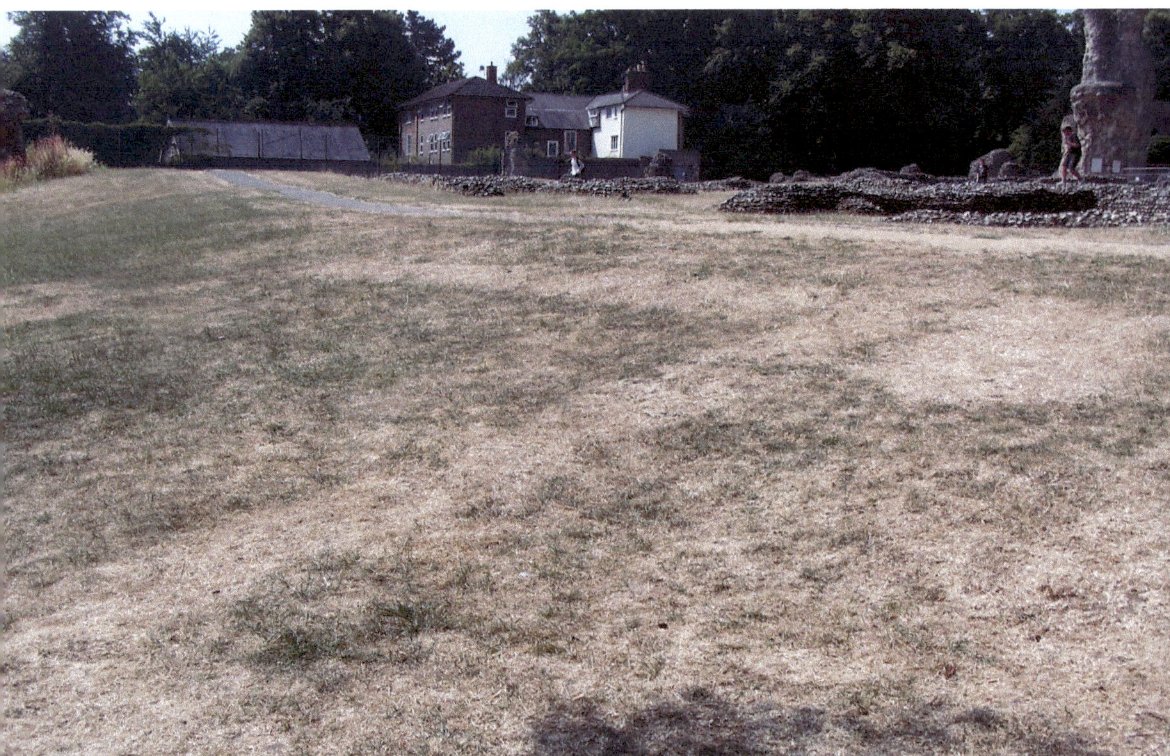

of the abbey site by Dr Richard Hoggett, which included a great deal of information never published before. It also dealt with a possibility of further excavations that could take place through ground-penetrating radar or remote-sensing technology called LIDAR, which uses the pulse from a laser to collect measurements that can then be used to create 3D models and maps of objects and environments. This would be invaluable in finding out what these parch marks are, a vestige of the very hot summer of 2018. It would seem from this photo there is a turret at the junction of two walls. According to Arthur Whittingham's 1951 abbey plan, the nearest building in that area is the former Priors House – could it be this?

Excavations in Tayfen Road

During 1121 to 1136 Abbot Anselm's sacrist, Hervey, undertook further defensive measures for the town, adding to those carried out by King Cnut (see Le Dycheweye, p. 86). In 1968, the Ministry of Public Building and Works were given the opportunity to investigate the possible location of Hervey's wall in Tayfen Road, as detailed in a paper published in the Proceedings of the Suffolk Institute of Archaeology by eminent archaeologist Stanley

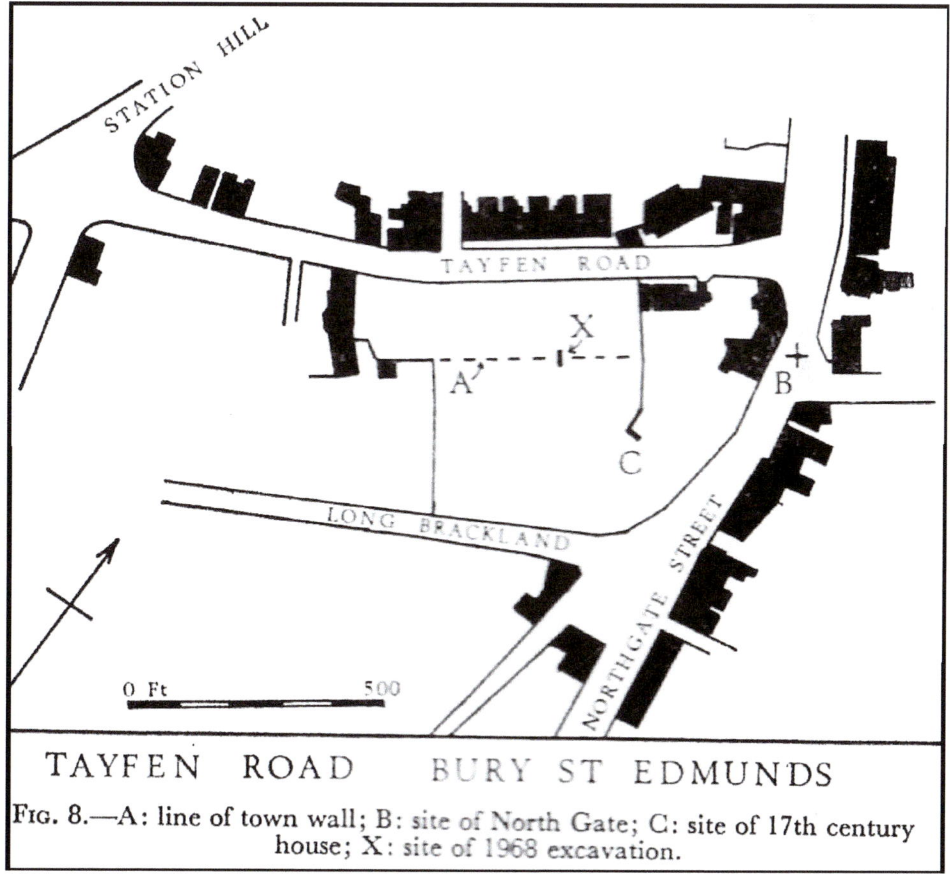

Fig. 8.—A: line of town wall; B: site of North Gate; C: site of 17th century house; X: site of 1968 excavation.

Map of Tayfen Road.

West in 1970. The excavation began with the demolition of a mixed rubble wall prior to redevelopment, then a 30 × 10-foot trench opened, cutting across the line of the town 'wall' (Fig. A). The foundation of the rubble wall actually cut into part of a rampart, which gave rise to the belief that it could be part of the original works of Cnut. The 'wall' was never constructed of stone, as there is no evidence to substantiate it and is in fact most probably a continuation of Le Dychewye. The Northgate was where today's roundabout is situated and is directly in line with the excavation. Interestingly, some brick remnants of a seventeenth-century house (now gone and not far from Long Brackland) is of the same type and date as the mixed rubble wall. For many years it has been propounded that the wall at the rear of the former gasworks and to the rear of Peckham Street was the actual town wall. This is not correct and may even be part of Fig. A. Excavation footnotes revealed that over 500 worked flints from the Middle Stone Age, some 8,0000 years ago, were recorded – the Tayfen was popular for fishing then!

Crosspenny Court, Cotton Lane

A tarmacked car park used by the NHS to the rear of Thingoe House in Northgate Street was lifted in advance of an archaeological dig in 2012. Fifty-six assisted living, one- and two-bedroom apartments called Crosspenny Court would eventually be built on the site by 2014 by developers McCarthy & Stone. The development is named after an early fourteenth-century silver long cross penny of Edward I, which was found on the site by archaeologists. A pedestrian access is by Northgate Street and a vehicular one by Cotton Lane, though this is now a no-through road.

The image shows the large amounts of earth removed before any archaeological investigations could go ahead. The discoveries were astonishing and added to the rich history of the town as part of the Historic Environment Records (HERs). Archaeologists from Oxford Archaeology East, employed by the developers, found evidence of a quarry dating to around the twelfth/thirteenth century, which may have provided the materials used to build the town. Other finds included a Roman coin, a prehistoric flint, two Boy Bishop tokens and a fine seventeenth-century tin-glazed apothecary jar known as an albarello. Aileen Connor of Oxford Archaeology East said, 'while individual finds could be exciting, archaeology is more about building a story.' Generally, the finds are medieval and early post-medieval. All of these smaller finds help to piece together the historical jigsaw that makes Bury St Edmunds so interesting. However, the most impressive and totally unexpected finds were red-brick structures, possibly from the eighteenth century and possibly in use as cisterns for storing water with the associated well as part of some ornamental garden. Though all recorded, these are no longer there because of the development.

Cotton Lane had different names in the past: Scurff Lane and Skoron Lane. The latter probably evolved from Scurun's Well where the cellarer (provisioner) of the abbey had property. The archaeological dig here uncovered medieval occupation, including a very fine well with curved limestone blocks, evidence of a high-status owner. The other image shows what may have been part of an ancient cellar, the timber-framed building it once belonged to now long gone.

The most unusual finds were the garden features possibly linked to No. 1 Mustow Street, aka Mustow House, as this property backed onto this site. Partly Dutch-gabled, in the early

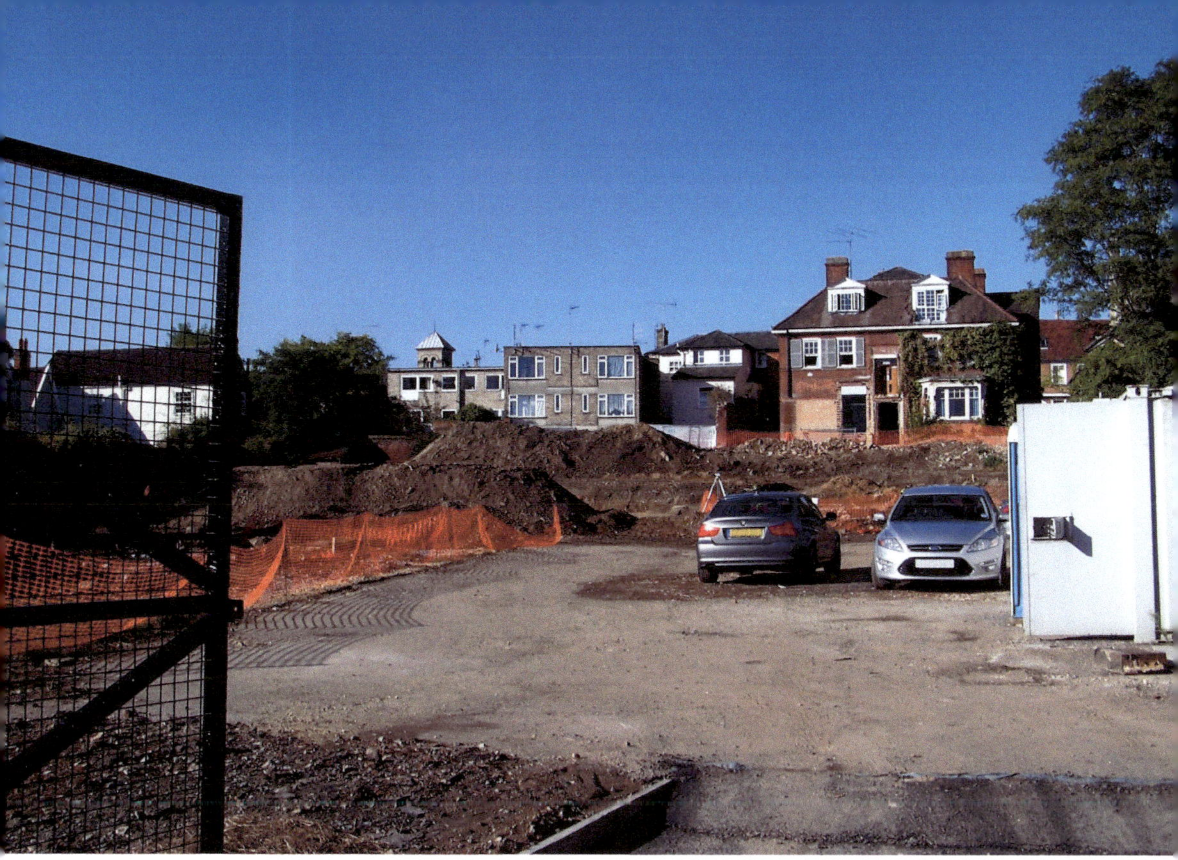

The car park that was to become Crosspenny Court.

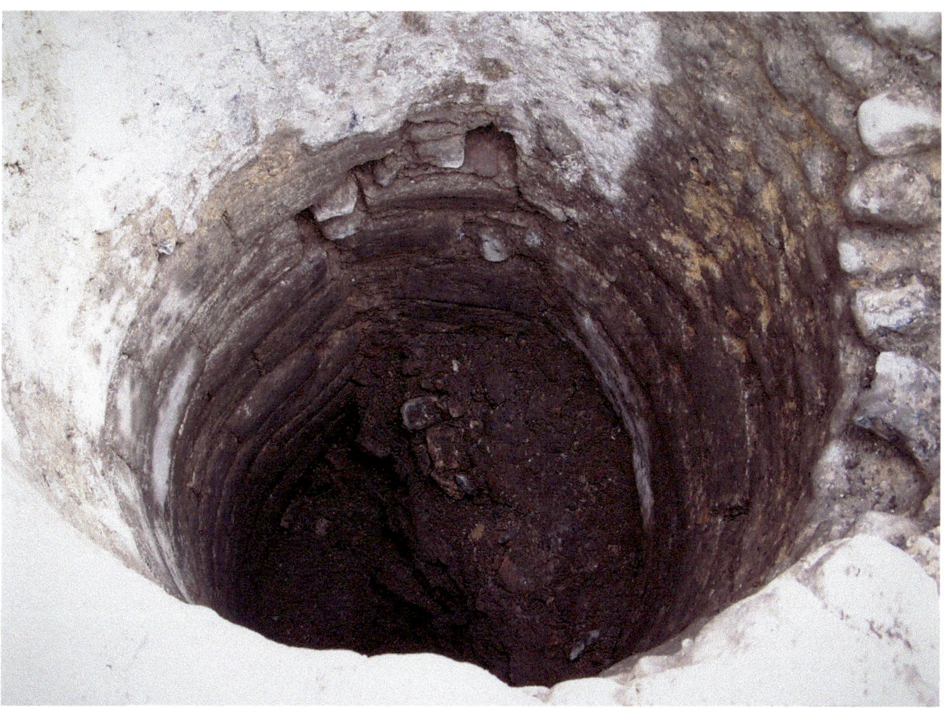

The medieval well uncovered on Cotton Lane.

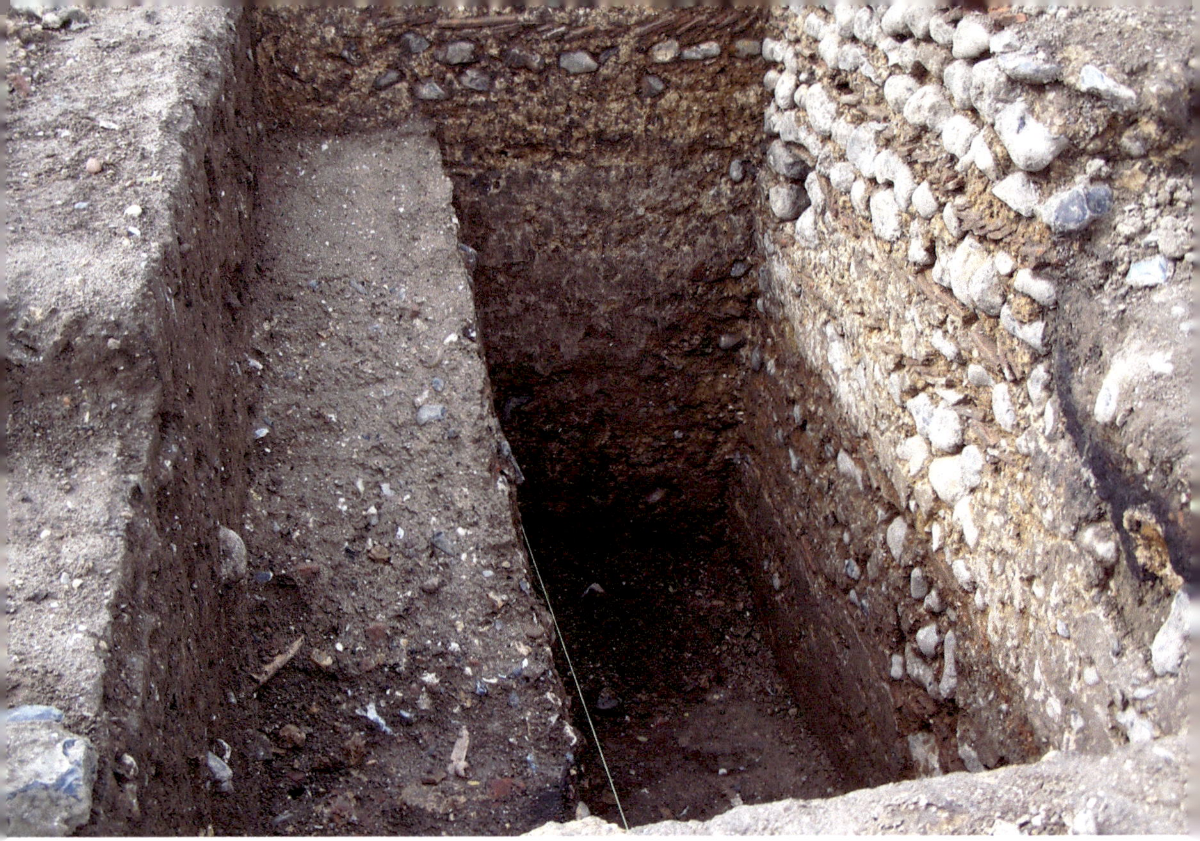

Above: Possibly a former cellar.

Below and opposite: Uncovered garden features possibly linked to Mustow House.

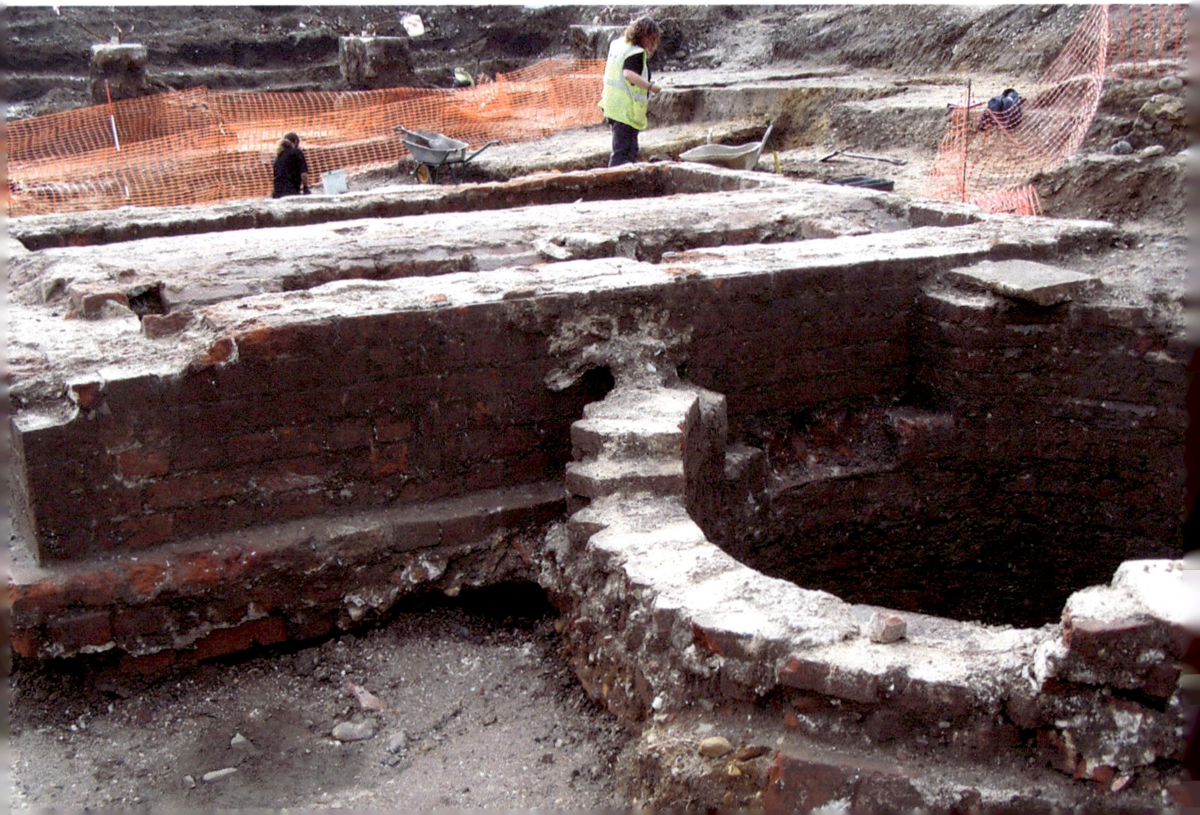

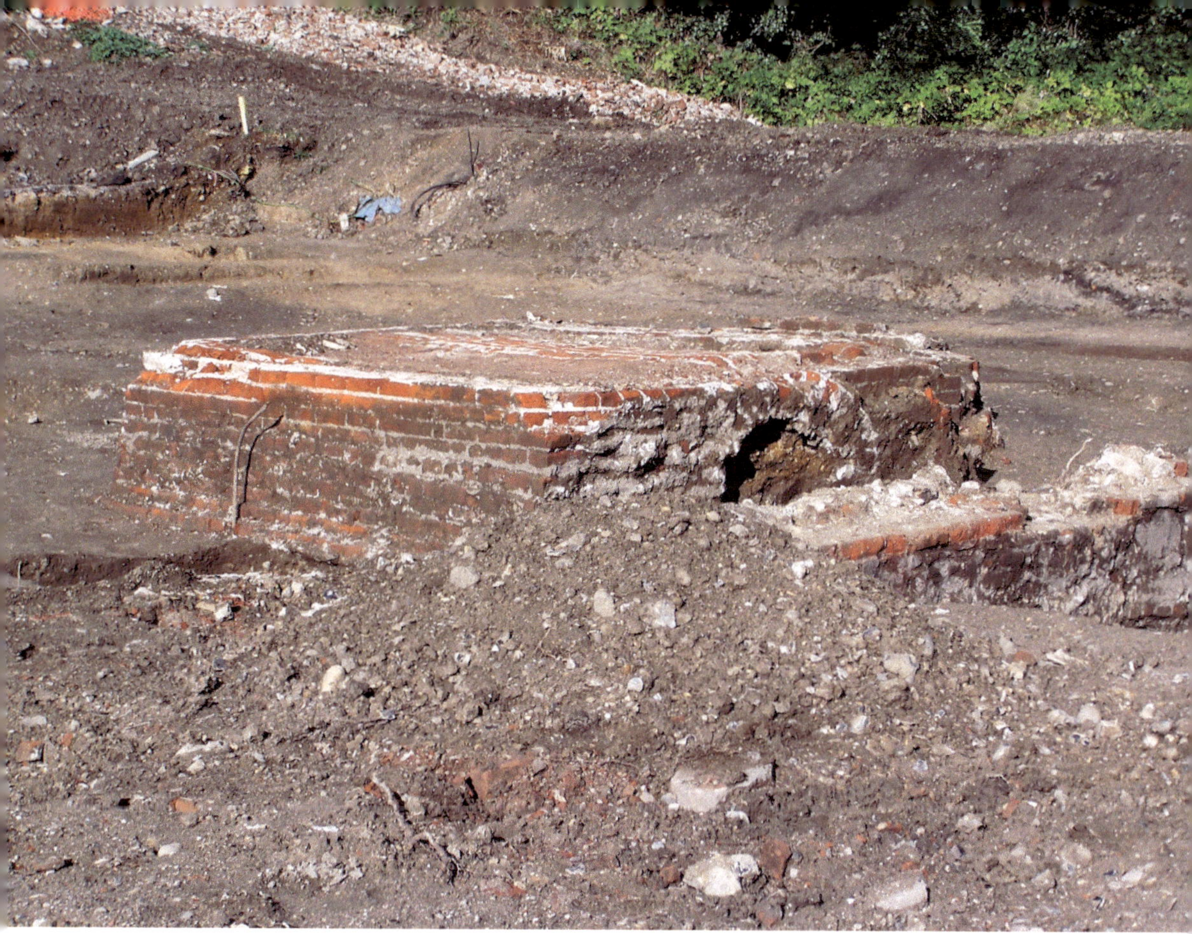

nineteenth century it was a day and boarding school run by Edward Lockwood and also the headquarters of the Red Cross during the twentieth century. Thomas Warren's map of 1747 shows formal gardens to the rear of this property in plan form. Bizarrely, they are similar in design to the later concentric layout of the abbey gardens used by Nathaniel Shirley Harness Hodson in 1831. However, he used the Royal Botanical gardens in Brussels for his template.

Woolhall Street Collapses

Woodhall Street did not exist until 1828, when a narrow path known as Woolpack Passage (adjoining a woolhall) was widened, giving better access to Field Lane (King's Road) and a new beast market in St Andrew's Street South. During medieval times, the town's economy thrived on the wool trade, but with its decline towards the end of the eighteenth century the woolhall ceased in 1805. The owner, John Green, was ultimately declared bankrupt in 1823. The Woolpack Inn on the corner eventually became Everards Hotel in 1864 when Michael Everard purchased it, which sadly closed in 1987. An article in the *East Anglian Daily Times* of 9 September 2010 reported that a large 12-foot hole appeared while Anglian Water were working on a water main in the street. Suffolk County Council archaeologist Colin Pendleton thought, 'it could be linked to a series of chalk mines in the town from the medieval period'. The street temporarily closed while the hole was dealt with.

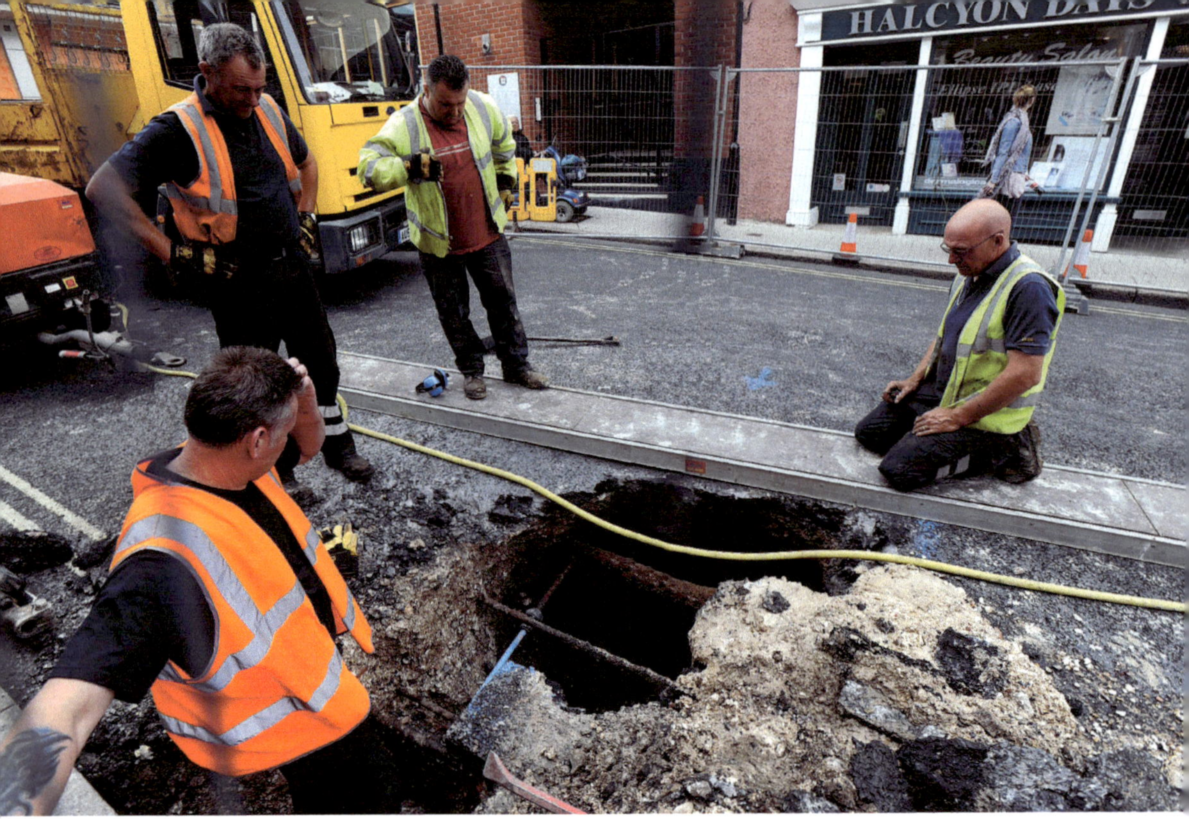

Woolhall Street. This photo was taken through the temporary Heras wire fencing and shows workmen wisely working on a 'Youngman Platform' in case of further subsidence.

Large holes have suddenly appeared at various times. Near the Cornhill corner, previously the town gaol, a 25-foot-deep hole appeared in 1969, which archaeologist Bob Carr considered was possibly caused by chalk workings. Quakers were once imprisoned at the town gaol. One, George Whitehead, spoke of the cruel treatment meted out by the gaoler: 'As a punishment two of them were put into a dismal dungeon that could only be reached by a ladder. It was four yards deep underground, at the bottom, in the midst an iron grate a foot distant from each other and underneath a pit or hole we knew not how deep!'

Le Dycheweye, St Andrew's Street South

Four years after King Cnut came to the throne in 1016, he built a stone rotunda church to house the martyred King Edmund's (AD 869) body. According to the medieval chronicler William of Malmesbury, Cnut also had defensive fortifications put in place to protect the town. Part of this was a deep ditch with an earthen rampart that ran all the way from the Westgate (Butts Corner), up St Andrew's Street South, down St Andrew's Street North until meeting the Tayfen. Then, as now, this part of the town was, as its name suggests, a waterlogged area, which acted as a natural defence along with the Lark and the Linnet – Bury's two rivers. During 2008/9, as part of construction work to erect a purpose-built public house, a basement at Oakes Barn in St Andrew's Street South was excavated for the pub to house toilets, stores and an office, all accessed via a staircase. This work allowed archaeologists to cut into a section of the medieval ditch. No longer required for its original purpose of protecting the western side of the town, the rampart and ditch had fallen into

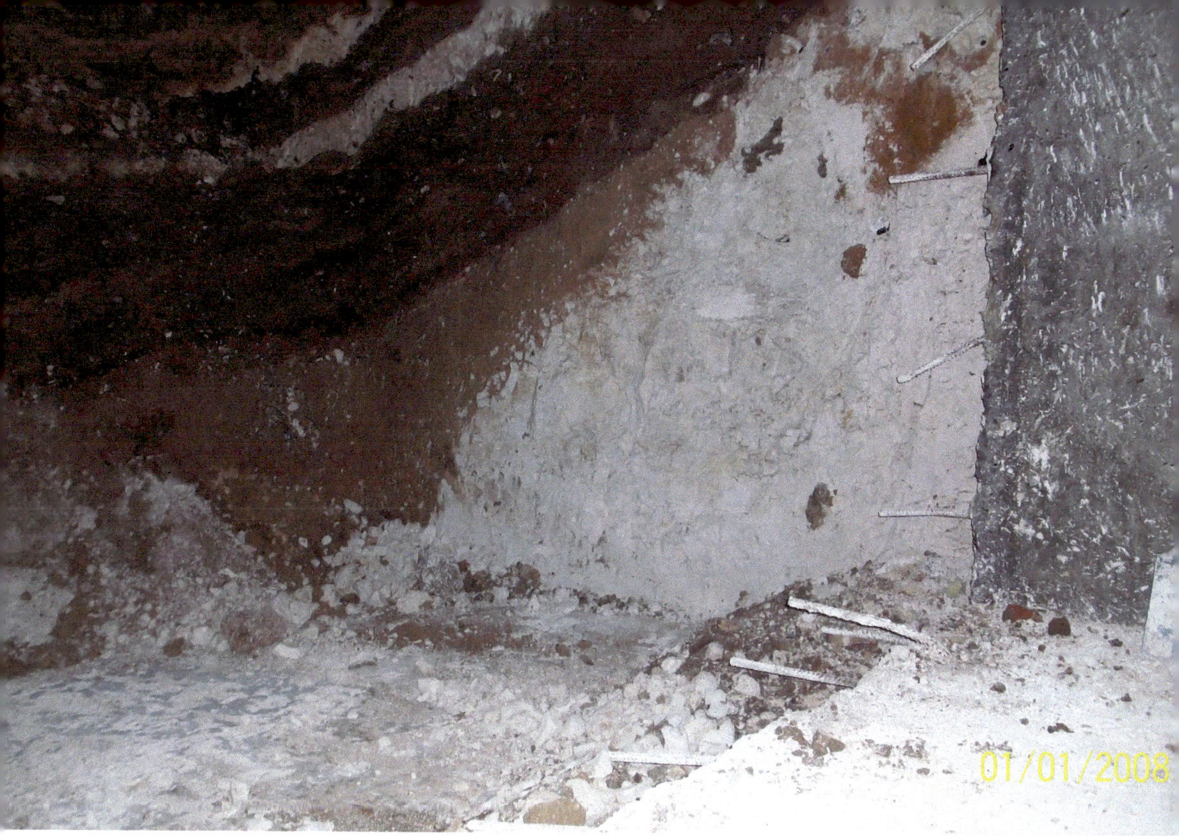

Above: You can gauge the depth of the chalk excavation by a shovel leaning against the wall. Vestiges of human waste, the brown and green colourings, tipped into the ditch over time.

Below: Oakes Barn public house, St Andrew's Street South.

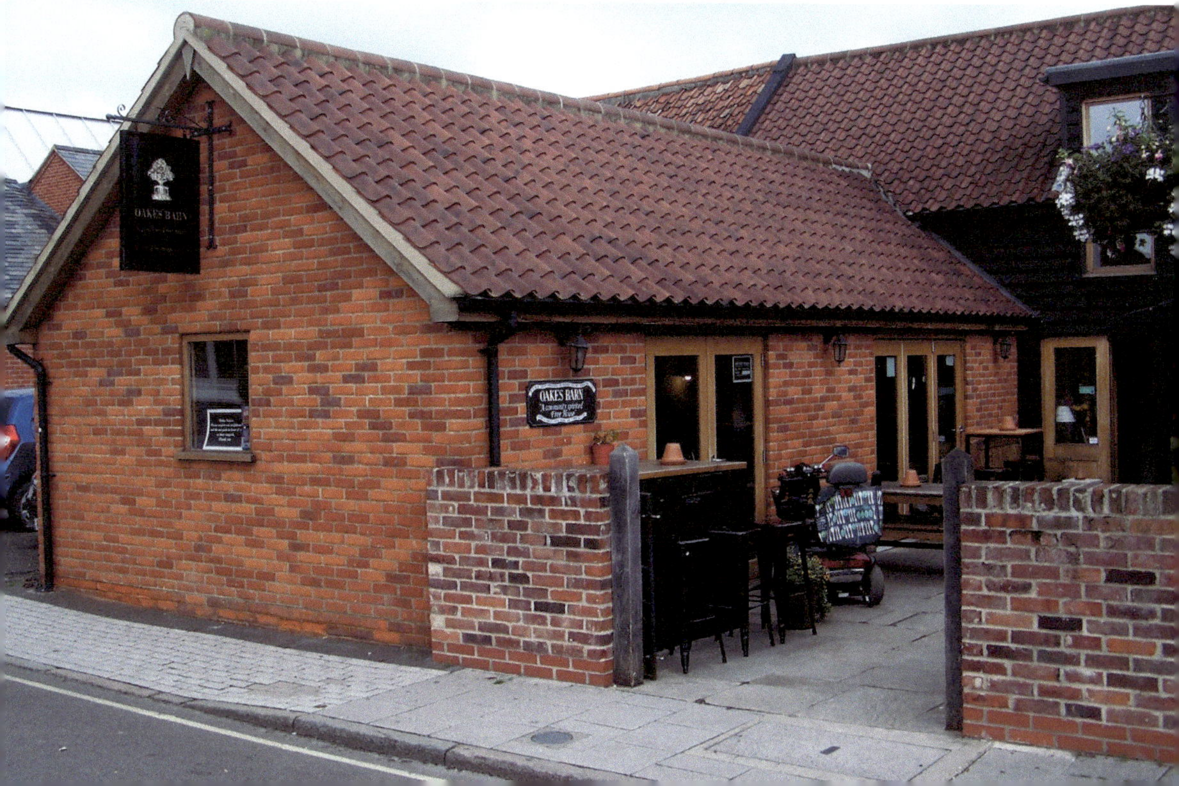

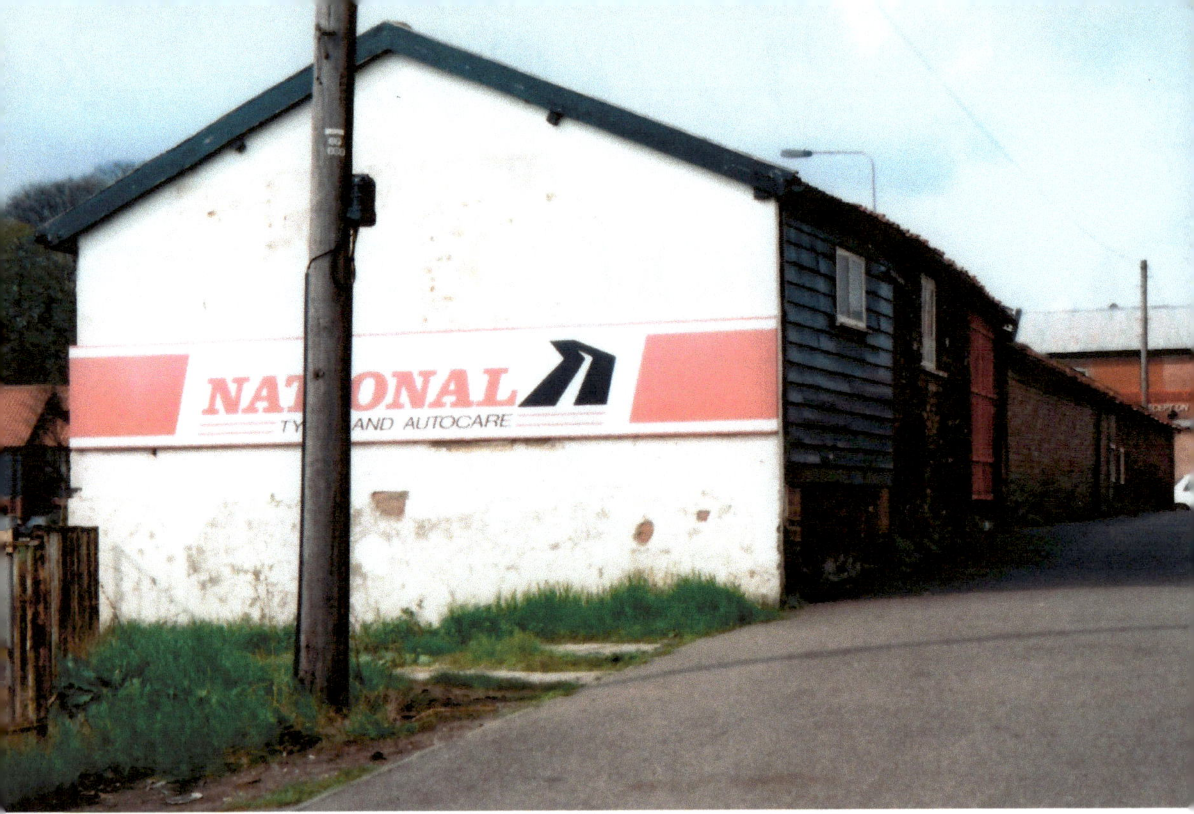

The Bungee, St Andrew's Street South.

disuse many years earlier. The ditch was used for the disposal of sewage and rubbish from the houses in Guildhall Street, which backed onto St Andrew's Street South. In fact, wool merchant-cum-banker James Oakes's house in Guildhall Street was the reason Oakes Barn was called thus, as some of his operation backed onto St Andrew's Street South itself.

The sloping forecourt shown here is known by locals as 'the Bungee'. It is from the former Currys shoe repairers, and it continues as such to the rear of the Hunter Club and Black Boy public house's yard. It was once part of the medieval western defences of the town, known as Le Dycheweye. As the Dycheweye was an earthen ditch and rampart, the slope is a vestige of this rampart – the ditch discovered in the Oakes Barn building works. Because the Dycheweye continued down St Andrew's Street North there is the same topography down the street via Sergeants Walk to St Johns Street and the Bushel public house car park.

Cycle King Excavation

Unbelievably, on the evening of Friday 29 September 2017, two bored employees of Cycle King on Angel Hill were in the rear store room trying to incinerate a dead rodent in a cardboard box. Thinking the fire had gone out they left to go into the front of the shop, but it soon became apparent that the fire was still very active. Only the professionalism of the attending sixty firefighters, with twelve fire engines, prevented the fire spreading to the adjacent Francella restaurant and the ancient One Bull public house. Subsequently, the two men were arrested and given suspended prison sentences for arson, but no penalties for their stupidity. Cycle King, formerly the premises of Burrells garage and very much an industrial-type building, subsequently submitted a planning application to rebuild after demolition of the burnt-out shop. With this carried out the archaeologists moved in and, with the existing surfaces within the shop stripped off, there were some quite remarkable finds beneath. As can be seen by the photograph, at the rear of Cycle King is the north curtain wall of the abbey, built during the abbacy of Abbot Anselm by his sacrist Herveus (Hervey), the officer or obedientiary of the abbey responsible for the abbey's infrastructure. Alongside this wall, on the abbey side, were the stables, cowsheds, brewhouse and bakehouse. But is this the true extent of the abbey? The image definitely shows two flint foundations of walls, one of which is certainly contemporary with the tall wall at the rear. Though purely hypothetical, could the abbey have once reached out further than what we accept today as its boundary?

The excavations under the demolished building posed more questions than answers. The Warren maps of the eighteenth century show buildings on the site of Cycle King and, at its rear, today's abbey's curtain wall – thought provoking! The flint foundations of the properties previously here indicate that they may have abutted the One Bull at some time in the past. The other adjacent building, Crescent House, on the corner, is early nineteenth century. The Cycle King shop has now been rebuilt – every cloud has a silver lining.

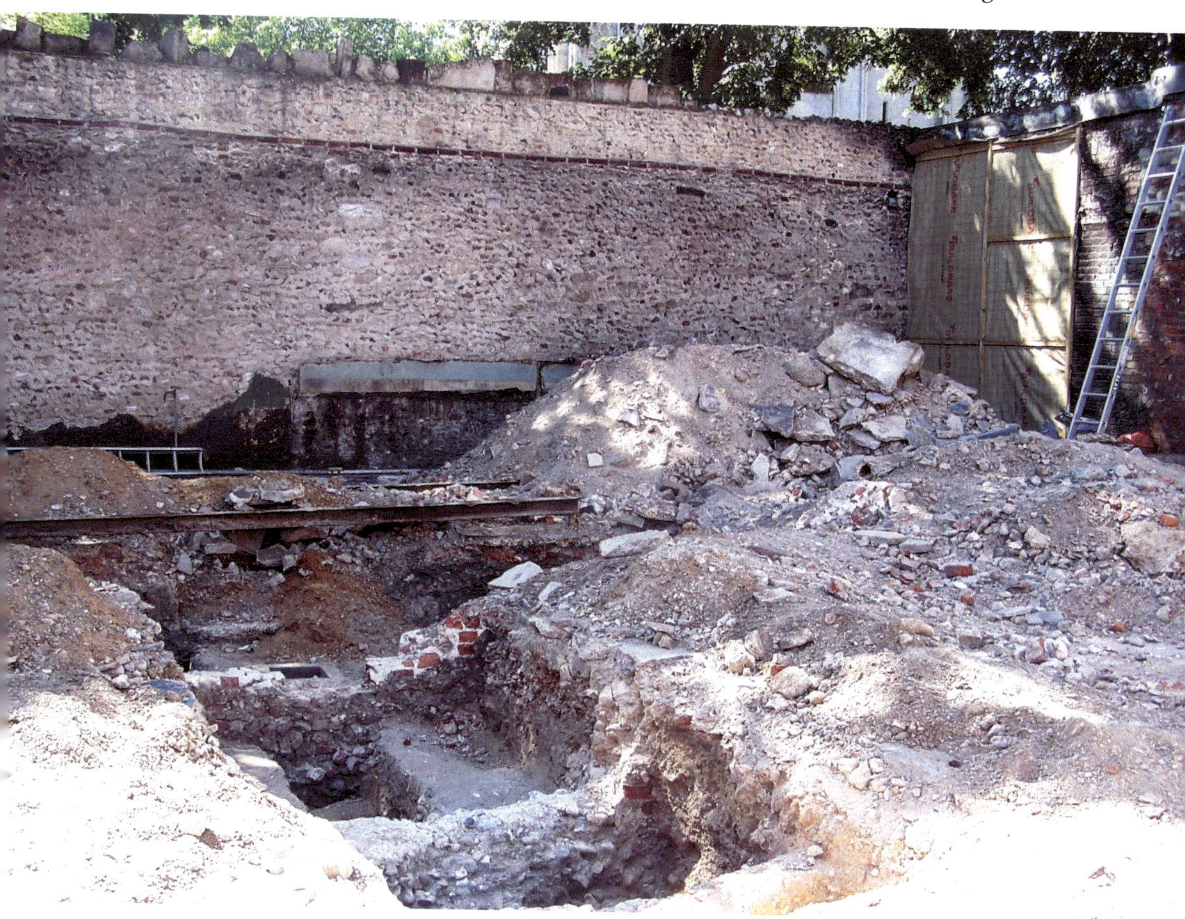

Above and overleaf: Cycle King excavations.

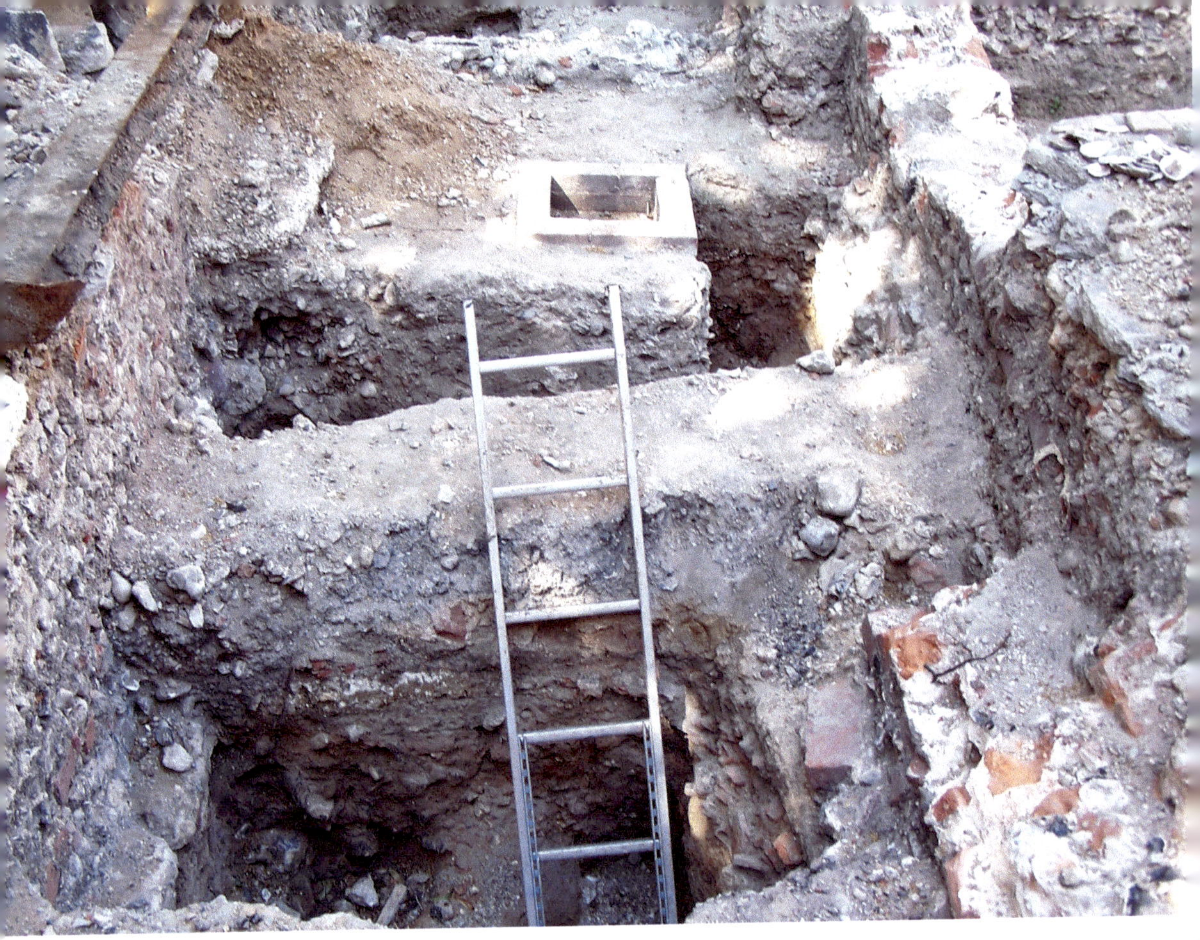

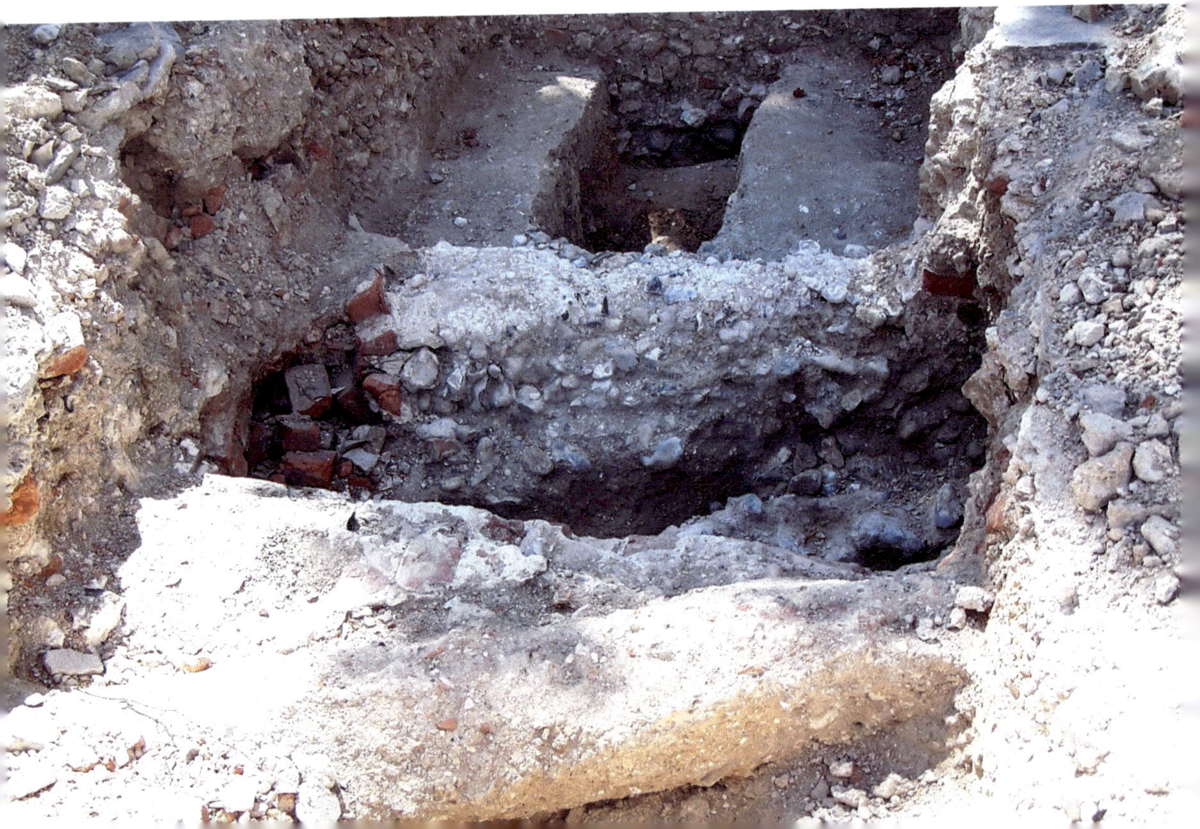

Bury St Edmunds Abbey Excavations

St Edmundsbury Abbey, as it was once known, celebrated 1,000 years of existence in 2020 and has seen numerous investigations into its past. Discoveries, such as the burial of Thomas Beaufort in 1772 and the unfortunate person finding bones (1844) in the Charnel House crypt, were due to luck more than judgement. People such as John Darkin, a local viticulturist, builder and also clerk of the works to St James, carried out excavations to the east of the abbey in 1849, and Gordon Hills, a notable academic, contributed to the understanding of the abbey site around 1865. The intervention of ghost writer supremo and academic par excellence M. R. James found in Douai, France, the whereabouts of abbot burials in the chapter house, making headlines in 1903. Between 1929 and 1933 the Ministry of Works, in collaboration with the town's corporation, cleared some of the site, which enabled Arthur Whittingham to define the outline of the monastic buildings in 1951, dating its best representation. Hundreds of years of neglect contributed to undergrowth covering much of the abbey church; a period of seven years, from 1957, saw this removed with metal railings encompassing the ruins. The Ministry of Public Buildings and Works, as it was then called, also revealed much of the abbey church (albeit a flint core) and removed rubble and detritus 14 feet down in the crypt. The most surprising were forty-three pieces of balusters, thought to be of Saxon origin. However, much of the nave has yet to be excavated.

What had long been thought a mere possibility was finally realised in 1988 after components of a Saxon road – possibly part of the town's ancient grid – were found when

Conservation work in the abbey's St Botolph's Chapel for the Ministry of Public Works, 1960s.

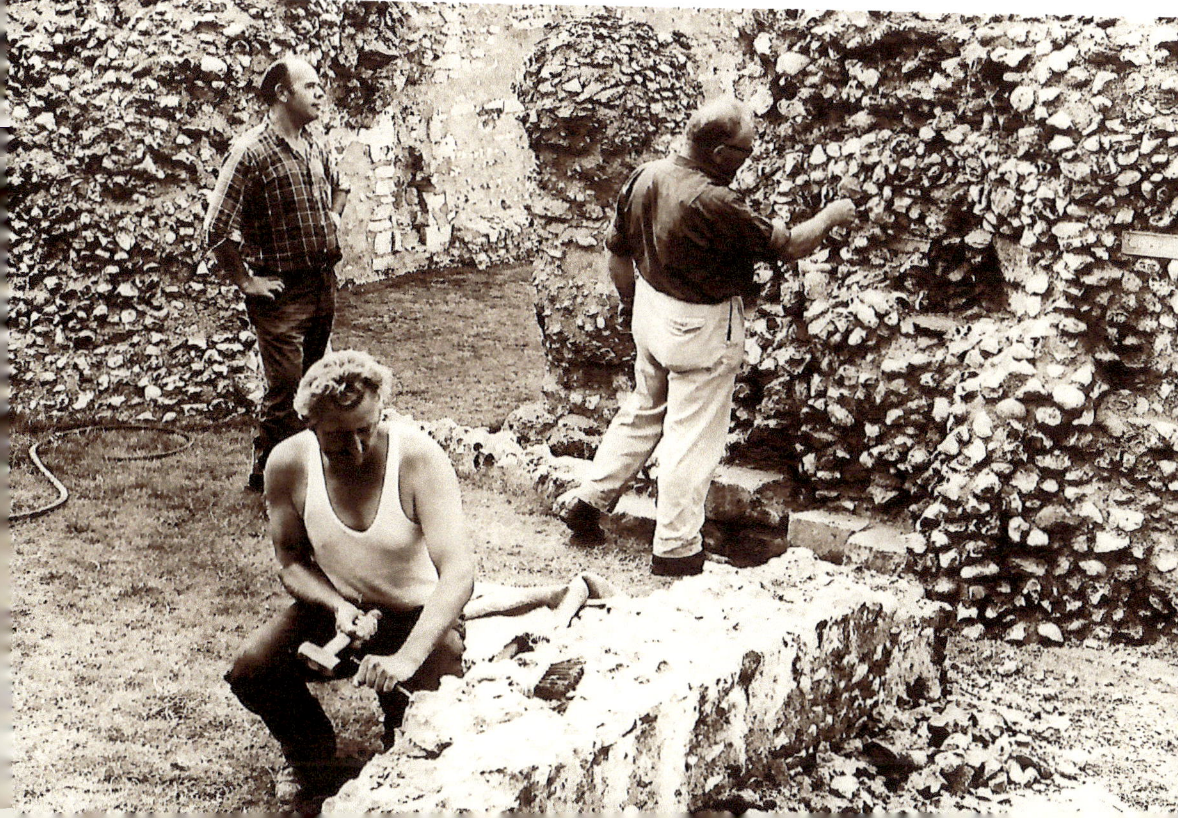

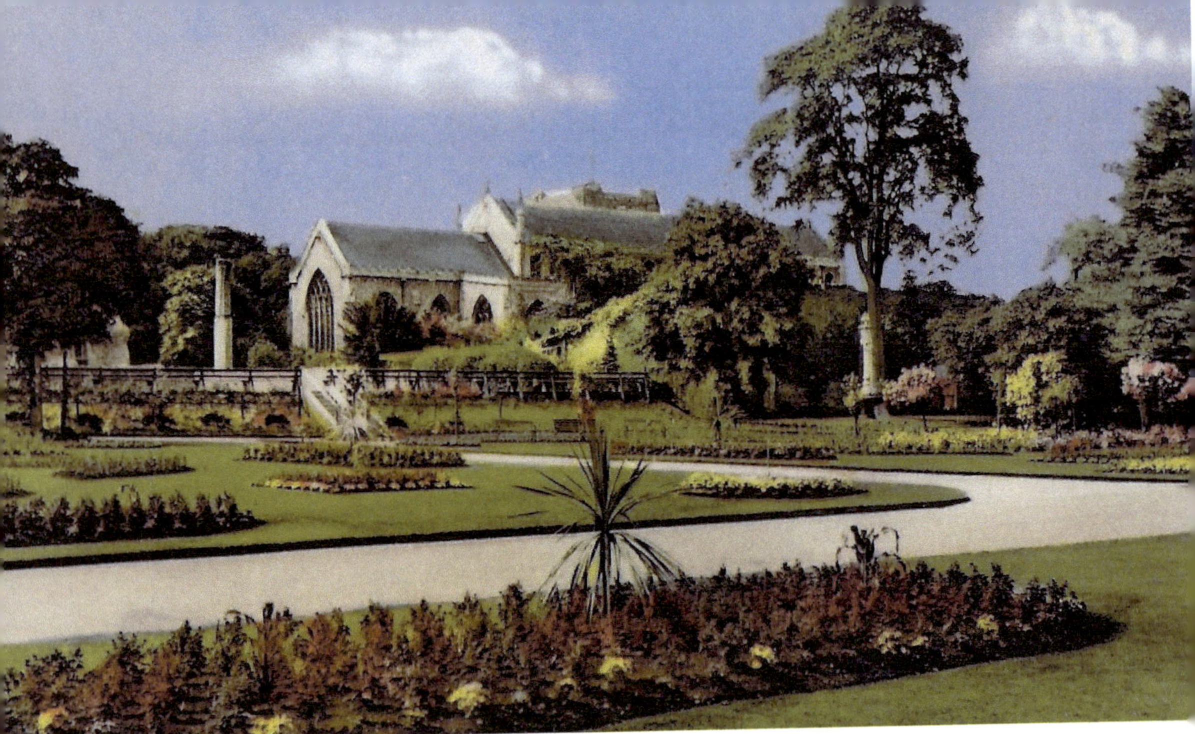

Abbey excavations.

excavations for the new Cathedral Centre were carried out. This road, on a south–north alignment, went from Southgate Street, St Mary's Square then via Spahawk Street across the west front of the abbey church to the High Street (today's Northgate Street) and consisted of a series of cobbled surfaces 5 feet down abutted by a ditch. St Mary's Square, once known as the Horse Market, was considered the market place in the Saxon era, so the discovery of this road became very relevant in the subsequent understanding of Bury St Edmunds as the oldest purposely laid out Norman town in the country. Further excavations in 1999 led Suffolk archaeologist David Gill to announce that a substantial eleventh-century secular building had been identified 1 metre under the floor – now part of the precinct of St James' Cathedral. This was an important discovery before the commencement (shown) of the building of the cathedral's Millennium Tower in 2000 (completed 2005), the culmination of diocesan architect Stephen Dykes Bower's vision. Many archaeologists have contributed much to our understanding of the abbey over the years, and January 2019 saw the Abbey of St Edmund Heritage Partnership publish a public consultation document titled *Past, Present and Future*. It is anticipated that the two studies they commissioned, a heritage assessment by Richard Hoggett Heritage and a conservation plan by Purcell Architects of Norwich, will be used as a blueprint for looking after the wonderful inheritance we have.

College of Sweet Jesus, No. 58a College Street

Jankyn Smyth, one of the town's great benefactors, founded the College of Sweet Jesus as a chantry to say prayers for his soul, under the terms of his will of 1480. Previously known as Barnwell Street, the college did not refer to a seat of learning, but a retirement home for priests from St James' and St Mary's. It was finished in 1549 – ten years after the dissolution. Gable-ended seventeenth-century buildings here were converted in 1748 to the Bury Workhouse by the town's corporation. Just one wing survived its sell off in 1884 –

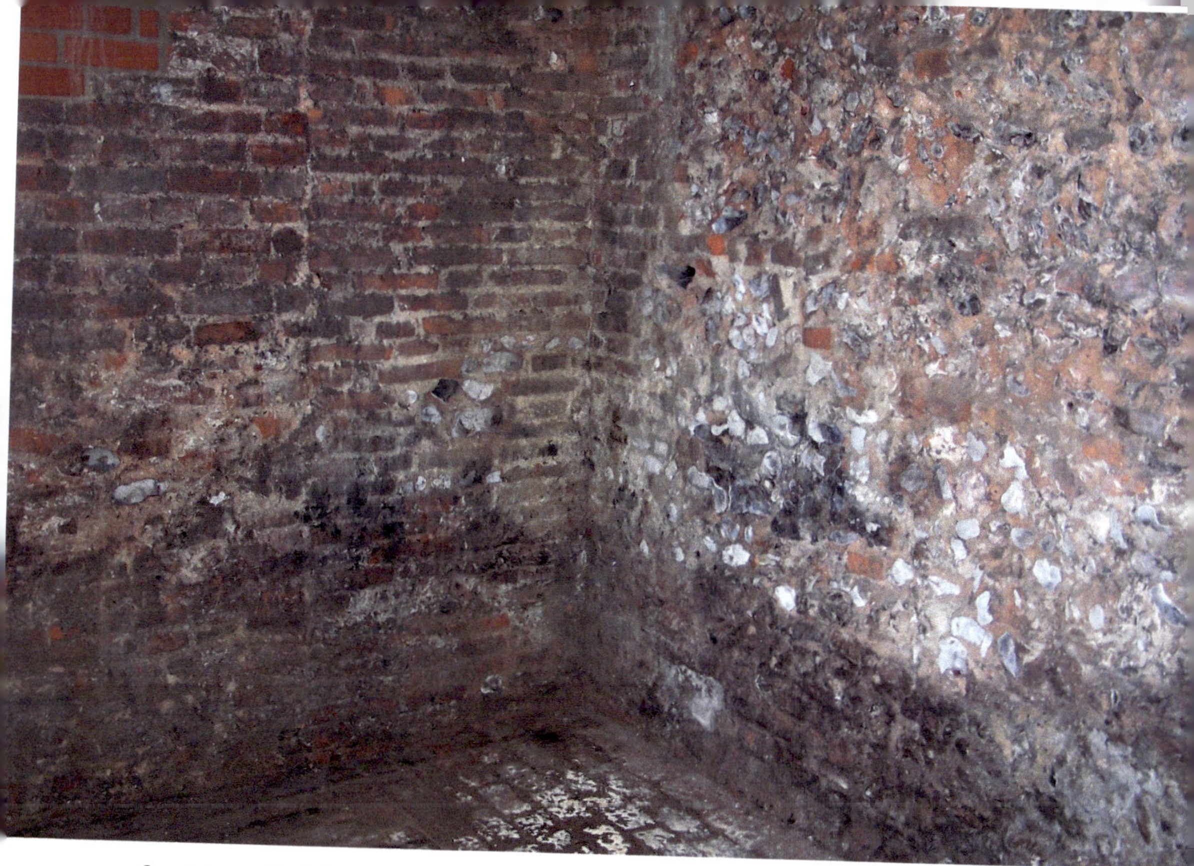

Surviving wall of the college of Sweet Jesus cellar.

today's Old Dairy Yard. Excavations in 2012, in advance of a housing development on land between Nos 57 and 59 College Street, identified a large 15 × 12-foot cellar, dated to the Norman period by its flint-coursed walls. Part of the detailed archaeological report says:

> Its original depth was in excess of 2m with a clay floor; a corridor appeared to descend into it from the west of the site. The corridor between 5ft to 6ft wide ran westward towards Whiting Street for 17ft before continuing beyond the excavation. The foundations of a stone buttress are evidential of a stone building above the corridor; probably the College as for many years the exact location of it could not be verified. It is uncertain how many stone lined cellars there are within our town, but it seems reasonable to suggest that this cellar is from a high-status pre-reformation building. Other remnants of a surviving medieval yard surface made of stone and chalk were found along with a sequence of brick foundations thought to be the remains of the former workhouse.

The new house, set back from the street, now incorporates the cellar.

Excavations at the Norman Tower

This fine, 80-foot-high, Grade I listed Norman belfry, or campanile, was also the religious gateway to St Edmundsbury Abbey. At different times water would cascade down Churchgate Street, flooding Paddock Pool (Chequer Square) and also going into the abbey church – hence why land was eventually built up around the tower. The original level is inside the

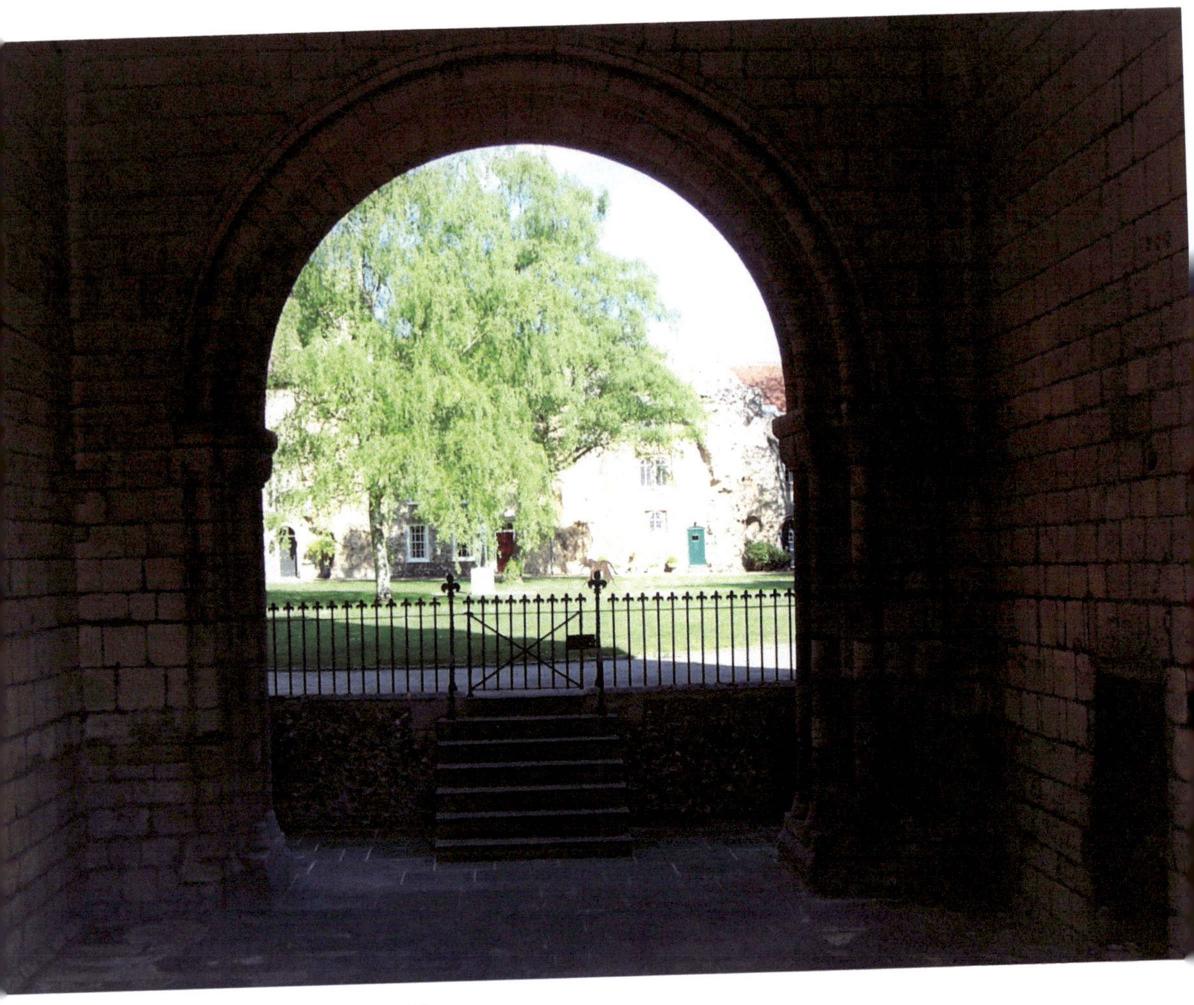

Excavations at the Norman Tower.

tower, which can be verified by the southern low-level cathedral doorways. During the mid-nineteenth century, houses abutting the tower were removed, along with accumulated earth, so builder Thomas Farrow could repair the tower. As the work was finishing in 1848, twenty animal skulls were found. These unusual finds were then sent to the foremost authority on animal anatomy, Professor Owen of the Royal College of Surgeons, who identified them as wolf skulls, except for one. It's hardly surprising then that a connection to the Edmund legend was made. In 1973 further work in and around the tower uncovered more animal bones, a well, the abbey precinct wall foundations, fragments of pottery and window glass. A large memorial brass matrix imprint from the late fifteenth century, on a Purbeck stone slab and relating to a bell-founder (possibly Reignold Chirche of the Bury Bell Foundry) was also found. Interestingly, the only complete set of bells put into a belfry in this country were put into the Norman Tower in 1785 by Thomas Osburn of Downham Market. Extraordinary, during cellar renovation work in 2000–01 in the adjacent Norman Tower House, twenty-seven burials were discovered, some with wall foundations of this property of 1846, across them proving that the Great Churchyard once extended up to Crown Street.

Is St Edmund Hidden Away?

Did Prince Louis, Dauphin of France, really kidnap Edmund's body in 1217 while rampaging through East Anglia during the Baronial Wars? Ending up in Toulouse, France, the alleged bones there have since been repudiated. The latest theory is that Edmund was snaffled away by monks and buried in an iron-bound chest in the monk's cemetery. Many years later tennis courts were built over this cemetery. The courts themselves were removed in 2020 and blinded with topsoil, ready for ground-penetrating radar sometime in the future. Currently a 36-meter-diameter wildflower labyrinth has been planted.

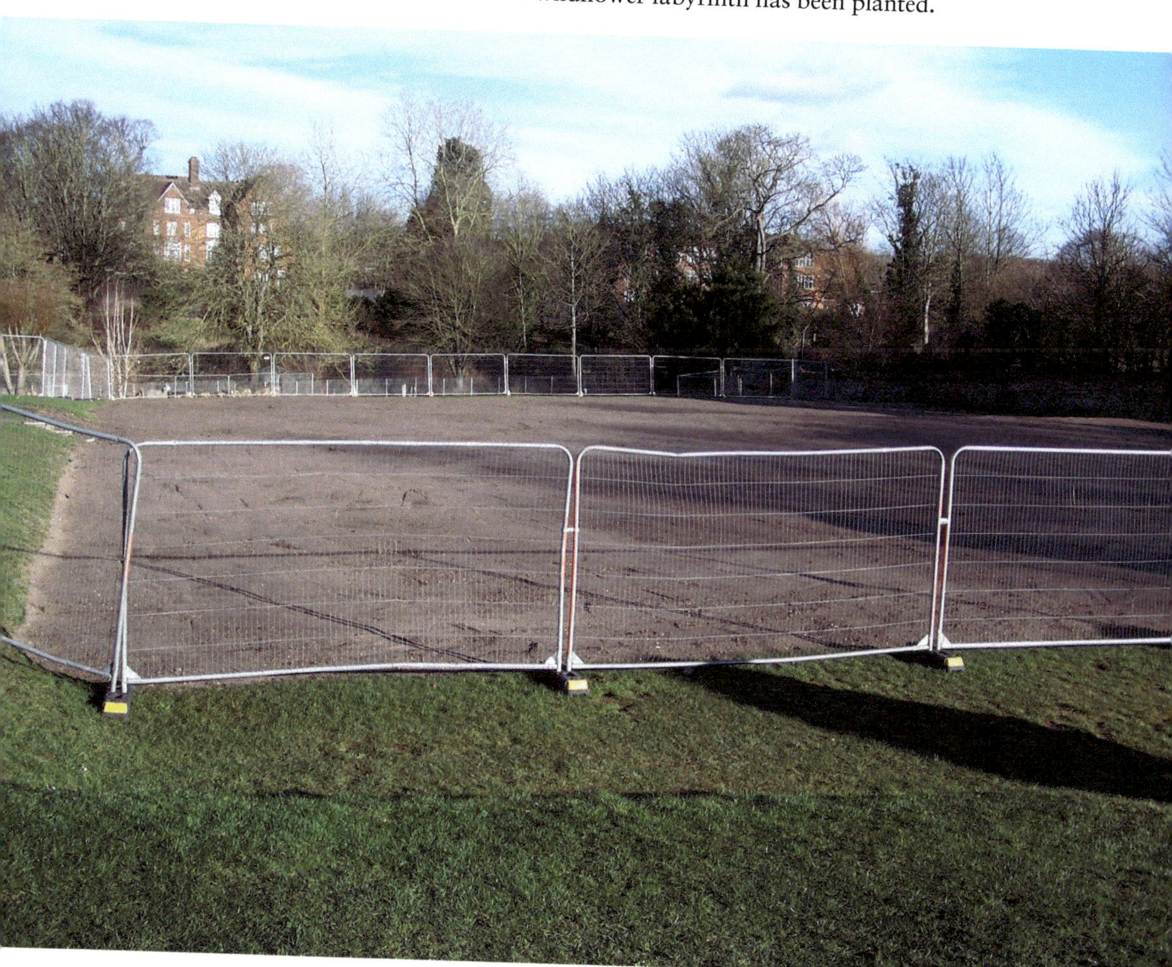

Tennis courts now removed.

ACKNOWLEDGEMENTS

My sincere thanks to all the following people, organisations and services for their contributions in the research for this book: Andy Abbott, Abbeygate Masonry, Abbey Hotel, Abby Antrobus, David Addy, Betty Barton, Margaret Beatty, John Brunskill, Rob Butterworth, Bury Free Press, Bury St Edmunds Past & Present Society, Edward Cobbold, Anne Cross, Susan Chisholm, Pat Church, Brad Jones and the EADT, Brian Fallows, David Gill, Graham Gosling, Darren Hempstead, Stuart Hogger, Richard Hoggett, Karen Hurden, Stephen Hurst, Nick and Birgitte Mager, Louise Martin, James Mellish, Gerry Nixon, Terry O'Donoghue, Rosy Payne, Kevin Pulford, Purcell Architects of Norwich, Jo Rayner, David Rees, Peter Riddington, Steve Ruthen, John Saunders, Michael Smith, Sarah Friswell of St Edmundsbury Cathedral, Suffolk Institute of Archaeology, Suffolk County Council Archaeological Services, SIAH, Suffolk Archives, Fiona Talbot, Shaun Thompson, West Suffolk Council Cemetery Services, Whatley Lane Estate Agents, Simon Whitnall, Whitworth Partnership, Richard G. Wilson (Greene King History), Sara Yaxley, Francis Young (*A Secret Disclosed*), and, of course, my wonderful wife, Sandie.